THE YOUNG GAIA

ATLAS OF

EARTHCARE

An illustrated reference guide
to looking after our planet

MILES LITVINOFF

Facts On File, Inc.

AN INFOBASE HOLDINGS COMPANY

Atlas of Earthcare was produced for Gaia Books by
BENDER RICHARDSON WHITE, UXBRIDGE, UK.

Acknowledgments
Editor Judy Garlick
Managing Editor Lionel Bender
Production Kim Richardson;
    Susan Walby, at Gaia Books
Publisher Liaison Hannah
    Wheeler, at Gaia Books

Designer Malcolm Smythe
Art Editor Ben White
Direction Pip Morgan, Patrick
    Nugent, and Joss Pearson,
    at Gaia Books

This edition was first published in Great Britain in 1996 by
Gaia Books Limited
66 Charlotte Street, London W1P 1LR
and 20 High Street, Stroud GL5 1AS

Copyright © Gaia Books Limited, London, 1996

The Young Gaia Atlas of Earthcare

ISBN 0-8160-3470-2
Library of Congress CIP data is available from Facts On File.

Jacket design by Smart Graphics

Printed in Spain
10 9 8 7 6 5 4 3 2 1

CONTENTS

Abbreviations
The following abbreviations are used in this book:

%: percent	m²: square meter	g: gram
cm: centimeter	ha: hectare	kg: kilogram
m: meter	m³: cubic meter	t: ton
km: kilometer	km³: cubic kilometer	kW: kilowatt
		kWh: kilowatt-hour

The Author
MILES LITVINOFF is a specialist writer and editor of books on the environment, development, and human rights for children and adults. He works as an editor for the Minority Rights Group, a human rights organization in London, and tutors the Open University Environment course. He is author and editor of many successful titles, including *The Greening of Aid: Sustainable Livelihoods in Practice* (coeditor, 1988), *The Earthscan Action Handbook for People and Planet* (1990), *Ancestors: The Origins of the People and Countries of Europe* (coauthor, 1992), the *Junior Cultural Atlas* series (1989–94), and *The World Minorities Directory* (1996).

ABOUT THIS BOOK

Corals are marine organisms *that live in large colonies in warm seas. Their skeletons – made from dissolved limestone (calcium carbonate) absorbed from seawater – accumulate to form reefs and even islands. This one is in Tonga in the southwest Pacific Ocean.*

The *Young Gaia Atlas of Earthcare* describes our place on Earth as members of a community of living things, how we have changed our surroundings, the problems we have created for ourselves and other species, and the challenges we face to make things right where they have gone wrong. The book shows how we can harm our environment, but also how people are working to reverse this damage. And it explains the changes we need to make — replacing waste, poverty, hunger, and violence with a fairer, more peaceful, sustainable society — to safeguard our future on the planet.

The Gaia theory states that the biosphere — the thin layer between the Earth's crust and outer atmosphere that contains all living things — is like a living organism itself. Life-forms have created and maintained the special conditions they need for survival. According to the Gaia theory, the biosphere too has "life-support" systems to ensure its survival, whatever human beings do to it. But humankind may not survive unless we safeguard the clean air and water, fertile soil, trees, and other natural resources on which we depend.

Structure of the book

This book provides a detailed, up-to-date picture of the challenges we face. Following a short Introduction, there are nine numbered chapters, dealing with the topics Land, Food and Farming, Oceans, Energy and Elements, Fresh Water, Plants and Animals, Humankind, Civilization, and Tomorrow's World.

Chapter 1, **Land**, describes plant and tree growth, soil damage and deforestation resulting from human activity, and how we can protect land and forests.

Chapter 2, **Food and Farming**, focuses on crops and livestock, traditional and modern agriculture, food distribution systems, world hunger, and the kind of farming we will need in the future.

Chapter 3, **Oceans**, looks at the importance of oceans and seas for climate, as the place where life began, and as a source of food. It considers problems linked to fishing, whaling, and sea pollution, and how we can tackle them.

Chapter 4, **Energy and Elements**, describes our dependence on the Sun and the Earth's fossil-fuel and mineral reserves. It explains, and offers solutions for, such urgent problems as the greenhouse effect and the Antarctic and Arctic ozone "holes."

Chapter 5, **Fresh Water**, is about the importance of rainfall and clean water in our daily lives. It looks at the severe water shortages that people in many countries face, and how these might be overcome.

Chapter 6, **Plants and Animals**, explains how the natural world has evolved, the way different living things interrelate, and the effects of human activities on other species. It closes with a discussion about conservation.

The subject of Chapter 7, **Humankind**, is human potential, human rights and needs, and how these may best be fulfilled. After considering such major problems as unemployment and overpopulation, the chapter makes suggestions for solving them.

Chapter 8, **Civilization**, looks at humanity as a whole. It considers both the benefits, such as rapid communications, and the problems of the modern world, including poverty and the threat of war, and ways to ease the problems.

Chapter 9, **Tomorrow's World**, suggests that the human race can learn from past mistakes. It shows many ways in which people are now working together to make a better world, and what more we can do.

More than half the world's people are expected to live in cities *by the year 2000. The heart of New York City offers all the excitement of modern city life — spectacular buildings, shops, entertainment, museums, and more — but it also suffers from most, if not all, of today's urban problems.*

Information is laid out in self-contained two-page sections, or "spreads." Each spread combines text, maps, diagrams, and sometimes photographs to focus on different aspects of the main topic, and takes one of three viewpoints: Resources, Problems, or Solutions.

Chapters 1 to 8 also include an illustrated "Gaia Watch" case study, showing how the chapter themes affect particular groups of people in their daily lives. Most case studies have been provided by Oxfam.

The numbered chapters have two further features. "Do you know?" boxes provide facts, figures, and examples in addition to those in the main text. "Home action" boxes suggest what we can do within our community to tackle problems.

The *Atlas* ends with a Reference Section that describes how maps are drawn up and explains how diagrams work. This section also lists official organizations and suggests national groups to join and support. In addition, there is a glossary of terms, a list of recommended reading and CD-ROMs, a note on sources, acknowledgments, and the index.

Terms used in the book
We have explained new, difficult, and important terms the first time they are used in the text. The glossary provides further help. However, some terms need a brief, further comment here.

We describe countries as "developed" or "developing." Developed countries are those where large-scale industry, based on burning coal, oil, and gas, is well established and usually the main source of jobs and wealth creation. These countries control most international trade and world money markets. Most developed countries are rich and in the North (see below). The main ones are the European Union countries (such as France, Germany, Italy, and the UK), the United States, Japan, Australia, and Canada. People sometimes include Russia and Eastern European countries under the term "developed."

Developing countries are those where farming is still the main way of life, and industry is building up only slowly. Most developing countries are poor and in the South (see below). There are many more developing than developed countries. Ranging from Afghanistan to Zimbabwe, developing countries make up almost all of Africa, Asia, the Caribbean, Central and South America, and the Pacific. Four out of every five of the world's people live in developing countries.

The terms "developed" and "developing" do not describe all countries equally well. In some developed countries, such as Portugal and New Zealand, farming is as important as industry. And some developing countries, such as Brazil and South Korea, are quite rich compared with many others and have a great deal of modern industry.

The book also uses the terms "North" and "South." These terms have been widely used since 1980, when the Brandt Report on world development suggested that they could mean roughly the same as "developed" and "developing," or "rich" and "poor." All industrialized countries, apart from Australia and New Zealand, are in the Northern Hemisphere, while most countries in the Southern Hemisphere are poor. Some of the maps in the book show the North–South divide as a physical gap between the two hemispheres.

Some maps refer to Australasia, others to Oceania. Australasia means Australia, New Zealand, and the islands of the South Pacific. Oceania includes not only Australasia but also the Central Pacific islands and the Malay islands of Southeast Asia.

We have used the US dollar as the standard measure of money, which is common for international comparisons.

INTRODUCTION

"At first I thought I was fighting to save rubber trees. Then I thought I was fighting to save the Amazon rainforest. Now I realize I am fighting for humanity."
FRANCISCO CHICO MENDES,
Brazilian rubber tappers' leader, shot dead in 1988

The Earth is a remarkable planet. Its old age and ancient beginnings, the fact that life exists at all, and the huge variety of life-forms: all are part of an amazing story. Humanity has become part of this story. At first we were just one kind of animal among many. With time, we came to consider ourselves something apart from the rest of nature. We behave as though we have conquered nature and forget we are a part of it. Much of this so-called conquest has produced bad results: polluted skies and waters, land stripped bare of trees, dwindling animal populations, and millions of people living in poverty. We need to learn from our mistakes, acquire a greater sense of responsibility toward our surroundings and our fellow human beings, and begin to repair the damage.

The world's tropical rainforests lie close to the equator where hot, wet conditions encourage dense plant growth. This aerial photograph shows the rainforest canopy, which hides a wealth of plant and animal species below. The world's rainforests are among the regions most at risk from human activities.

SPACESHIP EARTH

Space travel, though exciting, involves risk and danger. Astronauts must operate their equipment carefully, because mistakes can be fatal. Our planet is sometimes compared with a spacecraft, traveling with the rest of the Solar System through space. We need to understand how our "craft" works, and respect it.

DO YOU KNOW?

The biosphere and Gaia

Living things inhabit the Earth from the deepest sea to the highest mountain peak and the air above it. Yet, compared with the size of the planet, this layer of life is as thin as the surface dew on the skin of an apple. We call this living layer the biosphere (from the Greek *bios*, meaning life).

Plants, animals, and the environment they share depend on and affect each other. Even the ocean floor is constantly being created. The interrelated nature of all things on Earth means that the planet itself resembles a single, giant, living organism. The scientist James Lovelock coined the term Gaia (the name of the ancient Greek goddess of the Earth) to describe our world and all the life it contains.

Orbiting the Sun, our world seems small and alone. The way it supports its living "passengers" appears unique. Astronomers have not yet detected any other planet in the universe showing signs of life.

The Earth formed from gases and dust 4.5 billion years ago. The planet's center is white hot; at the upper edge of the Earth's atmosphere, the air is too cold and thin for our survival. Life began to evolve between these hot and cold extremes 3.7 billion years ago. The mix of gases in the air, and the Earth's surface temperature, probably changed when life began.

Global interaction

Plants and animals, humans included, have developed together and affect each other in more ways than we fully know. Living things also interact with the environment (our surroundings). From the tiniest soil microbe to the mightiest whale, we all depend on the flow of energy from the Sun.

Plants convert solar energy into forms that animals can use to breathe and eat. Water, oxygen, and carbon dioxide also flow through the "life systems." These flows take place during breathing, photosynthesis (the manufacture of carbohydrates by plants, using sunlight), feeding, and the decay of dead matter.

The Earth has survived major changes to its air, land and sea, climate, and life-forms over millions of years. Many species have evolved, and many have died out. A vast range of human activities has similarly, but much more recently, had a great impact on the planet.

THE LIFE-SUPPORTING PLANET

A layer of gases — the atmosphere — helps warm the Earth and shields living things from the Sun's harmful ultraviolet rays. Surfaces that reflect sunlight, such as ice, prevent overheating of the biosphere. Plants use energy from sunlight, carbon dioxide and oxygen, and water to make food. Animals get their food from plants, and oxygen from the air or water. Warm water rises from the sea as vapor, forming clouds that eventually water the land.

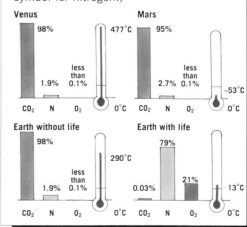

The Earth's atmosphere before life began was probably similar to that of Venus or Mars. The planet's surface was very hot. Early life-forms helped change the gas mixture by absorbing carbon dioxide (CO_2) and releasing oxygen (O_2). (N is the symbol for nitrogen.)

Venus — CO_2 98%, N 1.9%, O_2 less than 0.1%, 477°C / 0°C

Mars — CO_2 95%, N 2.7%, O_2 less than 0.1%, 0°C / −53°C

Earth without life — CO_2 98%, N 1.9%, O_2 less than 0.1%, 290°C / 0°C

Earth with life — CO_2 0.03%, N 79%, O_2 21%, 13°C / 0°C

Life on Earth depends on many complicated, interacting natural processes. For example, warm water rises from the sea as vapor, forming clouds that contribute to the natural "greenhouse effect," which warms the Earth. But the same clouds also reflect the incoming rays of the Sun back into space, cooling the planet. We do not fully understand how these processes affect each other.

Venus

Mars

Natural greenhouse effect warms Earth

Ozone layer shields Earth from Sun's harmful rays

Sunlight reflects from polar ice and other shiny surfaces

Earth before life began?

Oxygen

Nitrogen

Carbon dioxide

Stratosphere, 9-33 mi.

Lower atmosphere, up to 9 mi.

Plants grow by absorbing sunlight energy

Nitrogen

Carbon

Animals feed on plants

Oxygen

Clouds

Carbon dioxide

Water rises into air from sea

Temperature 60 mi. underground: 5432°F

Water flows back to sea in rivers

Water falls on land as rain, hail, sleet, or snow

OUR CHANGING PLANET

Imagine lilies growing on a pond. If they double in area every day, and take 30 days to cover the whole pond, when will they cover half the pond? Answer: the 29th day. This riddle shows what accelerating change is like: slow at first but frighteningly fast later on. Human beings have changed the face of Earth in much the same way.

The universe has existed since the Big Bang simultaneously created space, time, and energy about 15 billion years ago. Another 10.5 billion years passed before the Earth formed. The evolution of life began more recently still, first in the oceans and then on land.

Life has evolved over several billion years, creating a vast range of species. Over time, many new life-forms emerged that were more complicated than earlier ones. The most complicated species of all, the highly intelligent human being, is a recent arrival.

From the beginning of time, each new development in the history of the universe and, later, the Earth has happened faster than the previous one. Imagine the whole time span of the universe so far taking place during a 24-hour day. The Big Bang happens in a split-second at 12 midnight. Atoms, the infinitely tiny building blocks of all objects in the universe, come into existence after a few seconds. By 4:00 a.m. the first stars are

forming. Our own Solar System, including planet Earth, begins to take shape only in the late afternoon, at about 5:00 p.m.

Life begins in the sea in the early evening, at 6:20 p.m. The first land plants and animals appear only at 11:15 at night. The age of dinosaurs lasts from 11:40 p.m. till six minutes to midnight. The first humans walk upright 10 seconds before midnight. The modern industrial age, which brings huge changes to the planet, lasts for just one-thousandth of a second right at the end of the day.

OUR PLANET'S LIFE STORY
The five globes show the story of life on Earth. The spiral lines represent "time" winding down from past to present. The first globe (far left) illustrates the complete history of our planet — 4.5 billion years. Because the pace of change has speeded up over time, each of the other globes, from left to right, traces a period 100 times shorter than the previous one. The fifth globe (far right) shows only the last 45 years, a tiny one-hundred-millionth of the Earth's total life span.

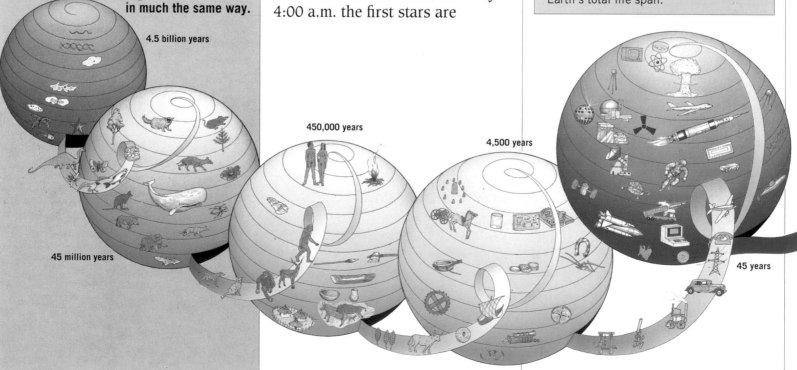

4.5 billion years

45 million years

450,000 years

4,500 years

45 years

The human impact

We believe that we are the most intelligent species on the planet. We can learn from our mistakes, make decisions affecting our fellow human beings, and plan for the future. We have changed our environment as our activities have become more complex.

Early humans made little difference to their environment. Feeding on plants and animals, they benefited from the way plants convert sunlight into food energy. Later — just 50,000 years ago — they learned to make fire, using the energy stored in wood. Only in the last 300 years have people burned coal, and later oil and gas.

Like our use of energy, human numbers have grown faster and faster. We have learned how to produce more and more food, control disease, and prolong life. Since the 1830s the population of the world has grown from 1 billion to 5.75 billion today.

The impact we have had on our surroundings has grown with time, and the speed of change has built up. More and more problems result from the growing use of coal, oil, and gas, the over-farming of soils and over-fishing of seas, the clearing of forests, and the mining of underground metals.

Unchecked, our growing impact will surely bring about disaster for us. Luckily, there are plenty of practical ideas available for slowing the pace of change and reversing the damage.

THE PACE OF CHANGE
Each graph shows how change has accelerated over time, as human beings have had more and more impact on their surroundings. For hundreds of years the number of people on the planet grew very slowly; the use of energy (animal and water power) changed little; few books and journals existed worldwide; and journeys from place to place were slow. In each of these areas there has been a steady increase in the rate of change in the last 300 years, and especially since 1900.

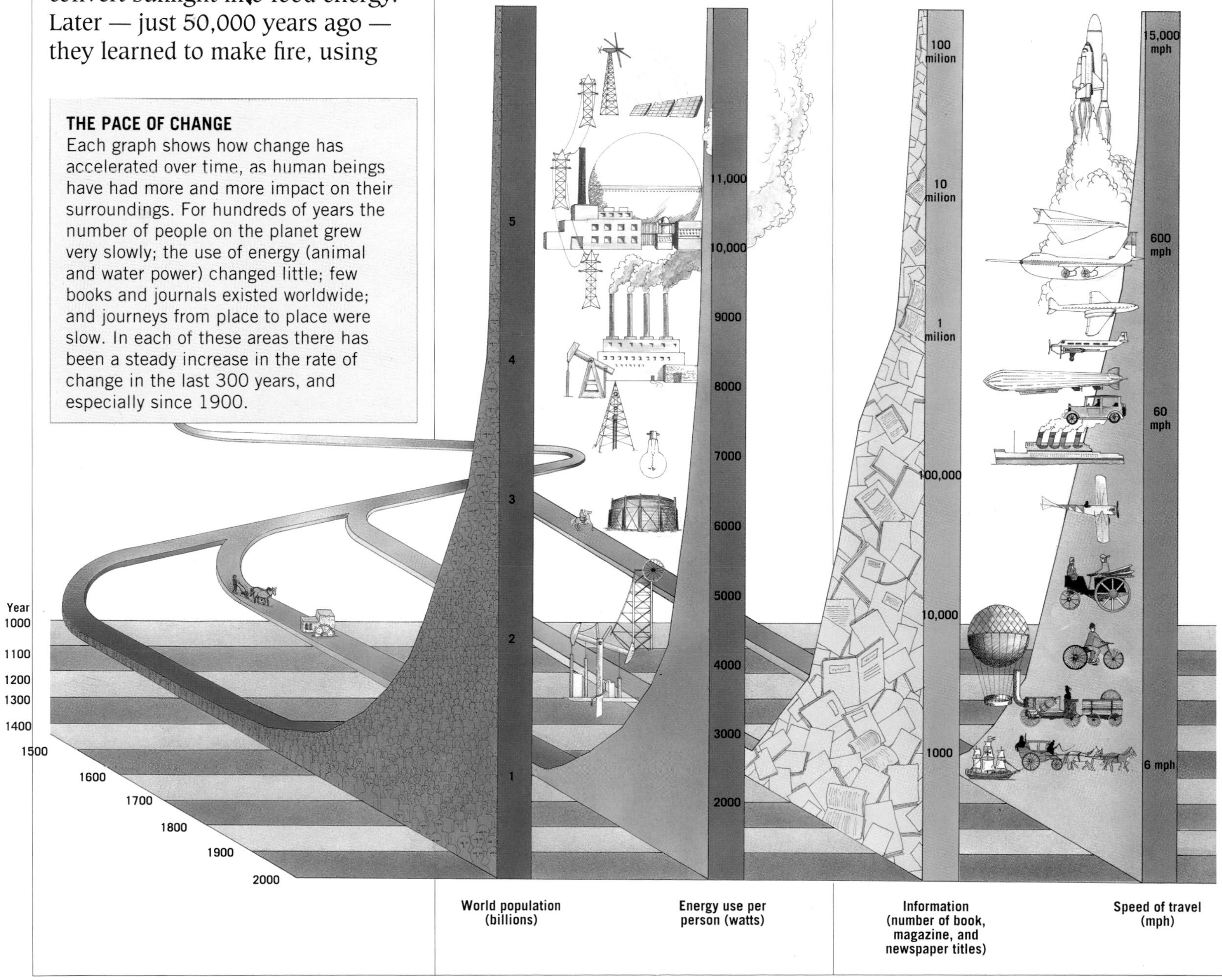

World population
(billions)

Energy use per
person (watts)

Information
(number of book,
magazine, and
newspaper titles)

Speed of travel
(mph)

11

CHALLENGE AHEAD

One person out of every four alive today lives in poverty so severe that they cannot enjoy their basic human rights. And one person in every five uses more resources than is good for the environment. True or false? If you agree that these statements sound true, you are ready to face the challenge ahead.

▶ **This mother-and-baby clinic** in Prampram, Ghana, was funded by the British Overseas Development Administration, an example of the developed world providing practical help for developing countries..

Modern society consumes vast amounts of the Earth's resources. Yet hundreds of millions of people are poor, hungry, sick, homeless, uneducated, and unemployed. Compared to the rest of the world's population, the richest 1.1 billion people, mainly in the developed countries of the North, live lives of luxury.

The wealthiest fifth of humanity causes much of the damage that our planet suffers. They overfarm the best land until soil washes and blows away in rain and wind. They destroy ancient forests in order to grow luxury foods; mine metals to make throw-away juice and soda cans; sweep the oceans for fish; guzzle oil in cars; and pollute the skies.

This way of life damages the human community as well as the environment. More and more people live in poverty — in both the developed and the developing world. More and more conflicts take place about land and limited resources. Sometimes these disputes lead to war. Facing all of us is the challenge to try to bring such problems under control. It will not be easy.

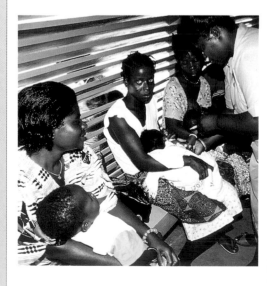

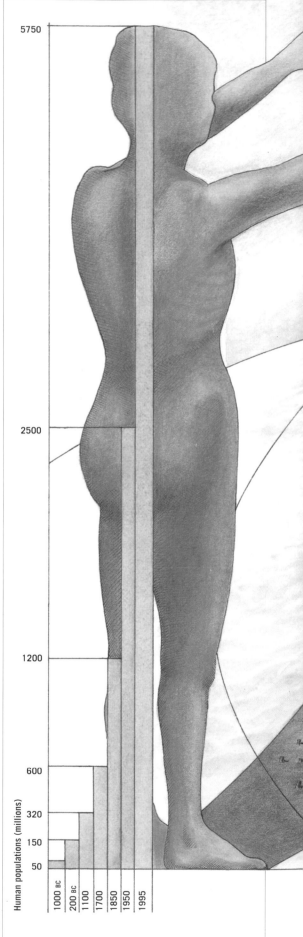

Human populations (millions)

5750

2500

1200

600

320

150

50

1000 BC
200 BC
1100
1700
1850
1950
1995

Early humans caused deforestation when they began to clear woodland to create fields. Badly managed farming by early civilizations turned fertile soils in the Middle East and North Africa into desert. Human suffering increased as stronger peoples conquered and ruled over weaker ones. Pollution began to affect rivers, coastal waters, and people living in cities.

With the Industrial Revolution in the 18th and 19th centuries we began to damage our surroundings even more. Belching chimneys, gushing sewage pipes, and other forms of waste disposal have polluted air, rivers, seas, and land ever since. Key resources such as timber and gas are going up in smoke at an alarming rate. The climate may be changing as a result of air pollution.

Many environmental problems seem to be near to crisis point. The evolution of life itself is under threat as we wipe out natural habitats and species. Where is the pattern of destruction leading us?

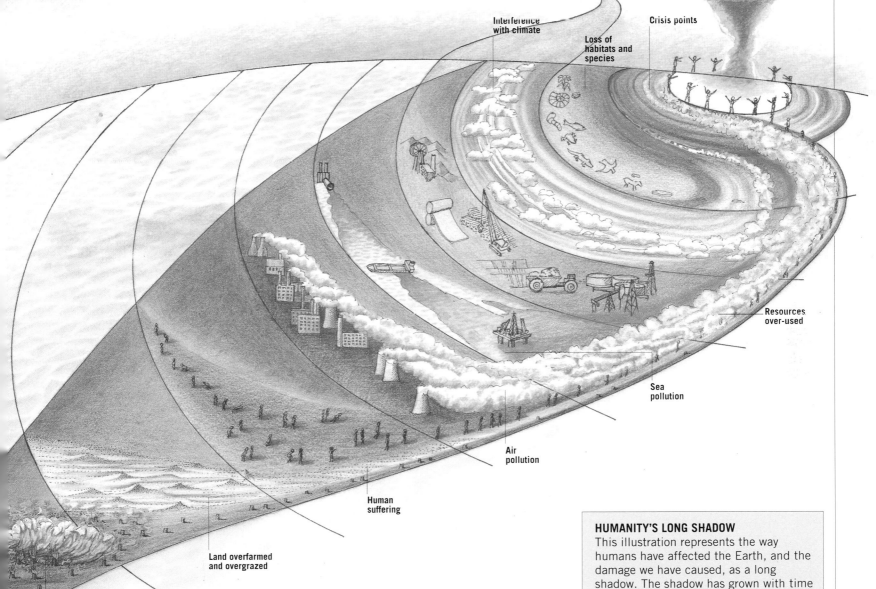

Final catastrophe?

Interference with climate

Loss of habitats and species

Crisis points

Resources over-used

Sea pollution

Air pollution

Human suffering

Land overfarmed and overgrazed

Forest destruction

HUMANITY'S LONG SHADOW
This illustration represents the way humans have affected the Earth, and the damage we have caused, as a long shadow. The shadow has grown with time as the human population has expanded and the power of our technologies has multiplied. At the far end of the shadow, disaster seems to wait for us, perhaps in the form of nuclear war. Surely we can change our ways in time to avoid catastrophe.

I
LAND

"Whatever befalls the Earth befalls the sons of the Earth . . . . The Earth does not belong to man: man belongs to the Earth . . . . Care for the land as we have cared for it . . . . Preserve it for your children and love it."

CHIEF SEATTLE,
leader of the Duwamish Native
Americans, 1854

We have no home other than the land. Its plants, animals, and fresh water maintain the air we breathe and provide our food and drink. The fuel and power we use for cooking and heating come directly from trees, or indirectly from the buried, fossilized remains of long-dead creatures and plants, in the form of coal, gas, and oil. Or we harness the power of the Sun, wind, rivers, and waves, using machines that we build from minerals taken from the ground. We also make our buildings, clothes, and possessions from materials on or below the land surface. In the end, everything we have and everything we need depends, in some way, on the land.

Terraces in Banaue, in northern Luzon in the Philippines, enable rice farmers to make intensive use of steep hillsides.

FERTILE SOIL

Next time you are out in a garden, in a park, or in the countryside, think about what is under your feet. Just boring old "earth," "dirt," or "mud"? Maybe. But this thin layer on the planet's surface is essential to all living things. Without the soil, there would be no plants or animals on the land. We had better learn how best to look after it.

LAND AND SOIL TYPES

Every continent has different types of soil. Some are well suited to growing crops, but many are not. The diagram shows the world divided into eight land "slices" (continents or regions), the size of each slice reflecting the relative size of that region. It shows six main types of soil and how much of each there is in each region. Of the six soil types, only one is fertile (suitable for growing crops). The percentages show how much of each soil type there is on Earth (excluding Antarctica and Greenland).

- Year-round frozen soil: 6%
- Dry and desert soil: 28%
- Waterlogged soil: 10%
- Soil lacking chemicals needed for plant growth: 23%
- Shallow soil: 22%
- Fertile soil, suitable for cultivation (crop growing): 11%

The pie chart for each continent or region shows how much of the land people use for crops and grazing animals, and how much is forest. It also shows the percentage of other kinds of land, such as waste land, wild land, built-up areas, and roads.

- Cropland
- Forest land
- Grazing land for animals
- Other land

▶ **In North and Central America** more than a fifth of the land is suitable for crops, but less than half of the fertile land is farmed. Buildings and roads cover much good soil in the USA.

North and Central America

13% / 16% / 32% / 39%

South America

▲ **South America** has large areas of soil lacking many of the chemicals needed by plants, especially in the forest regions. Farmers use less than half the area of fertile soil for growing crops.

7% / 26% / 54% / 13%

What is soil?

Soil is the uppermost layer of the land surface. It is made up of tiny grains of rock, water, and air. It also contains the remains of dead plants and animals – known as litter before rotting and humus after rotting. Humus is one of the most important ingredients of a fertile soil. Soil is essential for plant growth, providing many chemicals that plants need. The topsoil, nearest the surface, is rich in humus; lower down is the mineral-rich subsoil. Below this is the underlying rock. Roots grow between soil particles to get water, air, and chemicals.

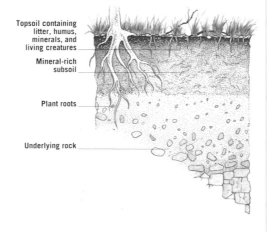

Topsoil containing litter, humus, minerals, and living creatures

Mineral-rich subsoil

Plant roots

Underlying rock

There is a lot more life in a handful of soil than at first meets the eye. At its best, soil is as full of activity and as fascinating as a rainforest or a coral reef. One acre of soil may contain up to 120 million mini-beasts such as earthworms, mites, and millipedes. It also contains a vast number of tiny bacteria, algae, and fungi – which are commonly known as microbes. All these living things help to convert complex chemicals in soil into forms that plants can

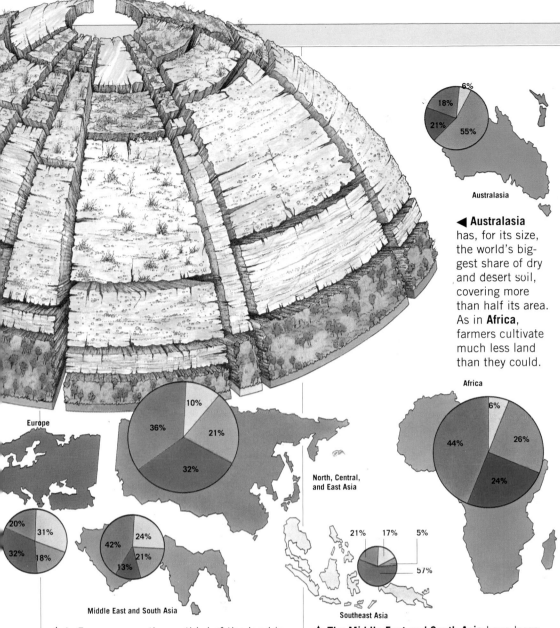

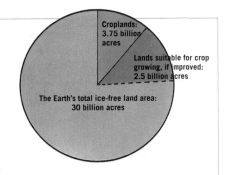

Croplands:
3.75 billion
acres

Lands suitable for crop
growing, if improved:
2.5 billion acres

The Earth's total ice-free land area:
30 billion acres

Australasia

▲ **Australasia** has, for its size, the world's biggest share of dry and desert soil, covering more than half its area. As in **Africa**, farmers cultivate much less land than they could.

Africa

Europe

North, Central, and East Asia

Middle East and South Asia

Southeast Asia

How much land do we cultivate?
People grow crops on just over a tenth of the ice-free land surface. With hard work, money, and the right tools we could perhaps double this area.

◄ **Much of Africa** suffers badly from a lack of rainfall, which makes almost half the land too dry for crops. But African farmers use only about a third of the area that is suitable for cultivation.

◄ **North, Central, and East Asia** make up a huge region, but much of the soil is unsuitable for cultivation. More than half the area is too cold or has very thin topsoil. Only a tenth of the land is good for growing crops.

◄ **Southeast Asia** has large areas of poor-quality tropical forest soil. Crops cover almost a fifth of the land, not all of which is naturally suited to farming.

▲ **In Europe**, more than a third of the land is suitable for cultivation. Crops are grown on almost all this land. Compared to its small size as a continent, Europe has the world's largest area of fertile soil.

▲ **The Middle East and South Asia** have large areas of dry land or desert and thin soil. Less than a fifth of the land is suitable for crops; but people use irrigation water to farm almost a quarter of the land.

take in to help them grow.

Soil varies in quality from region to region, even field to field. To be suitable for growing crops, all the nutrients (ingredients necessary for plants to thrive) must be present and in the right amounts. In some parts of the world the soil has too much water and not enough air (as in marshland) or too little water (as in desert) to be fertile. Other soils lack sufficient humus, topsoil, or living creatures.

In tropical forests nutrients do not stay in the soil but are quickly taken up by the lush vegetation. In places where people have used modern farming methods over a long period, the soil may contain too few microbes, or have lost important minerals after intensive use, or have been spoiled by too many human-made chemicals. In cold regions the soil may be frozen solid — known as permafrost — or be too shallow to allow plants to put down roots.

Soil loss and soil gain
Living and dead plants, animals, and microbes make up only a tiny fraction of soil's weight. Most of the soil consists of small grains of rock, which rainwater, wind, ice, gases in the air, and plant roots have broken down from larger rocks. When a river washes away material, it can deposit a sediment 12 in. deep downstream over 50 years. But when new soil forms by the erosion (wearing away) of rock, it can take 1000 years to create just 0.4 in. of soil. So 4 in. of soil could take 10,000 years to form — almost as long as recorded human history.

PLANT LIFE

Plants are very important to humans. They feed us, clothe us, and help make the air fit to breathe. Plants also help provide water to drink, materials for building and making things, and medicines to take when we are ill. Without plants, we could not live. But plants are not evenly distributed either on the land or in the sea.

Without the Earth's covering of vegetation (plants), there would be no animal life. Millions of years ago, the first plants began to change the gases around the Earth — the atmosphere — by increasing the amount of oxygen. All animals need to breathe oxygen to live.

Plants use the energy of sunlight to build up their own supplies of chemical energy, which in turn provide animals with food. All animals either eat plants or feed on other animals that do.

Plants protect the soil from being worn away by wind or rain, and from drying up in the sun. Their roots take up water from the ground and their leaves let it evaporate into the air. This calms or moderates local weather slightly — so conditions are not too dry or too hot — keeping it pleasant for animals and for people. Plants also give us useful materials, ranging from wood and straw for building, to textiles for clothing, and dyes and medicines.

Sparse, scrubby vegetation is typical of the landscape in much of North Africa, as here in northern Tokar, Sudan.

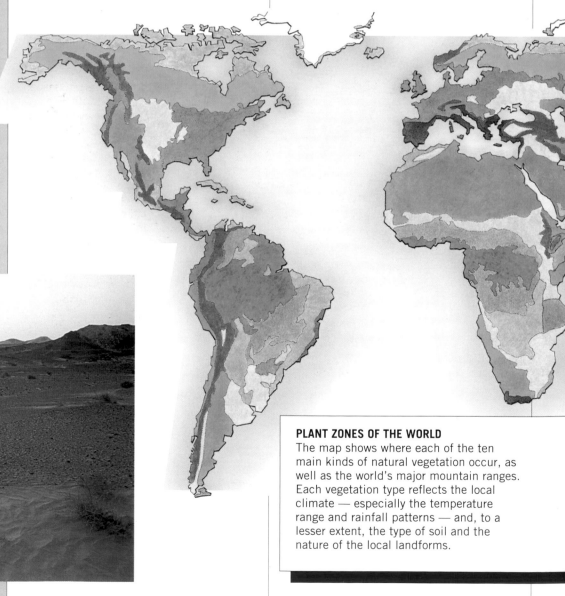

PLANT ZONES OF THE WORLD
The map shows where each of the ten main kinds of natural vegetation occur, as well as the world's major mountain ranges. Each vegetation type reflects the local climate — especially the temperature range and rainfall patterns — and, to a lesser extent, the type of soil and the nature of the local landforms.

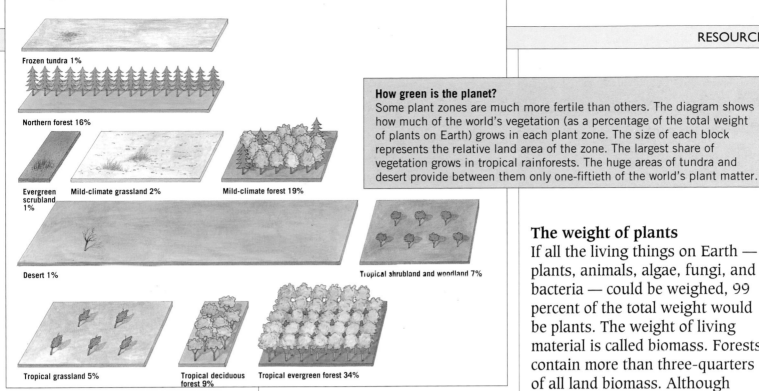

Frozen tundra 1%

Northern forest 16%

Evergreen scrubland 1%

Mild-climate grassland 2%

Mild-climate forest 19%

Desert 1%

Tropical shrubland and woodland 7%

Tropical grassland 5%

Tropical deciduous forest 9%

Tropical evergreen forest 34%

How green is the planet?
Some plant zones are much more fertile than others. The diagram shows how much of the world's vegetation (as a percentage of the total weight of plants on Earth) grows in each plant zone. The size of each block represents the relative land area of the zone. The largest share of vegetation grows in tropical rainforests. The huge areas of tundra and desert provide between them only one-fiftieth of the world's plant matter.

The weight of plants
If all the living things on Earth — plants, animals, algae, fungi, and bacteria — could be weighed, 99 percent of the total weight would be plants. The weight of living material is called biomass. Forests contain more than three-quarters of all land biomass. Although tropical forests cover less than a tenth of the planet's surface, they contain more than half of the land biomass. Farmers' crops make up only about 0.5 percent of the total weight of living plants.

Plants grow fastest in the tropical forests, which account for nearly a quarter of new plant growth every year. Tropical regions produce new plant material more than twice as quickly as mild-climate zones, and more than four times as fast as northern forests.

Understanding plant zones
The northern frozen tundra is close to the Arctic: few plants grow there. The northern forests of Canada, Europe, and North Asia have tall cone-bearing trees. Mild-climate forests, found mainly in North America, Europe, and North and East Asia, have a mixture of evergreen and deciduous (leaf-shedding) trees.

Mild-climate grasslands include the plains of North and South America, Central Asia, and South Africa. The dry evergreen scrubland zones of the southern USA, Mexico, and southern Europe have short, tough plants. The world's deserts — in the Americas, Africa, the Middle East, Central Asia, and Australia — are very dry zones where few plants survive.

The jungles of Central and South America, Central Africa, and Southeast Asia are tropical evergreen rainforest. In Southeast Asia's tropical deciduous forest, trees lose their leaves during the dry season. Tropical shrub and woodland have fewer trees and more open space than tropical forest. Tropical grassland has even fewer trees.

Photosynthesis and energy
Plant growth depends on a process called photosynthesis (literally, "building with light"). A green substance in the leaves – chlorophyll – absorbs energy from sunlight. Plants use this energy to combine carbon dioxide gas from the air, water from the soil, and small amounts of other chemicals to make carbohydrates, which include sugars and starch. From carbohydrates plants make fats and proteins, which are needed by them to stay alive. During the process of photosynthesis, plants give off oxygen into the air. Large areas of vegetation are therefore very good regulators of oxygen and carbon dioxide levels in the atmosphere.

Mountain ranges	Desert
Frozen tundra	Tropical evergreen forest
Northern forest	Tropical deciduous forest
Mild-climate forest	Tropical shrubland and woodland
Mild-climate grassland	Tropical grassland
Evergreen scrubland	

GLOBAL FOREST

Forests and woodlands are one of the planet's greatest natural resources. They provide us with wood to make into paper and to use as a fuel for cooking and heating, and as a building material. They even supply us with substances to make into medicines. Forests are also host to an enormous variety of animals and plants.

HOME ACTION

We need more trees everywhere, and trees need friends. Here are some ways you can help.

- Care for trees by watering them during dry weather and clearing away any weeds around them.
- Tell your municipal authorities if you think somebody is going to damage or destroy a tree.
- Learn more about trees.
- Collect seeds such as acorns, and raise seedlings in your own tree nursery.
- Plant native trees in your garden, at your school or community center, or on patches of waste ground.
- Buy or sponsor a tree for somebody as a birthday or anniversary present.
- Support an organization that campaigns to protect and plant trees.

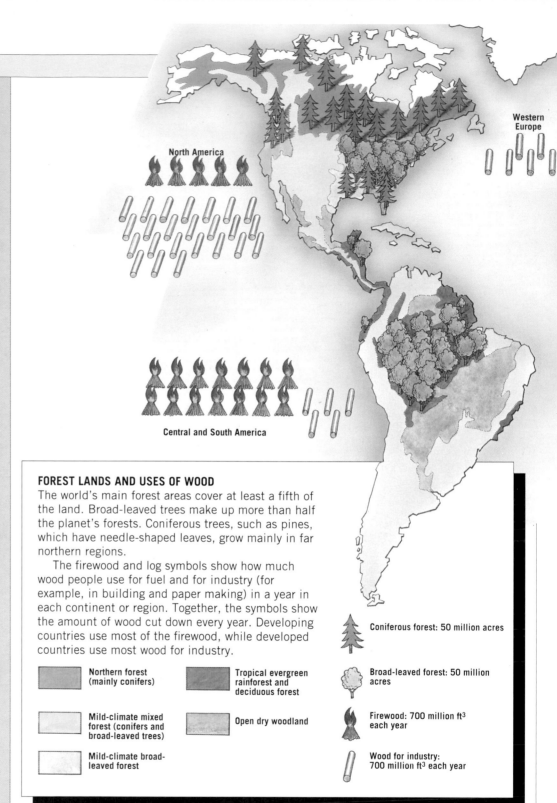

North America

Western Europe

Central and South America

FOREST LANDS AND USES OF WOOD

The world's main forest areas cover at least a fifth of the land. Broad-leaved trees make up more than half the planet's forests. Coniferous trees, such as pines, which have needle-shaped leaves, grow mainly in far northern regions.

The firewood and log symbols show how much wood people use for fuel and for industry (for example, in building and paper making) in a year in each continent or region. Together, the symbols show the amount of wood cut down every year. Developing countries use most of the firewood, while developed countries use most wood for industry.

- Northern forest (mainly conifers)
- Mild-climate mixed forest (conifers and broad-leaved trees)
- Mild-climate broad-leaved forest
- Tropical evergreen rainforest and deciduous forest
- Open dry woodland

Coniferous forest: 50 million acres

Broad-leaved forest: 50 million acres

Firewood: 700 million ft³ each year

Wood for industry: 700 million ft³ each year

Forests and woodlands cover about a quarter of the planet's land surface, ranging from the huge tropical rainforests of the Amazon in South America, to the equally impressive forests of coniferous (cone-bearing) trees in Siberia, North Asia. The Earth's forests contain the richest variety of plants and animals anywhere on land, and the oldest and largest living things — trees. Oak, redwood, and yew trees live for hundreds, sometimes thousands, of years. They may tower above us, or have trunks large enough for people to live in. Tropical forests are millions of years old.

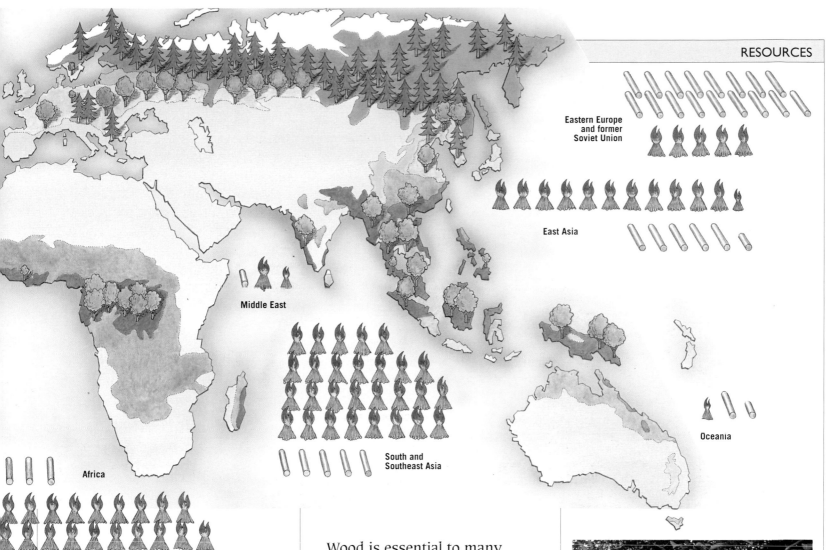

Eastern Europe
and former
Soviet Union

East Asia

Middle East

South and
Southeast Asia

Africa

Oceania

Tropical rainforest in Indonesia *displays the many levels of plant life that are typical of this vegetation zone.*

The value of trees

Besides being impressive in themselves, forests and their trees are important in very many ways. They are the world's great centers of photosynthesis, the process by which all plants grow. The roots and leaves of trees transport water from the soil to the air, helping to maintain a climate suitable for other living things, and to clean polluted air. They protect the soil from erosion and overheating, and feed it with their falling leaves. They protect the sources of rivers and help to prevent flooding. Finally, they shelter the nesting and breeding sites of many animal species, and forests are home to about 200 million people throughout the world.

Wood is essential to many aspects of our lives and probably more important for human civilization than any other material. Without it, we could not make all the paper we need. Trees provide fuel for cooking and heating for about half the world's people. Far less energy is needed to work with wood than cement, plastic, or metal. The walls of a wooden house provide better insulation (preventing heat escaping and cold air entering) than most other materials. Many everyday things that we take for granted — medicines such as aspirin, for example — also come from trees.

Forests hold secrets that we have yet to discover. Who knows how many new plant and animal species, and new uses for forest products, people will discover in the future — if forests survive?

SHRINKING FORESTS

As you read this page, an area of tropical rainforest larger than an Olympic Games sports stadium is being destroyed — by burning, being hacked down tree by tree with a chain saw, or being bulldozed out of existence. Most people agree that this destruction is wrong, but so far nobody has managed to stop it.

Every year people destroy about 43 million acres of tropical forest and woodland — an area twice the size of Austria — and badly damage another 12.5 million acres or more of tropical forest. Worldwide, trees are disappearing ten times faster than people are planting them.

People everywhere want more wood. In developing countries the main need is for firewood, and local communities take what they need for their own use. These developing countries also use their tropical forests to earn much-needed money. They sell timber to developed countries, which use enormous quantities for building and industrial activities. Even if big businesses, rather than local inhabitants, cut down the trees using careful methods of forestry, they can still cause serious damage.

A forest that has lost most, but not all, of its trees can usually grow back, given enough time. But this process may take 100 years or more, and often it is not given a chance. Once a logging company has built roads into a forest, poor people who have nowhere to live, or richer people greedy for more land, may move in and clear the remaining trees. All these activities also threaten the lives of the people originally living in the forest.

The need for wood does not tell the whole story. Huge areas of tropical forest disappear when countries build giant dams, set up large mining operations, or clear land for commercial farming. Most of these activities happen because developing countries see them as a way of making themselves richer. Yet these activities cause more problems than they solve.

Will forests survive?
The area of land covered by forest has shrunk dramatically during the last 45 years. In 1950, forest covered almost a third of the Earth's land surface, divided equally between tropical forest and mild-climate forest. By 1975, the area of tropical forest was noticeably smaller. By the end of the century, tropical forest will probably cover only a third of the area it covered 50 years ago. Forest in mild-climate regions has stayed about the same, mainly because the richer, developed countries of these zones are better able to protect and replant their trees than the developing countries of tropical regions.

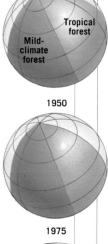

FORESTS UNDER ATTACK
The red zones show where human activity is destroying forests fastest. Forests are most at risk in Central and South America, Central Africa, South and Southeast Asia, and eastern Australia.

Cattle graze in Amazonas, Brazil, on land once covered with trees.

When the forests have gone

Tropical forest soils are unsuitable either for growing crops or raising cattle. Once the trees have gone, the heavy rains typical of these regions wash nutrients out of the soils, and there are no longer falling leaves to feed them. The soils become depleted and useless after just a few years of heavy farming.

Sometimes land never recovers from forest destruction. Stripped bare, the soil may bake to a hard, dry crust. In hilly or mountainous areas, the loss of trees can cause landslides, burying people alive or sweeping away their homes. With the trees gone, rivers may not flow as steadily. Their courses and volume of water may vary, causing floods, such as those that have killed hundreds of thousands of people in Bangladesh. Cities that depend on river water may find their supplies running dangerously low, as in some developing countries today, and local climates may change. The low rainfall in Africa in recent years may be connected to the loss of tree cover.

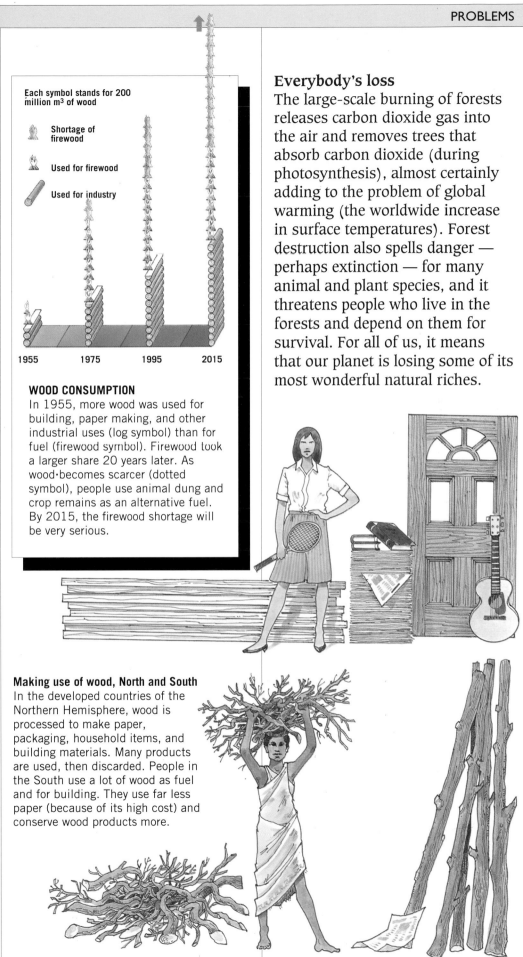

Each symbol stands for 200 million m³ of wood

Shortage of firewood

Used for firewood

Used for industry

1955   1975   1995   2015

WOOD CONSUMPTION
In 1955, more wood was used for building, paper making, and other industrial uses (log symbol) than for fuel (firewood symbol). Firewood took a larger share 20 years later. As wood·becomes scarcer (dotted symbol), people use animal dung and crop remains as an alternative fuel. By 2015, the firewood shortage will be very serious.

Making use of wood, North and South
In the developed countries of the Northern Hemisphere, wood is processed to make paper, packaging, household items, and building materials. Many products are used, then discarded. People in the South use a lot of wood as fuel and for building. They use far less paper (because of its high cost) and conserve wood products more.

Everybody's loss

The large-scale burning of forests releases carbon dioxide gas into the air and removes trees that absorb carbon dioxide (during photosynthesis), almost certainly adding to the problem of global warming (the worldwide increase in surface temperatures). Forest destruction also spells danger — perhaps extinction — for many animal and plant species, and it threatens people who live in the forests and depend on them for survival. For all of us, it means that our planet is losing some of its most wonderful natural riches.

23

SOIL LOSS

Sand can be fun at the seaside, and it has its uses in industry. But if you have ever tried to grow plants in sand, or have been in a sandstorm, you will know that if all our soil turned to sand we would be in serious trouble.

Rivers build islands
A large landmass is forming under the sea in the Bay of Bengal, south of Bangladesh, as a result of trees being chopped down on the lower slopes of mountains hundreds of miles away. Every year, thousands of tons of topsoil are washed off the Himalayan mountainsides and hills and carried by the Brahmaputra and Ganges rivers across India and Bangladesh to the bay. The landmass will surface above sea level in about 15 years.

In parts of North and Central America dry lands are becoming more desert-like as people raise large numbers of cattle on soils unsuitable for grazing.

Expanding deserts
There are five main regions of hot, dry desert in the world, colored gray on the map: the Atacama (South America), the Sahara and Kalahari deserts (Africa), the Arabian Desert (Middle East), and the Gobi Desert (East Asia). Lands nearby and elsewhere are becoming more desert-like. This occurs when people strip the land of trees and farm poor soils, growing crops and grazing animals too heavily.

Lands at risk of becoming desert

In South America many poor people are forced to grow their food on poor, thin soils without being able to improve their farming methods.

Atacama Desert

Ice-free land area: 33.75 billion acres (100%)

Existing desert: 2 billion acres (6%)

Medium risk of becoming desert: 4.375 billion acres (13%)

High risk of becoming desert: 4 billion acres (12%)

Very high risk of becoming desert: 1 billion acres (3%)

SPREADING SANDS
More than a third of the ice-free land surface (outer circle) is already desert or at risk of becoming desert-like in the future. The colors on the map reflect the same risk categories as the diagram.

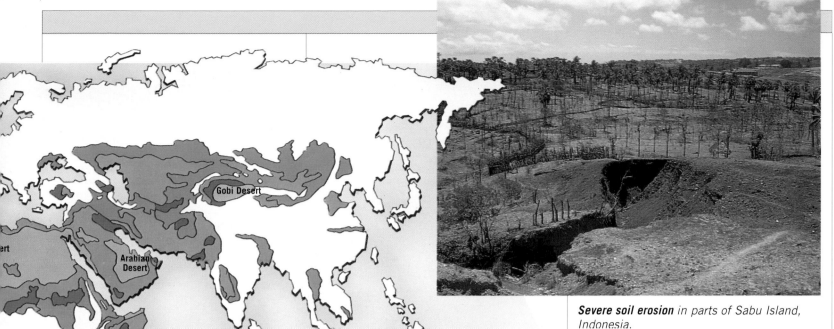

Gobi Desert

Arabian Desert

Kalahari Desert

In Asia about a third of the land is at risk of becoming desert, mainly because it is farmed too heavily and because irrigation water is badly managed.

In Africa land is becoming more desert-like in several very dry regions as people cut down trees, grow more food crops, and raise larger herds of animals.

Severe soil erosion in parts of Sabu Island, Indonesia.

In Australia the increase in desert conditions is happening only very slowly, but in much of the country grazing animals are seriously damaging the land.

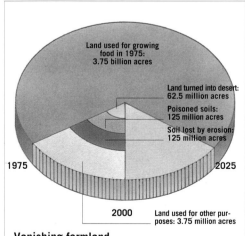

Land used for growing food in 1975: 3.75 billion acres

Land turned into desert: 62.5 million acres

Poisoned soils: 125 million acres

Soil lost by erosion: 125 million acres

1975

2025

2000

Land used for other purposes: 3.75 million acres

Vanishing farmland
By the year 2000, we may have lost almost a fifth of the land on which we grew food in 1975 (represented by the full circle), and who knows how much more by 2025? The main causes are the spread of deserts, soils harmed by salt and chemicals, wind and rain erosion, and changing land use.

The Earth's land surface is losing soil at a frighteningly fast rate. Every year, wind and rain erode millions of tons of earth worldwide, blowing it into the air or washing it into rivers, and finally dumping it in lakes and oceans, from where it cannot be recovered. This affects tropical regions more than others. Ethiopia, for example, loses as much topsoil each year as the USA, which is six times larger.

The felling of trees and other natural protection against wind and rain can lead to soil erosion. Seasonal flooding or the drying of local climates can also increase the risk of erosion. Farmers add to the risk by grazing large herds of animals on poor soils or by using

chemicals and machines that damage the soil. Farmland also suffers when farmers use irrigation (artificial watering) without good drainage. Soils may become waterlogged or damaged by salt and other chemicals.

In dry zones, large areas are becoming of poorer quality and therefore less suitable for cultivation. This is known as "dry land degradation" or "desertification." It happens when people try to grow more crops than the dry, semi-desert soils can sustain, or graze more animals on the land than it can support. The loss of land for growing crops was one cause of the famines in Africa's Sahel region in the 1970s and 1980s.

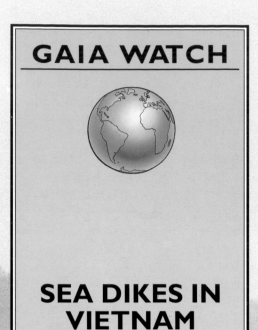
Every year the coast of Vietnam is lashed by tropical storms and typhoons. The area around Ky Anh, in central Vietnam, suffers badly, with the loss of lives, homes, crops, and animals. There is barely time to recover before the next typhoon season begins.

Nguyen Van Tu has vivid memories of Typhoon Becky, which struck in 1990: "All we could do when we saw how the sea was rising was to pick up our children and set out into the darkness towards dry land. I had to force my way through water that was up to my neck in places."

The rice paddies of Ky Anh lie in the narrow area of land between the mountains and the sea. Often they are flooded by the sea, making the soil salty and infertile. It takes years before the soil produces healthy crops, causing food

The long coastline of Vietnam is constantly battered by storms, during which the sea used to flood low-lying farmland between the coast and the mountains. Paddy fields and vegetable and fruit crops were destroyed.

▲ *People carried soil* to the site, where it was pressed firmly into position by machine. The slope facing the sea was covered with large, carefully placed rocks to protect it from waves. The landward slope was planted with grass.

shortages and hunger. An early-warning system helps to save lives, but the people of Ky Anh needed something to protect their land.

The answer was to build dikes along the coast to hold back the sea and protect the valuable soil. There had been dikes in the area before, but they had been bombed during the Vietnam War (1965–73) and neglected since. Now they were easily breached by the sea.

Redesign and a rebuilding program were much needed.

Help arrived in the form of engineers from Hanoi Water Resources University, who assessed the problems and designed a better, stronger dike. They trained local people in new building methods. The work was done by teams of volunteers, working on the dike nearest their community. Along much of the

length of the dikes on the seaward side, communities are planting mangrove trees. These will provide extra protection against the waves.

By 1995 nearly half the 39 miles of dikes had been rebuilt, protecting more than 35,000 people and their land. It will be 1999 before the soil has completely recovered, but people are able to plant crops again, knowing they are safe from the sea.

▲ *Once local technicians and workteam leaders had been trained, some 3000 people from local communities set to work rebuilding the 10-mile long embankment.*

▶ *Rice is the most important crop in Ky Anh. Flooding used to leave the paddy fields full of salt. This caused low crop yields, which in turn meant food shortages for the people of Ky Anh.*

27

GOOD USE OF LAND

If you have ever been in the open countryside on a hot day, you will know how important a shady tree can be. Trees need soil to grow in, and people need soil and woodland to survive. There are important ways to make sure that future generations have plenty of both.

Penan forest people protest against commercial logging in the rainforest of Sarawak in Malaysia.

One of the best ways to protect land and forests is to help local people look after them. Damage to soil and trees often happens when local people lose control over their land, such as when a government or company wants to clear land to grow food, usually to sell abroad.

Some people argue that the protection of forests in developed countries is less of a problem, as these countries can afford to buy wood from abroad. By recycling paper and using less tropical wood, however, developed countries can help conserve trees worldwide.

In developing countries, local people who have a fair share of the use of forests look after them well. Many governments encourage local people to protect the forests and replant them, using multipurpose trees that provide firewood, food for animals, building timber, and other useful materials. Replanting bare hillsides with trees helps stop floods and landslides, and stabilizes streams and rivers.

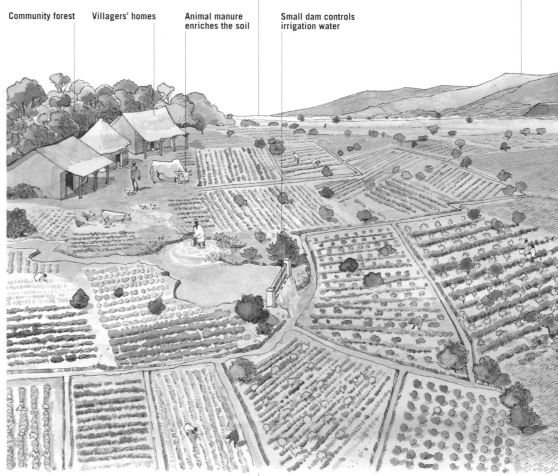

Community forest   Villagers' homes   Animal manure enriches the soil   Small dam controls irrigation water

Good soils allow people to grow a wide range of food crops, especially if they irrigate them with water, raise different crops together — often in the same field — and rotate (change around) the crops in each field each year. Organic material, such as crop remains and animal manure, enriches the soil. Trees and hedges (including fruit- and nut-producing varieties) can grow in the fields.

Medium-quality land is most suitable for crops such as legumes (peas and beans) and sweet corn. Farmers can grow peanut and cowpea (a tropical climbing plant with long pods containing pea-like seeds), which enrich the soil as well as providing fodder (food) for animals. Poorer-quality soils need fallow (rest) periods between plantings of crops to allow them to recover.

Community forest
In Kenya, India, and many other developing countries, local people are involved in raising seedlings and setting up plantations of new multipurpose trees. Many plans are supported by international development agencies. Local people are often the best protectors of existing forest in and around their village, as long as they can use it for their own needs.

On hillsides farmers can build terraces (narrow, flat areas, stepped up the slope) on which they grow crops. Terracing prevents the creep of soil downhill. Small numbers of hardy breeds of sheep and goats can graze dry hillsides without causing damage.

Conserving the environment
Local people need help from governments to prevent soil erosion and the spread of deserts. Some need money and machinery, others the advice of agricultural scientists or engineers. Planting trees, using irrigation on a small scale, farming organically (without artificial chemicals), and choosing the right crops and animals for their land, all help to conserve that land and create jobs.

If damaged or overused land is to recover, people in developed countries should not demand too much for themselves, while those in developing countries must have what they need to survive.

LOOKING AFTER THE LAND
This landscape, set in an imaginary developing country, shows ways of making good use of the land, while at the same time preventing the loss of soil and the spread of desert. The landscape ranges from fertile cropland (in the far left of the diagram) to dry, almost lifeless desert (far right). In each area — except for the natural desert, which people usually cannot farm — a good choice of crops and careful methods help farmers conserve and maintain healthy soil.

Dry grassland is better for grazing animals than growing crops. If people raise animals just to serve local needs, and move the herds from one place to another, the land is unlikely to become overgrazed and the soil poor. Planting clover and other such grasses feeds the soil. Carefully chosen tree species provide firewood and extra animal fodder, and protect the soil from erosion.

Rows of trees planted along tracks and roads protect the land from wind and rain, and provide other useful products, including firewood. At the edge of the natural desert (to the right of the diagram), suitable hardy trees and shrubs, including those that supply rubber, wax, and wood, will hold back the spread of the sand dunes and make the best use of poor-quality land.

29

2
FOOD AND FARMING

"Give me an oak forest and I will give you pots full of milk and baskets full of grain."
    Song of women in Reni, northern India, who are protecting forests

The demands made by ever-increasing numbers of people on the world's farmland have created a range of problems. Modern farming methods damage the soil and use up precious resources, such as fresh water that has taken thousands of years to collect in underground rocks. Large-scale, commercial farming makes some people enormously rich and overfeeds many on unhealthy diets, while leaving millions of others homeless, poor, and hungry. It relies on chemicals that pollute our world and depends on resources that may not last another century. It has led to a huge loss of wild species worldwide and to large areas of countryside becoming near-lifeless deserts or open-air food-production factories. But help is at hand in the form of different – but not always new – ways of growing our food. Can we meet the challenge and make the future of farming a success for everyone?

Large-scale, highly mechanized "prairie" wheat farming can cause severe soil erosion, and creates very few jobs.

CROPS & CROPLANDS

Much of what we eat today will become part of our bodies tomorrow; and, apart from fish and seafood, it all comes from the land. Using the land wisely is therefore as important as looking after our physical health, because unhealthy land cannot produce good food. How healthy is the land today and how much food can we grow on it?

DID YOU KNOW?

What are cereals?

All cereal crops are members of the grass family of plants. People grow them for their large edible seed-heads, called grains, which provide over half the food energy in the human diet. People use cereals in many different ways. We can cook them (rice, for example) or grind them into flour to make pasta or bread (wheat and rye, for example). We can give some grains, such as corn, barley, and oats, to animals to eat, and process others, including barley and rice, into cooking oils and drinks.

THE WORLD'S MAIN CROPS

Most of our food grows in the Northern Hemisphere. The lighter-colored areas of the map show the location of the better croplands. Each food symbol represents a harvest of 10 million tons a year, and the different foods are identified at the foot of the page. Asia is the leading producer of wheat, rice, and pulses such as soybeans; Europe grows the most potatoes; and North America produces the most corn. South America, Africa, and Oceania are less productive regions. The pie charts show how much land on each continent could be farmed, and how much actually is cultivated. Barrels and sacks represent quantities of fertilizer used and the size of harvests.

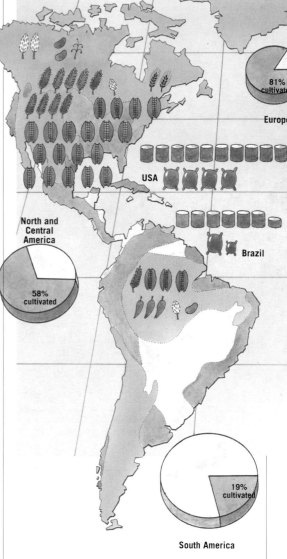

Farming began about 10,000 years ago in the Middle East and parts of Asia, as people started to settle along the river valleys and to grow crops and raise animals. This was one of the most important changes in human history. Croplands now cover 3.7 billion acres worldwide (about one-and-a-half times the area of the USA). Differences in soil and climate allow food crops to grow better in some places than in others. The milder climates and richer soils of much of Europe, North America, and Asia make them more suitable for farming than the dry, harsh conditions of much of Africa, the Middle East, and Oceania.

Modern technology can bring water to dry regions, and there are good traditional methods of making poor soils more fertile. But many people in developing countries cannot afford to pay for the improvements their land needs.

Feeding the world

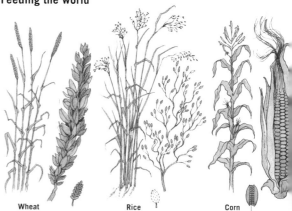

Wheat, the world's biggest cereal crop, grows best in mild areas. **Rice** is Asia's main crop. By growing it in semi-flooded fields, farmers produce food all year. **Corn** is a major part of the diet in South America and Africa. Most US corn is fed to animals.

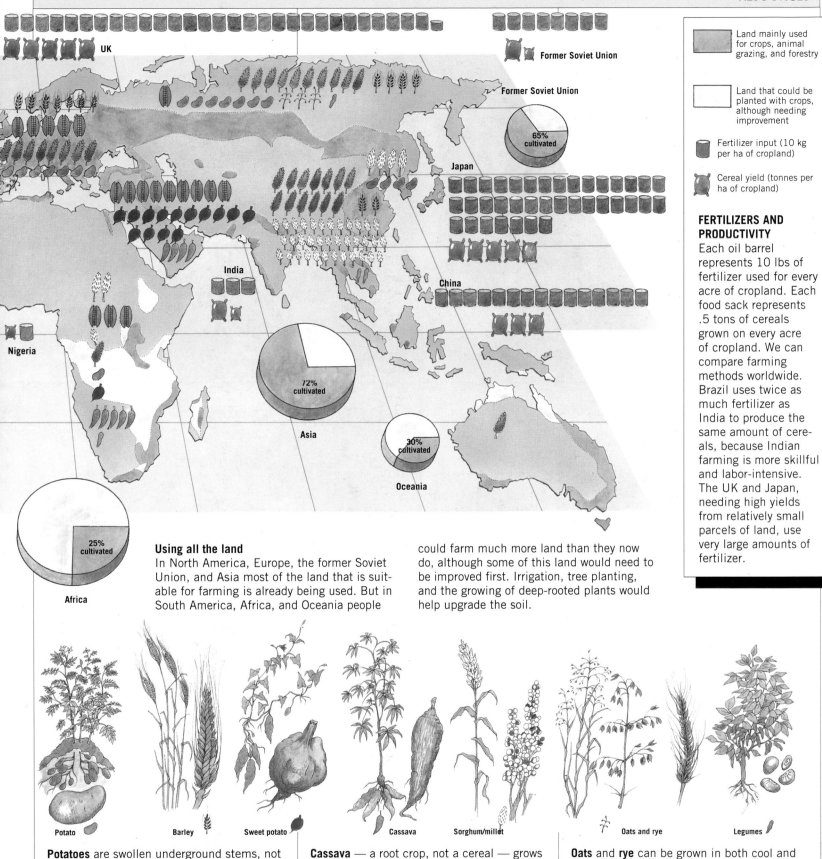

UK

Former Soviet Union

Former Soviet Union

65% cultivated

Japan

India

China

Nigeria

72% cultivated

Asia

30% cultivated

Oceania

25% cultivated

Africa

Legend:

Land mainly used for crops, animal grazing, and forestry

Land that could be planted with crops, although needing improvement

Fertilizer input (10 kg per ha of cropland)

Cereal yield (tonnes per ha of cropland)

FERTILIZERS AND PRODUCTIVITY

Each oil barrel represents 10 lbs of fertilizer used for every acre of cropland. Each food sack represents .5 tons of cereals grown on every acre of cropland. We can compare farming methods worldwide. Brazil uses twice as much fertilizer as India to produce the same amount of cereals, because Indian farming is more skillful and labor-intensive. The UK and Japan, needing high yields from relatively small parcels of land, use very large amounts of fertilizer.

Using all the land

In North America, Europe, the former Soviet Union, and Asia most of the land that is suitable for farming is already being used. But in South America, Africa, and Oceania people could farm much more land than they now do, although some of this land would need to be improved first. Irrigation, tree planting, and the growing of deep-rooted plants would help upgrade the soil.

Potato

Barley

Sweet potato

Cassava

Sorghum/millet

Oats and rye

Legumes

Potatoes are swollen underground stems, not cereals. They grow best in cool, mild climates. **Barley,** a major cereal crop, is used mainly for animal feed and to make beer and whiskey. **Sweet potatoes** grow in warm, damp areas of Africa, the Caribbean, and Asia.

Cassava — a root crop, not a cereal — grows well in dry climates, but is much less nutritious than most cereals. **Sorghum** and **millet**, two closely related cereals, grow well in hot, dry regions. The grains lack gluten and cannot be used for bread-making.

Oats and **rye** can be grown in both cool and damp climates. Oats are mainly fed to animals, and rye is used mostly for making bread. **Legumes** — beans and peas that form in pods — are important in developing countries. Soybeans are a major crop in Asia.

ANIMALS FOR FOOD

People all over the world rely on farm animals for meat, milk, and eggs that are rich in nutrients, as well as for other products such as wool. Worldwide, the area of land used by grazing (grass-eating) animals is double the area we use to grow crops, although some animals, such as goats, can survive on poor-quality food.

By converting plants that people cannot eat into useful energy, domesticated animals provide a valuable contribution to the human diet. Yet there are problems. Some grasslands are overgrazed: too many animals strip the land bare, making it vulnerable to erosion.

Do you like burgers? Lots of people do. In many countries the beef for burgers comes from cattle fed on soybeans. Much of the soybean crop — which people, as well as cattle, can eat — is grown in Brazil, where hundreds of thousands of children go hungry. Raising animals for food brings benefits for many people, but problems for others.

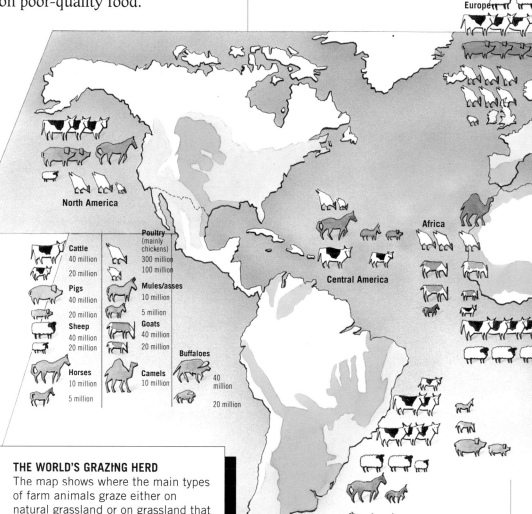

THE WORLD'S GRAZING HERD
The map shows where the main types of farm animals graze either on natural grassland or on grassland that people have planted or cleared. These regions are distributed quite evenly between the northern and southern hemispheres. Only nine types of domesticated animal provide nearly all the animal protein in the human diet. The size of the symbols reflects the number of animals in each region.

Natural grassland

Planted or cleared grassland

Worldwide distribution
Domesticated animals (those kept under human control) graze and forage for food over almost half the ice-free land surface of the Earth — about 15 billion acres. This includes some forests, semi-deserts, and mountain areas.

On the high plains of Bolivia, llamas are reared for meat, milk, and hides.

Animals reared intensively on "factory farms" not only lead confined lives, but often consume food that people could have eaten. Land used to provide meat for rich people far away could provide farms on which poor local people could grow their own food.

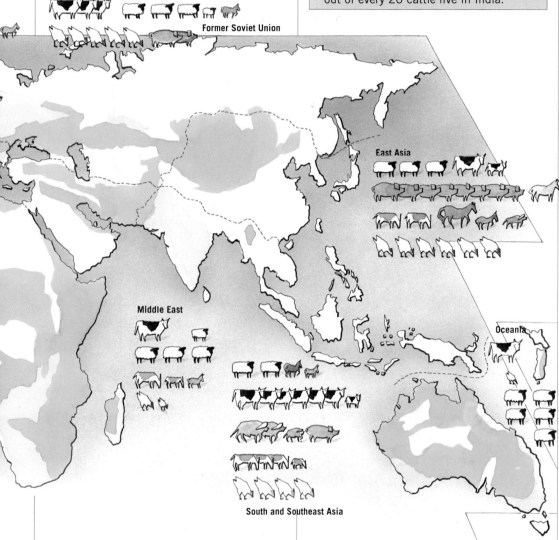

Former Soviet Union

East Asia

Middle East

Oceania

South and Southeast Asia

Low-grade feeders, such as camels, goats, upland sheep, and free-range chickens, can survive on poor-quality land and food scraps, converting them into useful food energy.

Medium-grade feeders, such as most Western cattle and lowland sheep, need good-quality grassland, but can also eat the remains of crops after harvesting and other plant matter.

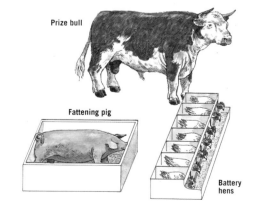

High-grade feeders, such as factory-farmed cattle, pigs, and chickens, need concentrated foods, including cereal grains, that are often suitable for people to eat.

Working animals, wool, and hides
Many of the animals that people raise have other uses besides providing food. Camels are a common method of transport in North Africa and the Middle East. Millions of farmers in developing countries use oxen (neutered male cattle) and buffalo, instead of tractors, to pull plows and carts. India uses 80 million animals for this form of transport.

People ride horses and use the pulling power of horses in most parts of the world, while mules and donkeys are used to carry loads in Central America, Africa, and East Asia. Among some African peoples, a person's position in society depends on the number of cattle that person owns. And people worldwide use non-food animal products, such as wool and hides (leather).

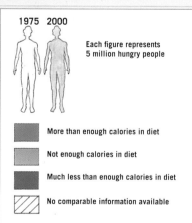

HUNGRY FOR CHANGE

Every year, 40 million people — half of them children — die from hunger and from the diseases related to it. If 300 jumbo jets crashed every day, leaving no survivors, people would be horrified — yet the number of deaths would be no greater. We seem to accept death from hunger as a fact of life.

The main cause of world hunger is not that we do not produce enough food to feed everyone. In fact, there are enough basic foods available to feed about 1.5 billion more people than are alive today. The problem is that not enough food reaches those who need it most. People in rich countries are supplied with too much. They suffer the illnesses caused by overeating, and waste a lot of food. As much as a quarter of the food available to North Americans rots in the supermarket or the refrigerator, or is thrown away uneaten after a meal. People in developing countries do not get enough food. Millions of children in poorer countries have a worse diet than the pet animals of people in developed countries.

More people are hungry in the world than ever before, and the numbers are growing. The situation is worst in Africa, where there is less food available for each person now than 25 years ago.

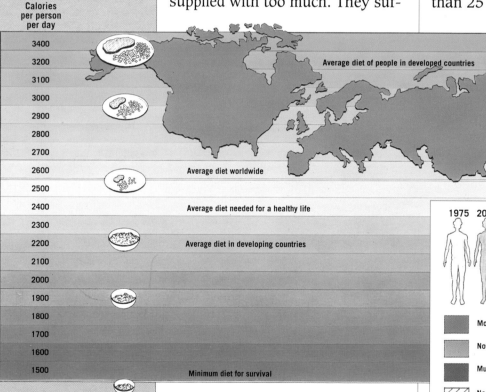

Calories per person per day

3400	
3200	Average diet of people in developed countries
3100	
3000	
2900	
2800	
2700	
2600	Average diet worldwide
2500	
2400	Average diet needed for a healthy life
2300	
2200	Average diet in developing countries
2100	
2000	
1900	
1800	
1700	
1600	
1500	Minimum diet for survival

1975 2000

Each figure represents 5 million hungry people

More than enough calories in diet

Not enough calories in diet

Much less than enough calories in diet

No comparable information available

For those of us lucky enough not to be poor, hunger lasts only as long as it takes to get to the kitchen, restaurant, or grocery store. But for millions of poor people around the world, hunger can mean days, months, years, or even a lifetime of suffering. All hungry people have a right to eat.

Energy for life
Each person needs an average of 2400 calories (units of food energy) daily to stay healthy. Most people in developed countries have much more than this: people in developing countries usually have less than they need, so many of them die from hunger and related illnesses.

THE HUNGER GAP
Many people in the developing world receive fewer calories each day than they need, unlike most citizens of the developed world. Even more people may be undernourished by 2000.

Hundreds of millions of people in Asia, and many millions in Central and South America, also eat much less than they should.

Hunger causes more than physical suffering and misery. A badly nourished person cannot work properly and gets sick easily. Hungry children are unlikely to develop to their full potential.

Hunger and poverty go hand in hand. Even within developing countries rich people eat more and better food than poor people. Even so, some developing countries, such as China, Sri Lanka, and Costa Rica, have managed fairer-than-average food distribution and few of their people actually starve.

The solutions do not come easily. But most concerned people agree that hunger will never be defeated without a huge effort to rid the world of poverty. Nevertheless, according to the United Nations Children's Fund, UNICEF, many of the 15 million babies and young children who die every year in Africa, Asia, and Latin America could be saved for just $5 each. This would cover the cost of a simple sugar and salt solution to treat diarrhea, and provide for improved nutrition and child health. In some places, it would also pay for extra food when it is needed. Is this too high a price for people in rich countries to pay?

Greed versus need?
Unhealthy eating habits in rich, developed countries are perhaps as much part of the world's food problems as hunger is in developing countries. Eating too much sugar, fat, salt, and animal products results in major illnesses, including obesity (the medical problem of being very overweight), heart disease, and diabetes. In countries in Western Europe and North America, people spend at least four times more money on diet aids than they do on support for hunger-relief organizations such as Oxfam, Save the Children, and Christian Aid.

HOME ACTION

We can challenge hunger and poverty by:
- eating less meat and dairy products — a field of cereals feeds 12 to 30 times more people than a field of cattle;
- eating only as much as we need to stay fit and healthy — labels on most foodstuffs provide details of daily requirements of nutrients and energy;
- buying "fair-traded" foods to help poor farmers;
- taking part in World Food Day activities, promoted by the UN Food and Agriculture Organization, on October 16 every year;
- supporting campaigning, relief, and development organizations that work for a fairer, less hungry world.

China's war on hunger
China has been successful at sharing a limited supply of food among its people. Starvation was once common in this heavily populated country, but now it is rare. For many years the government controlled the production and distribution of food. In recent years, however, it has relaxed its control over farming and food production, allowing market forces to operate more freely. This has tended to widen the gap between rich and poor, and between well-fed and hungry.

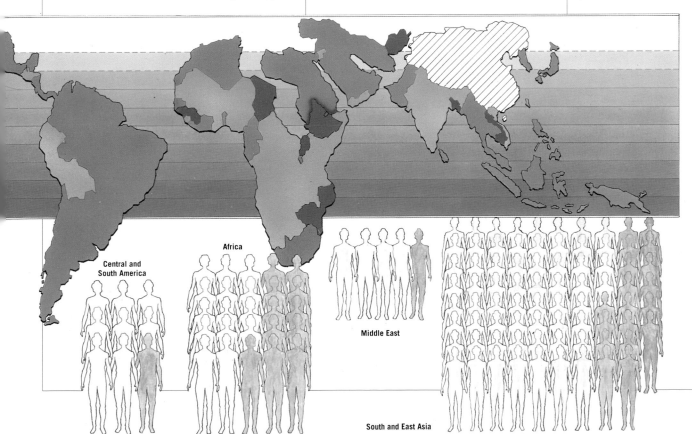

Central and South America

Africa

Middle East

South and East Asia

More and more people are going hungry. In 1975, about 435 million people worldwide had less than 1500 calories a day, the very minimum needed for survival. By the year 2000, there could be 588 million severely under-nourished people.

GLOBAL SUPERMARKET

People in developed countries can buy a huge range of foods from many lands, but their food is not always healthy or very natural. Farmers who supply supermarkets with apples, for example, have to produce standard-sized fruit that will stay fresh for long periods and look good on the shelves. No wonder apples are often tasteless and contain traces of the chemicals used in pesticides or preservatives.

Low supermarket prices have an environmental cost. Farmers may damage the land to produce food more cheaply and efficiently. They remove hedges and trees to enlarge fields, for example. Large quantities of fuel are used to make pesticides and to transport food and keep it fresh. Transportation also has an environmental cost. And supermarket packaging consumes enormous amounts of cardboard, paper, and plastic. Consideration of the true costs of sending food around the world might encourage local production.

Cheap food has human costs too. Low prices may be fine for large-scale farms, but small-scale farmers need fair prices. Many developing countries grow "cash crops" such as tea, coffee, and

Most Western farmers rely on large companies for seeds, fertilizers, and machinery, and to process their crops and sell the products. They grow as much food as they can, as quickly as possible, often helped by government grants.

A few giant companies produce and sell most of the seeds and chemicals that Western farmers use. In the USA fewer than 100 companies control food processing and marketing for the whole nation.

Large company, selling fertilizers and other farming chemicals, and processing and marketing food

Seeds   Pesticides   Fertilizer   GIANT F

THIS

● sells
● buys
● proce
● marke

Food "inputs" (from company to farmers)

Food "outputs" (from farmers to company)

Large-scale Western farmer, with powerful oil-guzzling machines and computer technology

FROM FARMER TO CUPBOARD
Farming is a worldwide industry. It takes raw materials from the field — shown by the produce coming on to the conveyor belt from the large-scale Western farmer's harvester (above left) and from the small-scale developing country farmer and Western farmer (right) — and processes and packages them, via the supermarket (above right), into food for your dinner table.

Farmer in developing world

Small-scale Western farmer

Have you ever thought about how much of your food comes from abroad? Look in your kitchen or on the supermarket shelves. The bananas are probably from the Caribbean or Latin America, the rice may be from India, the pasta from Italy, and the apples and oranges from Australia or South Africa. We enjoy eating food from all over the world, but the global supermarket has its drawbacks too.

Farmers in developing countries
often grow export crops, such as coffee, instead of food that local people need. Others are too poor to buy fertilizer and machinery.

sugar for export on the best land, while their own people go hungry.

Western farmers are encouraged by government grants to produce as much food as possible, not only for the home market but also for export. The European Union, under its Common Agricultural Policy, pays more than $20 billion each year to farmers. Some are subsidized (supported financially) to help maintain their livelihood. Overproduction has resulted in "lakes" of unwanted milk and "mountains" of surplus butter.

When unwanted food is sold off cheaply to developing countries, local suppliers have to lower prices below costs in order to compete. Local cattle farmers in West Africa have been badly hit by imports of low-cost European beef.

A small-scale farmer in Bolivia ferments cacao beans to produce fair-traded chocolate for sale in Europe.

Where the money goes when coffee is not "fair-traded"

20% to food shops

25% to processors and shop suppliers

28% to traders and shippers

19% to coffee-producing countries

8% to coffee growers

Fair shares? Profits from coffee

World trade in coffee is worth billions of dollars each year. Yet only a small fraction of this money goes to the people in developing countries who grow and pick coffee beans. Huge profits are made by shippers, wholesalers, retailers, and processing companies that make dried instant-coffee powder from the beans. Today, however, "fair-trade" brands of coffee, which give local farmers a better share of the profits, are on sale in more and more shops.

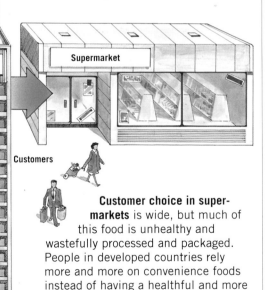

Customer choice in supermarkets is wide, but much of this food is unhealthy and wastefully processed and packaged. People in developed countries rely more and more on convenience foods instead of having a healthful and more natural diet.

The food production line involves both small- and large-scale farmers around the world. But the developed countries benefit most from the low-cost food and cash profits.

Small-scale Western farmers do not produce as much food per worker or per acre as large-scale farms. Many small, family farms cannot compete and go out of business.

A small number of giant companies, including financial institutions, have gained control over much of the world's food business, often working with large-scale farmers or by managing large commercial farms from a distance. Those local farmers who work on smaller areas of land find it harder to survive, although they usually farm more carefully.

Changes are needed so that everybody benefits from the global supermarket. More food should be produced locally, with less waste. Small-scale farmers and developing countries need better prices for their produce. Governments, customers, and producers need to work together to prevent damage to the environment. There are hopeful signs in our shops, such as organic (chemical-free) foods and "fair-traded" coffee and chocolate.

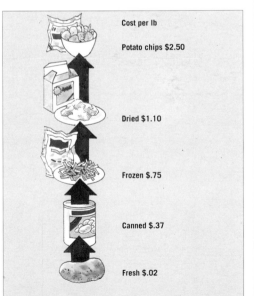

Cost per lb

Potato chips $2.50

Dried $1.10

Frozen $.75

Canned $.37

Fresh $.02

Healthy profits?

Fresh potatoes are usually cheap, but processing them into convenience snacks adds a lot to the price. Huge amounts of energy are needed for processing and packaging. Potato chips are the most expensive form of processed potato, the most wastefully produced, and the least healthy. Ads that persuade us to buy them make big profits — but not for farmers.

GREEN REVOLUTION

In the 1940s, scientists began to breed new varieties of rice, wheat, maize, and other crops. Farmers in North America and Europe who grew these new cereals using large amounts of chemical fertilizers and pesticides, and often using plenty of irrigation water, produced record grain harvests.

Soon after, farmers in Africa, Asia, and Latin America used the new seeds with similar success. In India, for example, cereal production tripled between 1950 and 1987. Throughout the world, people were able to grow more of their own food, and so relied less on costly food supplies imported from other countries.

These new crop plants had large seed-heads and grew quickly. Many farmers found that they could harvest two or three crops a year. But success was neither certain nor never-ending. Sometimes the crops failed because farmers used too much or too little fertilizer, pesticide, or water.

World food production doubled between 1950 and 1980, largely because new cereal seeds produced bumper crops when grown in the right conditions. But these "miracle seeds" of the Green Revolution have not really solved the world's food problems.

The Muda valley project

A large, expensive river dam providing irrigation water, together with the new rice seeds of the Green Revolution, promised bigger harvests and better living standards for the people of the Muda valley in northern Malaysia. At first, farmers' harvests nearly tripled, and people were better off. But rice production stopped increasing after a few years, although more and more fertilizer was being used, because the soil had reached its natural limits. Also, fertilizer prices rose during the 1970s and farmers started to lose money. Some of them became so badly off that they sold their land in the valley to their richer neighbours, and tried to farm poor-quality forest land. The valley landscape changed as plots were combined.

Muda before the Green Revolution was a valley of small, tree-filled, family-run farms.

Muda after the Green Revolution had just a few large, treeless farms, and some families had lost their land.

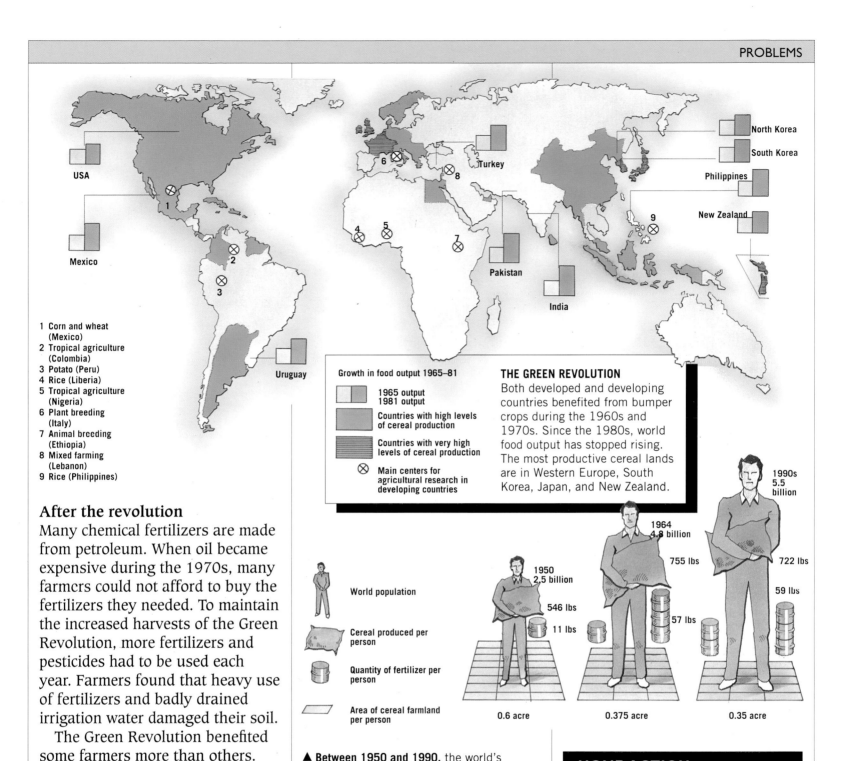

1 Corn and wheat
 (Mexico)
2 Tropical agriculture
 (Colombia)
3 Potato (Peru)
4 Rice (Liberia)
5 Tropical agriculture
 (Nigeria)
6 Plant breeding
 (Italy)
7 Animal breeding
 (Ethiopia)
8 Mixed farming
 (Lebanon)
9 Rice (Philippines)

Growth in food output 1965–81

☐ 1965 output
 1981 output

▨ Countries with high levels
 of cereal production

▤ Countries with very high
 levels of cereal production

⊗ Main centers for
 agricultural research in
 developing countries

THE GREEN REVOLUTION
Both developed and developing
countries benefited from bumper
crops during the 1960s and
1970s. Since the 1980s, world
food output has stopped rising.
The most productive cereal lands
are in Western Europe, South
Korea, Japan, and New Zealand.

World population

Cereal produced per
person

Quantity of fertilizer per
person

Area of cereal farmland
per person

1950
2,5 billion
546 lbs
11 lbs
0.6 acre

1964
4,8 billion
755 lbs
57 lbs
0.375 acre

1990s
5.5
billion
722 lbs
59 lbs
0.35 acre

After the revolution

Many chemical fertilizers are made
from petroleum. When oil became
expensive during the 1970s, many
farmers could not afford to buy the
fertilizers they needed. To maintain
the increased harvests of the Green
Revolution, more fertilizers and
pesticides had to be used each
year. Farmers found that heavy use
of fertilizers and badly drained
irrigation water damaged their soil.

The Green Revolution benefited
some farmers more than others.
The seeds, fertilizers, and other
chemicals necessary were expensive, so only wealthy farmers could
afford them. As they bought land
from poorer neighbors with the
profits of bumper harvests, the gap
between rich and poor widened.

Harvests do not have to keep
increasing. If we change the way
we produce and distribute food,
and the kind of food grown, everybody can have enough to eat.

▲ **Between 1950 and 1990,** the world's
population doubled. Farmers planted larger
areas of land with cereals and used much
more fertilizer to increase food production.
But since 1984, they have not been able to
increase food output as fast as the world
population has grown, and the environment
has suffered under the strain of being used
ever more heavily for crop production. Less
food is available in the 1990s for each
woman, man, and child on the planet than
there was in the mid-1960s.

HOME ACTION

*Help ease the environmental problems
caused by modern farming by:*
● choosing local produce instead of
 food that has been shipped long
 distances;
● eating fresh, rather than processed,
 fruits and vegetables;
● buying environment-friendly whole-
 foods and organic produce;
● cutting down on meat and dairy
 foods, so less grain is used for
 animal feedstuffs;
● growing your own food in a garden or
 on a small plot.

PASTORALISTS IN WAJIR, KENYA

Habiba Abdi and her family live in Wajir District in northeast Kenya. They are pastoralists, which means they rely on livestock — goats, cattle, and camels — for their livelihood. They are also nomads, migrating with their herds, following the rain in order to find good grazing land for their animals. They move on before each area is overgrazed. Another reason for moving on is to avoid tick-borne diseases, which spread among animals and can be passed on to people when herds are kept in one area for too long.

Habiba Abdi's day begins at dawn. The goats are milked and then taken out to graze. "We have to stay close to water with the goats and cattle, but we keep the camels away farther from the homestead so that they don't compete with the other animals for grazing land. One of my sons looks after the camels with his family; they go wherever the rains fall.

▲ **Habiba milks goats in her homestead** *near Tarbaj in Wajir District. When she has finished milking each goat, its kid (young goat) is released from a pen so that it can come to suckle.*

▲ **Fatima, one of Habiba Abdi's daughters,** *splits palm fronds to make* dufuls, *the mats that are used to cover the home. Children are taught how to build houses from local plant material and how to milk goats from the age of about six. They must be able to earn their keep a few years later.*

▶ **The goats are brought to a water hole to drink,** *led by Fatima. Many of the water holes dry up within a month or two after the last rainfall.*

There's plenty of grazing land if we just follow the rain."

Habiba lives with a group of families in a homestead. The homestead occupies an area about 264 feet in diameter, surrounded by a fence of thorn branches. Each family has one or two *herios*, houses made from branches bent to make a dome, and covered with *dufuls* – mats made from grass or palm leaves. *Herios* are quick to put up and take down, which makes it easy to move on. The thorny enclosure keeps out thieves and protects the goats from predators such as lions.

Everyone must help others when times are hard, for example during droughts. This means lending animals to friends and relatives who are not as well off. This debt may be carried on for generations but will be paid off eventually.

When Habiba's family needs income, it sells some goats, which are also exchanged for cattle and camels, instead of using money.

Pastoralism works well in areas like Wajir where there is not enough rain to grow crops. But this way of life is under threat. Many governments think pastoralists are primitive because of their ancient way of life. They like people to be settled, and to own land, not just use it. All over the world, pastoralists are under pressure to settle down and grow crops, even where the land is not good for farming.

Moving home in the Kenyan bushland (main photograph) takes no more than an hour or two, especially when everything you own — including the house, furniture, and cooking equipment — can be packed on the back of a couple of camels.

FUTURE FARMING

What kind of countryside would you like to see in 50 years' time? Wide-open treeless prairies managed by people with computers and farmed by huge oil-guzzling machines? Or a varied landscape of smaller-scale wooded plots, dotted with family households?

Farming with trees
More and more farmers are experimenting with agroforestry – growing trees and other crops together. Chinese farmers grow trees among wheat and tea plants. British and French farmers have planted cherry and nut trees among their cereals. The trees provide a home for small mammals and birds, helping control insect pests. In hot climates trees shade the crops, and some trees fertilize the soil with their leaves. Wood and other products from the trees help farmers earn more.

To feed the world's population adequately and protect the environment from damage, tomorrow's farming methods need to be different from today's. Many scientists, governments, and large farming businesses that produce, process, and distribute farm products favor modern, high-tech (using the latest technology) solutions. These include the "gene revolution" — the scientific breeding of food plants that grow well without lots of fertilizers.

Small-scale and organic farmers (who use natural

Better scientific research (6) will help tomorrow's farmers grow food with less harmful effects on the environment.

No-dig farming (1) saves energy and protects the soil. Farmers leave plant remains (called mulches) on the land after harvesting and do not turn over the soil before planting. **More natural pest control** reduces the farmer's reliance on chemicals (2). By mixing and rotating crops, encouraging the natural enemies of pests, as well as laying bait, farmers can keep pests down.

Plants that are well adapted to harsh conditions may be useful in future. **The hairy wild potato (3)** has a natural scent that keeps away insects (4). This feature could be bred into crops. **The yeheb bush (5)** has edible seeds and grows well in deserts.

methods as much as possible) prefer to combine a few new ideas with traditional, low-tech methods (using very little modern technology). They plant trees and hedges to encourage birds and beetles, which help to control insect pests, and in dry regions they build small rock walls to conserve water. Low-tech farming can succeed if land is shared fairly, so that all the people in a community can grow their food locally.

This is especially important in developing countries, where small-scale farmers are the key to producing enough food. If less land is used to grow crops for export, more land can be used for food for local people. Small-scale farmers need fair market prices, loans for investment, grants to improve their farming methods, and reliable transport to local markets.

Women produce half the world's food. Their knowledge and skills

Mixed cropping (7) means growing different crops (including trees) together, or one after the other. The choice of crops, or the order in which they are grown, is designed to to help conserve moisture, enrich and maintain the goodness of the soil, and keep the number of pests at a manageable level.

Local seed banks (8) will store different plant varieties and allow farmers to choose the most suitable types for their needs.

A BETTER KIND OF FARMING

Farming needs to change for the better. Plenty of good ideas and methods are available, many of them working toward the benefit of the environment, the farmer, and the consumer. They involve scientific research, careful land management, and the conservation of resources.

Greenhouses (9) and plastic tunnels (polytunnels) help farmers grow food on land that might otherwise not be suitable.

Trickle-drip irrigation (10) uses less water than other methods, and reduces the amount of salt left in the soil.

DID YOU KNOW?

A better way to feed the world
It takes almost 1760 lbs of cereals — used as feed for animals — to produce the meat that an average North American eats in a year. This is nearly five times more grain than a reasonably well-fed African eats in a year. A change in the meat-rich diet of one could help provide an adequate diet for several others.

Spirulina (11), a protein-rich algae, will grow in salt lakes in arid regions. **The winged bean (12)** was originally from the forests of New Guinea. Now farmers in 50 countries raise this nutritious crop for its high levels of protein and vitamins.

The pomelo (13) is the largest citrus fruit (in the same plant family as oranges and lemons). Originally from Southeast Asia, it is a good source of vitamins and food fiber, and could be a major new fruit crop in the future.

as small-scale farmers, especially in developing regions, will be important in the future.

In the developed world, more people need to adopt a less wasteful diet. By returning to the reduced-meat diets of just 30 years ago, they could improve their health and release food and land to cater to other people's needs. Soils in these regions that are over-worked today will benefit from more gentle farming methods.

Permaculture: making the most of nature
Permaculture (short for permanent agriculture) is a labor-saving form of organic farming that combines as many different food plants, fruit and nut trees, and animals as possible. Plants are grown close together to squeeze out weeds. Chickens and ducks are reared among the plants. Their droppings improve the soil, and they eat any weeds that do appear. Permaculture farmers collect rainwater for use in fishponds and grow fruit bushes as hedges. The aim of this method of farming is to feed people, avoid pollution, and save energy: it works.

3
OCEANS

"The death of the oceans would . . . lead to the death of most higher life forms on Earth, including humans."

Dr. Rosalie Bertell,
nun, scientist, and
environmental campaigner

The ocean was our beginning, the source of life on Earth. Today it still has wonderful gifts to offer that we often take for granted: food, minerals, energy resources, and climate control, for example. Imagine what could happen if we go on mistreating the planet's seas for another 100 years the way we have done for the past 100 or so. The results could be terrifying: many species of fish, seabirds, and sea mammals wiped out or reduced to tiny local populations; coral reefs and natural coastlines destroyed; and waters choked with invisible poisons and all-too-visible garbage. But there is hope. In the last 30 years, more and more people have come to understand the dangers. At work and in the home, in campaigning groups, businesses and governments, millions of people are searching for better ways to care for our seas.

Trawlermen sort the catch as their vessel heads for home and a future in which larger fleets fish for dwindling stocks.

SEAS & OCEANS

From space our planet appears largely blue rather than brown, yellow, and green: it is a watery planet. The first living things evolved in the sea; and water makes up about three-quarters of the weight of the human. Water is vitally important to us; there can be no life without it.

Greenpeace's ship Rainbow Warrior *has campaigned the world over, drawing attention to environmental issues concerning the quality and resources of our oceans.*

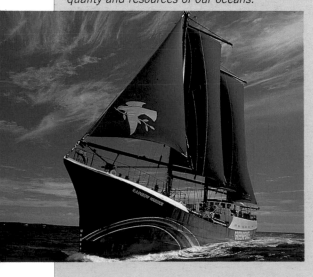

THE GLOBAL OCEAN

The world's oceans and major seas are interconnected, forming a huge global ocean. Warm and cold currents carry vast amounts of water over great distances. Cold water flows from the poles toward the equator; warm currents move in the opposite direction.

→ Warm currents
→ Cold currents

Warm currents
1 Irminger
2 Norway
3 Gulf Stream
4 North Equatorial
5 Equatorial Counter-Current
6 South Equatorial
7 Brazil
8 Kuroshio
9 Alaska
10 Agulhas
11 East Australian

Cold currents
12 Labrador
13 Canary
14 Benguela
15 Falkland
16 West Wind Drift
17 West Australian
18 Oyashio
19 Californian
20 Peru (Humboldt)

Depth of ocean

0–4000 m

4000–5000 m

5000–7000 m

Places where largest numbers of people live

Arctic Ocean

North Atlantic Ocean

South Atlantic Ocean

Southern Ocean

Seawater covers more than two-thirds of our planet's surface: perhaps we should call it Planet Ocean rather than Planet Earth. All the world's oceans and seas are interconnected (except for inland seas such as the Caspian). Their waters are always on the move as a result of the Earth's rotation, the tides, and the winds. Polluting materials dumped in the sea in one place often end up thousands of miles away.

Although large areas of the ocean floor are as flat and smooth as any plains on land, elsewhere it is uneven and rugged. Even close to the land there are long, deep canyons and trenches. Farther out, there are undersea valleys deeper than Mount Everest is high.

Mighty mountain ranges extend for thousands of miles, and island peaks rise steeply from the depths. The Earth's outer layer, or crust, is made up of great slabs of rock called plates — either oceanic or continental (land) plates. The movement of these plates results in

Our watery world
Two unusual views of Earth show how much of it is covered by sea. Each view is a hemisphere ("half-sphere"), showing half the planet. If we "look down" from a point in space above Western Europe (the land hemisphere, top), most of the planet's land surface is in view, yet we still see an equal area of water. Seen from above the same point on the opposite side of the globe — the ocean to the south of New Zealand (the sea hemisphere, bottom) — seawater covers an astonishing nine-tenths of the surface.

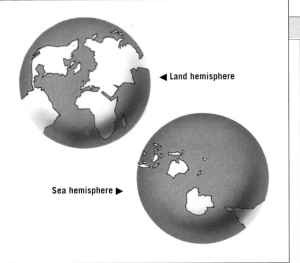

◄ Land hemisphere

Sea hemisphere ►

DID YOU KNOW?

What do currents carry?
Ocean currents make a big difference to the lives of millions of people. Without the Gulf Stream bringing warm water across the Atlantic, Northwest Europe might be as cold as Siberia. The Peru (Humboldt) Current along the west coast of South America brings deep-sea waters to the surface. They are rich in minerals and the remains of dead sea life, which provide a feast for ocean plants and creatures, making these waters important fishing grounds.

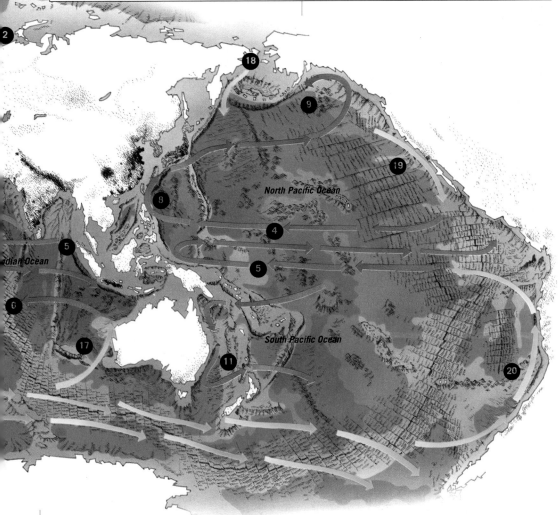

seasons, more slowly than temperatures on land. The sea therefore has a moderating effect on maritime climates — those within range of the sea's influence — making them less extreme. Large numbers of people live close to the ocean because, among other reasons, coastal climates are more pleasant than those inland.

Variety of life and resources
Oceans absorb gases, regulating the composition of the air and keeping it fit to breathe. They also supply much of our food, and certain places within them, such as coral reefs, are among the most species-rich regions on Earth. The seabed is a source of minerals and fuel such as oil.

Along the coastlines are narrow continental shelves. Shallow waters here are rich in minerals washed off the land, and are feeding and breeding grounds for fish, providing fishing grounds for people. From the continental shelves the seabed slopes away into the deepest ocean reaches. These are still largely a mystery to us, and may contain undiscovered species and mineral resources.

molten rock pushing up through gaps from the Earth's interior to form new undersea ridges, or in one plate diving beneath another, forming deep trenches.

The sea is where life began and it still plays an important role in the "workings" of our planet. The

circulation of air together with the movements of ocean currents give the world's climate zones the features they have. In effect, the oceans can be thought of as a giant "weather machine."

The temperature of the sea rises and falls each day, and with the

LIFE IN OCEANS

Where land meets sea there are fascinating shorelines full of surprises: crabs under rocks, unusual seaweeds, rock pools that come and go with the ebb and flow of the tides. Deep waters also have their share of the unexpected, and they support a huge number of plants and creatures.

Life in the ocean is as varied as life on land, ranging from the largest creatures on Earth – blue whales – to the smallest, and including some of the strangest. While many fish and sea mammals live near the surface of the sea, other species live on, or buried in, the seabed. The deepest, coldest waters are home to such eerie-looking creatures as the angler fish, which carries its own light. The regions that have the most abundant life are coastal marshlands, mangroves, estuaries, and coral reefs.

In certain places at the boundary of land and sea, the motion of the tides produces wetlands. These are the coastal marshes of mild-climate regions, and mangrove swamps, which include trees and shrubs, of the tropics. Seagrasses are the main vegetation in each, flowering beneath the water and providing food for shellfish, turtles (in mangroves), and ducks and geese (in marshes), among other creatures.

Estuaries, where the fresh water of rivers mingles with the saltwater of the sea, receive a rich flow of minerals from upstream. Vast numbers of worms, crabs, lobsters, and shellfish live in estuaries, and many ocean creatures travel to these waters at certain times of the year to give birth to their young.

As offshore winds blow over shallow water, turbulence makes cooler, mineral-rich water rise to the surface. Tiny phytoplankton grow here. A huge variety of tiny zooplankton (floating animals) feed on the plants and on each other. Also in these waters are the larvae (the young) of shore- and bottom-dwelling creatures such as crabs and worms.

Larger creatures feed on smaller ones. Squid, jellyfish, small fish such as herring and anchovies, and some whales and sharks eat zooplankton. Tuna and other medium-sized fish feed on smaller species and in turn provide food for larger sharks and marlins. Seals also eat small fish and are prey for sharks and leopard seals.

THE SEA-LIFE CYCLE
Countless millions of tiny, floating sea plants are the basis of all sea life. These phytoplankton (the name means "drifting plants") absorb the Sun's energy, minerals in the water, and carbon dioxide, using the same process (photosynthesis) by which land plants grow. All sea creatures depend on phytoplankton for their food (directly or indirectly), just as land animals need land plants.

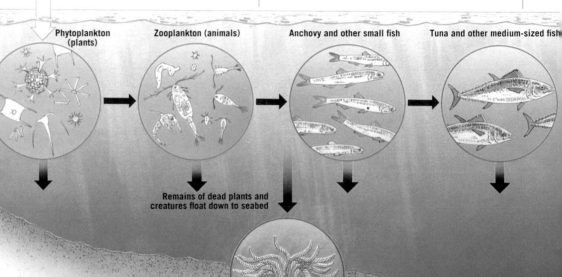

Light

Upper zone of the sea – enough sunlight for photosynthesis

Cooler, mineral-rich waters rise to the surface

100 m deep

Phytoplankton (plants)

Zooplankton (animals)

Anchovy and other small fish

Tuna and other medium-sized fish

Remains of dead plants and creatures float down to seabed

Dead plants and animals sink to the seabed where their remains provide food for crabs, sponges, sea urchins, and other creatures that live and feed there.

Bottom-living creatures feed on remains

The ocean food store: who should own it?

The sea zones that are richest in animal life are mostly near the coasts. Here rivers wash minerals down from the land, while wind-blown currents bring up more minerals from the seabed. This provides phytoplankton with the food they need. And where there are plenty of phytoplankton, there will also be many fish feeding on them – as well as other, larger fish species, seabirds, and marine mammals that feed on the plant-eaters. Coastal countries have claimed a right to control many of the oceans' most productive food zones.

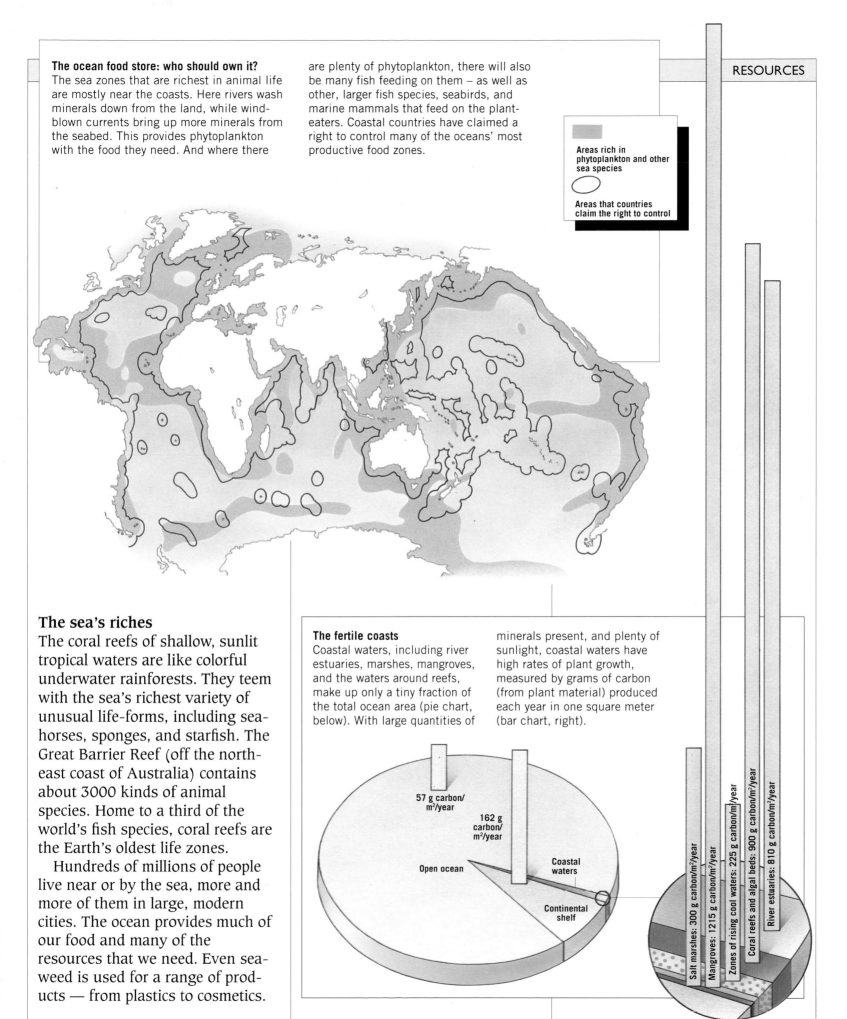

Areas rich in phytoplankton and other sea species

Areas that countries claim the right to control

The sea's riches

The coral reefs of shallow, sunlit tropical waters are like colorful underwater rainforests. They teem with the sea's richest variety of unusual life-forms, including sea-horses, sponges, and starfish. The Great Barrier Reef (off the north-east coast of Australia) contains about 3000 kinds of animal species. Home to a third of the world's fish species, coral reefs are the Earth's oldest life zones.

Hundreds of millions of people live near or by the sea, more and more of them in large, modern cities. The ocean provides much of our food and many of the resources that we need. Even sea-weed is used for a range of products — from plastics to cosmetics.

The fertile coasts

Coastal waters, including river estuaries, marshes, mangroves, and the waters around reefs, make up only a tiny fraction of the total ocean area (pie chart, below). With large quantities of minerals present, and plenty of sunlight, coastal waters have high rates of plant growth, measured by grams of carbon (from plant material) produced each year in one square meter (bar chart, right).

57 g carbon/m²/year

162 g carbon/m²/year

Open ocean

Coastal waters

Continental shelf

Salt marshes: 300 g carbon/m²/year

Mangroves: 1215 g carbon/m²/year

Zones of rising cool waters: 225 g carbon/m²/year

Coral reefs and algal beds: 900 g carbon/m²/year

River estuaries: 810 g carbon/m²/year

FISHING & WHALING

Do you keep fish as pets or enjoy fishing as a sport? Probably, like millions of others, you eat fresh or processed fish. We may take for granted the fish on our plate, and give little thought to the balance of marine life in the oceans, but there could be trouble in store unless we begin to conserve, rather than just consume, the world's fish resources.

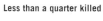

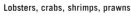

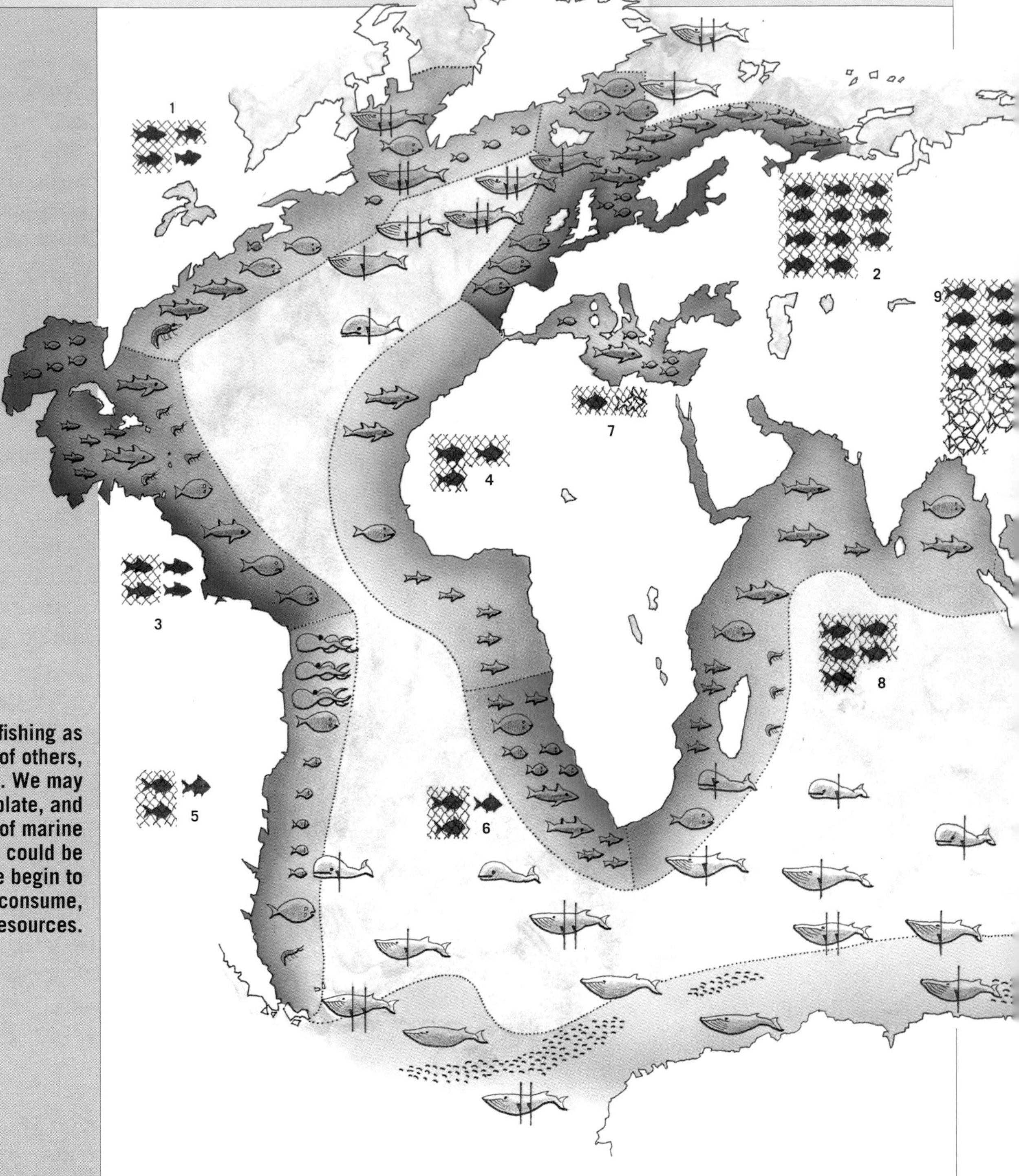

The world's catch

Fishing is based on five groups of species: bottom-dwelling fish such as cod and haddock; surface-dwelling species, including herring, mackerel, tuna, and anchovy; crustacean shellfish — crab, lobster, shrimp, and prawn; tentacled creatures such as octopus, squid, and cuttlefish; and marine mammals such as whales, dolphins, and porpoises, although the killing of whales has decreased since a ban in 1985. The large-scale harvesting of krill would threaten many other species in the marine food chain.

Estimated possible catch each year without reducing future stocks

- 1,000,000 tons

Size of fish catch each year

- 1,000,000 tons — no damage to future stocks
- 1,000,000 tons — damage to future stocks
- Swarms of krill

Catch in tons each year

Bottom-dwelling fish
- 1,000,000
- 100,000

Surface-dwelling fish
- 1,000,000
- 100,000

Lobsters, crabs, shrimps, prawns
- 1,000,000
- 100,000

Octopus, squid, cuttlefish
- 100,000

Whale stocks and whale kills each year before 1986

Sperm whales	Filter-feeding whales
More than three-quarters killed	
A quarter to three-quarters killed	
Less than a quarter killed	

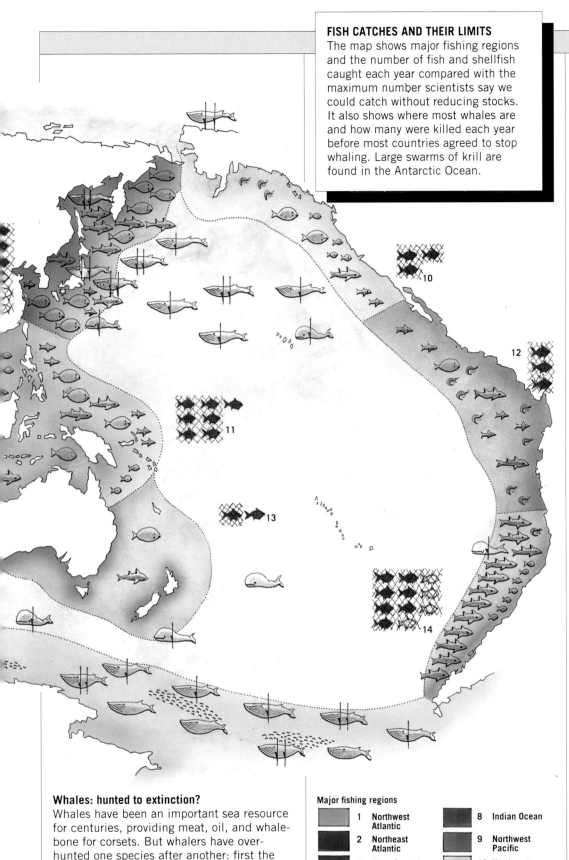

FISH CATCHES AND THEIR LIMITS
The map shows major fishing regions and the number of fish and shellfish caught each year compared with the maximum number scientists say we could catch without reducing stocks. It also shows where most whales are and how many were killed each year before most countries agreed to stop whaling. Large swarms of krill are found in the Antarctic Ocean.

People have eaten fish and shell-fish for thousands of years. In the last 45 years the world's catch has grown enormously as new fish stocks have been discovered and exploited, and modern technology has helped us harvest more fish.

The advantage is that more people have fish to eat (although much of the catch goes into animal feed or fertilizers). But there are serious problems with modern fishing. One is overfishing: we take fish from the sea faster than they can replace their numbers naturally. This has caused sudden large reductions in some stocks, such as those of North Sea herring, which once seemed limitless. People have overhunted whales, which are mammals, in the same way. Many years of killing them for meat, oil, and whalebone have resulted in the near-extinction of several whale species.

Wider problems

Another problem is that modern fishing methods threaten other sea creatures besides the fish we eat. Dolphins, seabirds, and turtles often get caught and die in nets meant for tuna or salmon.

There is also a human aspect. Many small-scale fishing communities worldwide have seen their way of life destroyed by big businesses with their huge sea-sweeping nets and factory ships. So far governments have done little to help them.

To ease these problems — falling fish and whale stocks, loss of other species, and poverty within small fishing communities — we need a much more careful approach to the way we take our food from the sea.

Whales: hunted to extinction?

Whales have been an important sea resource for centuries, providing meat, oil, and whale-bone for corsets. But whalers have over-hunted one species after another: first the right whale, next the bowhead and humpback, then the sperm, and later the blue, fin, and sei whales. Now only the minke survives in large numbers, although it is still hunted by a few countries. Despite the international whaling ban that came into force in 1985, countries such as Japan, Iceland, and Norway continue to kill whales.

Major fishing regions

1	Northwest Atlantic	8	Indian Ocean
2	Northeast Atlantic	9	Northwest Pacific
3	West Central Atlantic	10	Northeast Pacific
4	East Central Atlantic	11	West Central Pacific
5	Southwest Atlantic	12	East Central Pacific
6	Southeast Atlantic	13	Southwest Pacific
7	Mediterranean	14	Southeast Pacific

ENERGY FROM OCEANS

The age of ocean technology may be only just beginning, although modern industry already uses resources from the sea on a large scale. Much of the world's oil and gas, for example, come from off-shore drilling rigs on continental shelves, which may hold half the Earth's resources of these fossil fuels. The dredging of coastal waters for useful minerals began more than 100 years ago, off the coast of California, and is now widespread.

Factories around the world process seawater to obtain salt, magnesium (a valuable lightweight metal), and other materials; several Middle Eastern countries with a drinking water shortage meet their needs by removing the salt from seawater.

These activities are not problem-free. Dredging for gravel can disturb fish breeding grounds, and oil exploration close to the shore can spoil the peace and beauty of natural landscapes. It also brings the threat of pollution. Some people believe that we should concentrate on conserving oil stocks by using less fuel, rather than opening up new oilfields close to untouched coastlines.

Scientists and engineers have given us the means to explore the deep ocean and exploit its riches. But they do not always agree about the possible consequences of our activities at sea, or how to solve the problems created. With so much uncertainty about the way technology affects the ocean, "handle with care" should be our motto.

In 1995 Greenpeace campaigners took over Shell's Brent Spar oil platform in the North Sea, challenging Shell's plans to dispose of the rig in deep waters off northwest Scotland. These plans were shelved after a wave of public concern about possible sea pollution from the rig. The platform was towed to a deep fjord in Norway (right), where it awaits a decision about the best way of dismantling it.

Dredging for sand, gravel, shells, and even diamonds is an established way of getting seabed materials. Huge amounts of gravel are dredged up for roadbuilding.

Wave power may be an important future energy source. The technology has been developed in Britain and Norway.

Future wave-power machines based on this US design cou[ld] provide power to clean up oil spills and remove salt fro[m] seawater, as well as generating electricity.

TECHNOLOGY AT SEA: PRESENT AND FUTURE
As ocean technology has progressed, we have ventured into deeper waters to take advantage of the sea's mineral and energy resources. But many of the techniques are too expensive for use by developing countries, and some — such as dredging and oil production — cause serious damage to the sea environment.

Future possibilities

The ocean offers good possibilities of producing electricity without much pollution, and of helping to meet the world's future energy needs. France, for example, has a large tidal power station in northern Brittany that generates energy from the rise and fall of the sea in the Rance river estuary. Engineers have tried out wave-power machines on the Scottish and Norwegian coasts, and in the Pacific Ocean, and have set up wind-power machines in the sea near Denmark and Sweden. Wave power and sea-based wind power operations are still very costly to construct, but they should become cheaper in the long term.

In the future we may find new and better ways of using the sea's mineral and energy resources. As much as $7 billion worth of silver, copper, and zinc deposits may lie on the muddy bed of the Red Sea, for example. But modern ocean technology is at present costly to design, build, and operate. And it is important to work out how developing countries can get a fair chance to use and benefit from today's and tomorrow's inventions.

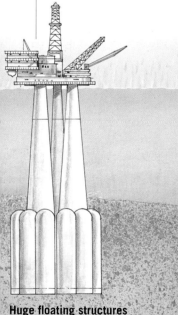

Huge floating structures like the North Sea Stratford B platform — the heaviest object that people have ever moved — take oil from the seabed and store it deep under water in concrete tanks until it is needed.

Deep-water oil platforms operate in the Gulf of Mexico and elsewhere, anchored to the sea floor by long cables.

Thermal energy converters take advantage of the difference in temperature between warm surface waters and cold deeper waters. These converters work like a refrigerator in reverse, evaporating a liquid as it is warmed, which drives a turbine and produces electricity. Thermal converters are not yet widely used.

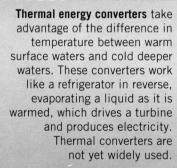

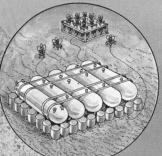

Gas-powered machines may enable us to extract oil from the deepest parts of the seabed in the future.

Deep-sea mining is one method of getting valuable minerals from the ocean floor. The technology has worked in tests but is very expensive, and countries have yet to agree about who can use the deepest zones of the seabed.

POLLUTING THE SEA

Do you enjoy a swim in the sea? If you do, be warned: even on the cleanest-looking beach the sea may be invisibly polluted with sewage, and you may suffer vomiting and diarrhea after you swim in it. Some beaches now have information signs about the water quality. A lot more polluting materials enter our seas than most people are aware of.

DID YOU KNOW?

The cost of losing wetlands
Almost two out of three people live near the coast, and nine of the world's ten largest cities — Tokyo, São Paulo, New York, Shanghai, Calcutta, Buenos Aires, Seoul, Bombay, and Rio de Janeiro — are on or close to river estuaries. The spread of many of these huge cities — home to more than 125 million people — has destroyed natural wetlands (coastal marshes and mangrove swamps) that once filtered out pollution and provided feeding and breeding grounds for fish. The loss of wetlands costs the USA more than $80 million a year because there is a much reduced fish catch.

We treat the oceans like a giant garbage can, dumping huge amounts of waste in them every day, often by way of rivers, drains, and outflow pipes. This pollution includes human sewage and domestic waste water, factory outflows of acids and poisonous metals, engine oil from roadside drains and garages, farm chemicals washed off the land by rain, building-site rubble, nuclear waste from power plants, and oil from wells, refineries, and tankers. The daily flow of materials into the sea also includes a million plastic items, such as bags, nets, and bits of packaging.

The oceans break up, disperse, or dissolve large quantities of waste. But there are limits. Most plastics never break down but just wash around coasts and islands for years. And there is no known way of getting rid of deadly substances such as the pesticide DDT (now widely banned) and PCBs (a group of chemicals used in factories) once they enter the water.

Most sea pollution occurs near the coast, where many species live, although traces of harmful chemicals have been found in the

deepest parts of the ocean, and even in Antarctica. Plankton in the shallows take polluting materials into their bodies, and they are passed on to the fish and shellfish that eat plankton, to larger fish, sea mammals, and seabirds, and eventually to humans who eat fish and seafood. At each stage of the food chain, the poisons can become more concentrated and therefore more deadly.

Ocean pollution results in smaller catches of fish all over the

Oil in the sea
More than three million tons of oil end up in the sea each year, the result of a variety of human activities, most of which take place on land. More than a third is waste oil from city drains (1) — mainly from cars — and from factories (2): this is carried to the sea by rivers. Some oil evaporates off the land into the air and reaches the sea via weather systems in the circulation of the atmpophere (3). More comes from tankers, either during cleaning or from accidental spills (4). Leaks at oil wells are another source, and some oil seeps naturally from the seabed.

Pollution in rivers
Rivers collect polluting substances from human activities along their banks. Rivers in developed countries pick up many chemicals and waste substances, which they carry downstream. Most of these wastes and poisons end up in the estuary waters that are so important to many ocean life-forms, causing serious problems for fish, seabirds, and other species.

Chemicals from farmland

Sewage and other wastes from cities

Dangerous chemicals from factories

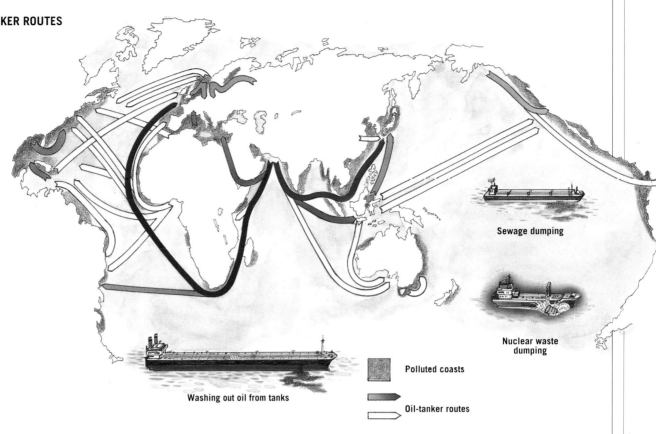

POLLUTED COASTS AND TANKER ROUTES

The worst pollution is along coasts where large numbers of people live or where there are industrial sites. These areas include the east coast of North America, around the North Sea in Northwest Europe, and the East Asian coastline. Major oil-tanker routes link the continents. Oil spills, such as the *Exxon Valdez* disaster off the coast of Alaska in 1989, usually happen close to land in busy shipping lanes. Other pollution at sea results from tankers washing out their tanks, from sewage dumping, and from the disposal of nuclear waste in drums or other containers. Nuclear dumping at sea stopped in the 1980s, but some drums have begun to leak their waste into the sea.

Sewage dumping

Nuclear waste dumping

Washing out oil from tanks

Polluted coasts

Oil-tanker routes

world, either by killing fish directly, preventing them from breeding, or causing birth abnormalities. It affects breeding in seabirds and poisons whales. It also seems to have led to a previously unknown disease among seals. Without even

being swallowed, plastic can kill seabirds, turtles, and other creatures by trapping them.

A shocking example of the effects of sea pollution happened in Japan in the 1950s. A local factory had poured waste water containing

a metal, mercury, into Minamata Bay for 20 years. Tuna in the bay absorbed the mercury, and people ate the tuna. Many children were born with deformities, people lost their hearing or sight, and thousands eventually died.

Nuclear waste from nuclear plants

Oil pollution from oil refineries

The dirty Mediterranean

The Mediterranean is one of the world's dirtiest seas, yet around its shores are some of the world's most popular holiday resorts. It has just one small opening to the larger ocean, at Gibraltar, where polluted water escapes into the Atlantic and clean water enters. Coastal towns and cities — such as Barcelona, Marseilles, Genoa, Naples, and Piraeus — where almost 50 million people live, produce masses of sewage and industrial waste. The worst oil pollution is from North African oil refineries and tanker ports.

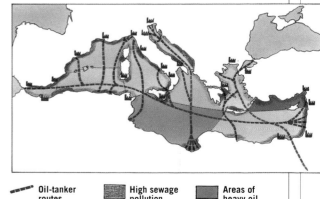

Oil-tanker routes

High sewage pollution

Industrial centers

Areas of heavy oil pollution

You may not realize it, but you could be using seaweed products every day. You walk on them, eat them, rub them into your skin — you may even wear them. Extracts from seaweed, such as agar, are used in the manufacture of cosmetics, tinned meat and fish, ice cream, jellies, other foodstuffs, artificial fabrics, plastics, floor coverings, and many more.

▲ **When the seaweed has been harvested** it is spread out on the shore and left to dry in the sun.

Sabu Island is surrounded by a reef, which has created an area of shallow, calm water between the reef and the island's shoreline. This lagoon provides ideal conditions for the cultivation of seaweed.

▲ **Young seaweed** is picked from the reef and attached to ropes or stones. It is then returned to the water and left to grow for another three weeks or so before being harvested.

Sabu Island is in Indonesia. The island is too small, and the soil too poor, to grow enough food to feed everyone who lives there. One thing the islanders have plenty of is seawater. A reef runs around the island and protects the shoreline from rough waves, creating a sheltered area of water.

Families work together to collect young seaweed from the reef. They tie it on to nylon ropes that are firmly anchored to the shore, or on to stones, and leave it in the calm water for about three weeks, to grow bigger.

When the weed has been harvested and dried, it is taken to a storeroom where it is kept until there is enough to sell to an exporter. The families are paid when they deliver the dried weed to the storeroom.

Seaweed farming is a good way of using Sabu Island's natural resources, and it supports a lot of people because, on average, two acres of sea can be worked by a group of ten families. It provides them with an income and takes the pressure off the land, giving the islanders a chance to terrace fields and plant trees to help the farmland recover.

◀ *The dried seaweed* is packed into sacks and taken to the storeroom, where it is kept until there is enough to sell.

MAKING SEA STOCKS LAST

A wide range of delicious fish and seafood is available to most of us wherever we live and not just from local waters. Yet the greater our choice, the fewer fish stocks there seem to be in the sea, and the more fishing communities have the source of their livelihood put at risk. Action is needed to correct the situation.

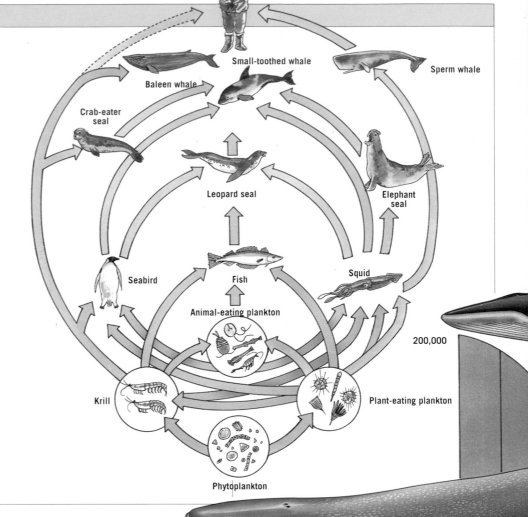

Human

400,000

Small-toothed whale

Sperm whale

Baleen whale

Crab-eater seal

Leopard seal

Elephant seal

Seabird

Fish

Squid

Animal-eating plankton

200,000

Krill

Plant-eating plankton

Phytoplankton

Krill: food of the future?
The waters of the Antarctic are home to a rich variety of sea life. Many species depend on small, shrimp-like krill for food. The weight of krill in the Antarctic Ocean reaches 650 million tons in summer. Small catches are taken for human consumption. They could be an important food source in the future, but should not be overfished.

DID YOU KNOW?

Life or death fishing
Large, deep-ocean fishing ships use huge nets with tiny holes to sweep the sea. All sorts of sea creatures get caught in these nets. Out of every ten fish that trawlers catch, they may throw back nine as unwanted, but these creatures usually die anyway. When trawlers come inshore they sometimes hit small fishing boats, cutting their nets and injuring or even killing the local fisherpeople. Stricter controls on large-scale fishing would help protect fish stocks and people too.

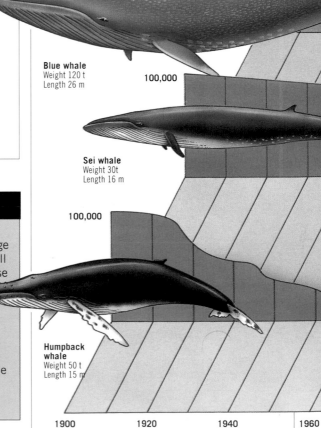

Blue whale
Weight 120 t
Length 26 m

100,000

Sei whale
Weight 30t
Length 16 m

100,000

Humpback whale
Weight 50 t
Length 15 m

1900   1920   1940   1960

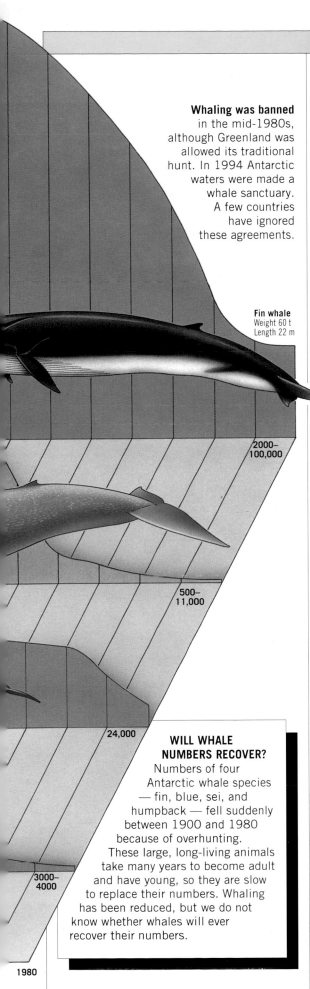

Whaling was banned in the mid-1980s, although Greenland was allowed its traditional hunt. In 1994 Antarctic waters were made a whale sanctuary. A few countries have ignored these agreements.

Fin whale
Weight 60 t
Length 22 m

2000–
100,000

500–
11,000

24,000

WILL WHALE NUMBERS RECOVER?
Numbers of four Antarctic whale species — fin, blue, sei, and humpback — fell suddenly between 1900 and 1980 because of overhunting. These large, long-living animals take many years to become adult and have young, so they are slow to replace their numbers. Whaling has been reduced, but we do not know whether whales will ever recover their numbers.

3000–
4000

1980

Community fish ponds make fishing a group activity on Hatiya Island in Bangladesh. The ponds are formed in very large, dug-out hollows, which are created when soil is removed to build large raised platforms. Houses are built on these platforms to protect them from flooding during the rainy season.

We need to improve the way we harvest the sea so that future generations will inherit well-stocked oceans. We should catch fewer fish today so there are enough fish to eat tomorrow.

In the last 60 years many countries have signed agreements and set up organizations to look after stocks of fish, whales, and other species. But some agreements to stop overfishing have come too late, when the fish have almost disappeared. This happened with the Peruvian anchovy and the North Sea herring.

Future agreements should come into force early enough to allow fish numbers to recover quickly. According to some experts, once a species has lost a quarter of its numbers in one part of the sea, fishing there should stop. In the long run this will give us a steadier flow of food from the sea.

To avoid overfishing, countries could agree to use a larger-sized mesh (the gaps in the net) in their fishing nets in certain sea zones.

Nets with larger gaps allow the smaller, younger fish to escape. This means more fish live longer, breed, and maintain numbers.

Food from the sea should go to those who need it most. The way of life of fishing communities in developing countries needs to be protected. Here fish usually feed poorer people who have few other food sources. Developed countries could manage with far less of the world's fish catch, some of which goes into animal feed. This would allow developing countries a fairer share of fish from their regions.

Fishing in the future needs to be based on a conserving approach that makes sure no sea zone suffers serious damage. We should monitor the use of the latest fishing technology that disturbs the seabed, where many fish breed, and fishing methods that kill unwanted fish or mammals. Perhaps some ocean zones should be made into nature reserves, in which fishing is banned and sea life protected.

THE BIG CLEANUP

Have you ever helped clear garbage from a local stream, a park, or a school playground? It can be fun, but even a small-scale cleanup operation is usually hard work. When it comes to clearing the world's oceans of 100 years or more of poisons and other polluting substances, the job is enormous. But it is well worth doing, and it has to be tackled.

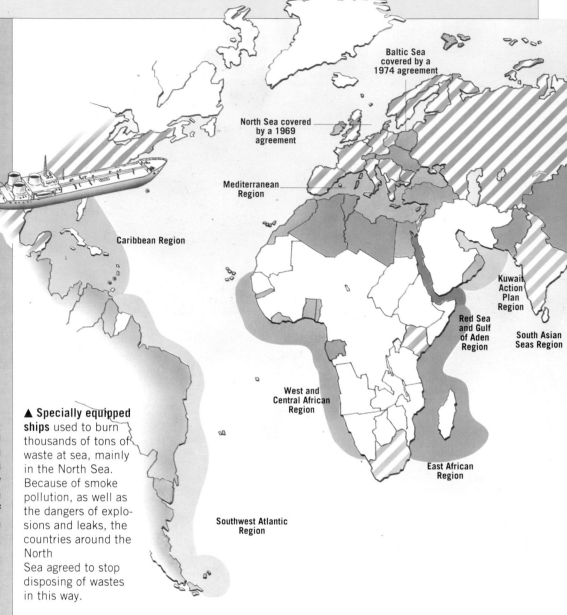

Baltic Sea covered by a 1974 agreement

North Sea covered by a 1969 agreement

Mediterranean Region

Caribbean Region

Kuwait Action Plan Region

Red Sea and Gulf of Aden Region

South Asian Seas Region

West and Central African Region

East African Region

Southwest Atlantic Region

▲ Specially equipped ships used to burn thousands of tons of waste at sea, mainly in the North Sea. Because of smoke pollution, as well as the dangers of explosions and leaks, the countries around the North Sea agreed to stop disposing of wastes in this way.

MARPOL: preventing pollution

MARPOL (the International Convention for the Prevention of Pollution from Ships) aims to protect coasts and seas from heavy pollution from ships. Under MARPOL's rules, ships must not dump treated rubbish nearer than 3 nautical miles (1 nautical mile is equal to 2037 yds) from the coast.

Other rules cover treated sewage, poisonous waste, untreated rubbish and sewage, and waste oil. Ships of more than 400 tons must have tanks for waste-oil storage. MARPOL does not allow ships to release oil into the Baltic, Black Sea, Mediterranean, Persian Gulf, or Red Sea.

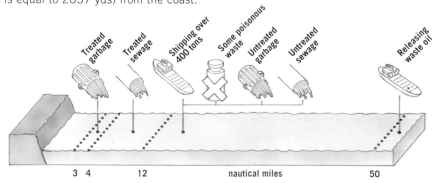

Treated garbage · Treated sewage · Shipping over 400 tons · Some poisonous waste · Untreated garbage · Untreated sewage · Releasing waste oil

3 4   12   nautical miles   50

We cannot go on polluting the seas as we have done, and more needs to be done to clean them up. A hopeful sign is that many countries have agreed to work together to improve the situation.

More than 90 countries have now signed the International Convention for the Prevention of Pollution from Ships (or MARPOL, from **mar**ine **pol**lution), which was first set up in 1973. MARPOL limits the amounts of oil, sewage, poisonous waste, and garbage that ships can release into the sea.

Several other agreements signed during the 1960s and 1970s are

Oil-tanker washing
There is a new way of cleaning out the large oil tanks on tanker ships without polluting the sea with dirty water. The new system uses a high-pressure jet of oil to clean the empty cargo areas. The resulting dirty oil is then disposed of on land.

HOME ACTION

Help reduce sea pollution and clean up our rivers and coasts.
- Do not dump garbage in streams, rivers, or the sea, or on beaches.
- Dispose of all plastic carefully.
- Reduce waste: reuse and recycle as much as you can.
- Ask your family to use safer household cleaning products containing fewer harmful chemicals.
- Before you swim in a river or the sea, check that it is clean.
- Tell the municipal authorities if you see river or beach pollution.
- Help a conservation group clean up local rivers and beaches.
- Join an organization that is campaigning against river and sea pollution.

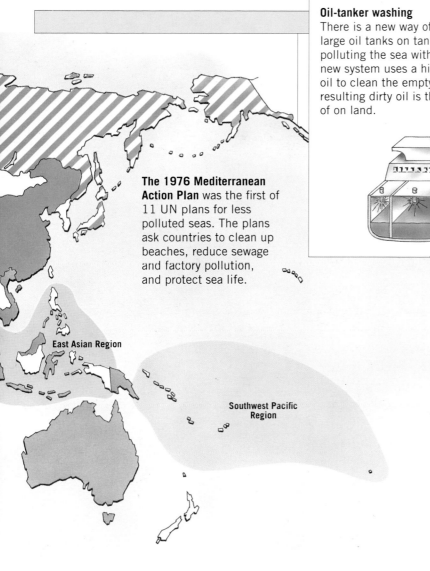

The 1976 Mediterranean Action Plan was the first of 11 UN plans for less polluted seas. The plans ask countries to clean up beaches, reduce sewage and factory pollution, and protect sea life.

East Asian Region

Southwest Pacific Region

Southeast Pacific Region

WORKING FOR CLEANER SEAS
Many areas of ocean are now protected by countries that have signed UN action plans since 1975 to reduce pollution. The plans are a good start, but countries must spend a lot of money to make them a success. Many countries have agreed to reduce pollution from ships. Sites on land dispose of oil from ships so that it does not end up in the sea.

 UN Regional Seas Program action plans since 1975

 Countries that have signed the MARPOL agreement on pollution from ships

Countries that have sites on land to dispose of oil from ships

 Countries that have signed MARPOL and can dispose of oil on land

still important today. The Bonn Agreement (1969) aimed to protect coastal areas around the North Sea, and the Helsinki Convention (1974) did the same for the Baltic Sea. The London Dumping Convention (1972) banned the dumping of fuel oil, chemical weapons materials, nuclear waste, and other dangerous substances.

Another step in protecting the ocean came when the United Nations started its Regional Seas Program as part of the UN Environment Program. This program has set up "action plans" for 11 areas of the sea and involves 130 countries. Its main idea is that we should protect the sea from possible pollution even before we know how bad the damage might be.

The Mediterranean Action Plan, which began in 1976, was the first plan under the UN programme. Countries around the Mediterranean have installed equipment to treat sewage before it enters the sea, share research into sea pollution, and are working to protect coastal wetlands and reduce pollution from rivers. This plan has been successful, but the Mediterranean is still seriously polluted.

Other forms of action include current efforts by the UK and other European Union countries to clean up their bathing beaches. To make a long-term success of the ocean cleanup, however, governments need to spend more money on it.

GLOBAL OCEAN

Even the best of friends argue sometimes. Different countries, with populations of millions, are much more likely to quarrel. But agreements between countries are possible, and they will be more and more important if we are to protect the oceans and Antarctica for future generations.

Adelie penguins and the research ship **World Discoverer** *explore Moubray Bay off Victoria Land in Antarctica.*

Oceans cover 144 million square miles of the Earth's surface, a huge area that needs protection from human damage. Between 1973 and 1982, 160 countries worked on a big package of agreements to safeguard the ocean: the Third Convention on the Law of the Sea. Under this agreement, coastal countries control inshore waters and must look after them.

One aim of the Law of the Sea agreement was that all the world would share in the benefits of seabed mining. But countries such as the UK, the USA, and Germany, which have the money and skills to mine the seabed, do not want to share the profits with other countries, and therefore refused to sign the agreement.

In the future, satellites and other technology will help countries to "police" the ocean environment, keeping track of ships that cause pollution, for example, and other rule-breakers. It will be just as important to make sure that people who live near the sea or earn their living from it have a say in what we do to protect coastal waters and how we use the ocean.

Protecting Antarctica

Antarctica is a huge ice-capped continent that covers one-twelfth of the Earth's land surface. Many people believe that we should preserve this great wilderness as it is, although the nearby Antarctic Ocean contains a wealth of sea resources, and Antarctica probably has large amounts of oil and other minerals under the ice. Some countries have claimed parts of Antarctica for themselves, and this could lead to serious problems.

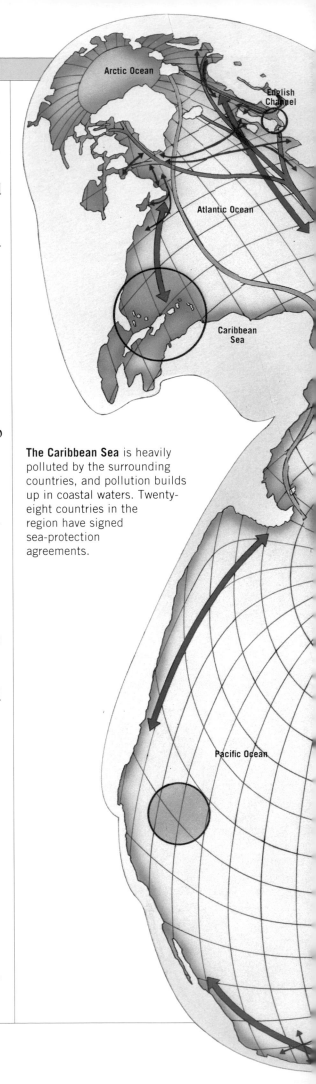

The Caribbean Sea is heavily polluted by the surrounding countries, and pollution builds up in coastal waters. Twenty-eight countries in the region have signed sea-protection agreements.

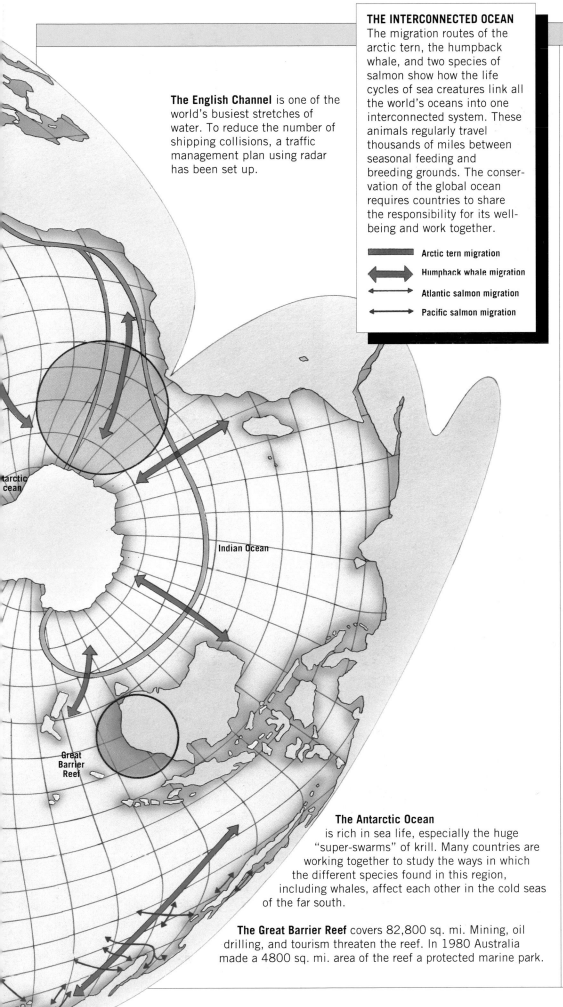

The English Channel is one of the world's busiest stretches of water. To reduce the number of shipping collisions, a traffic management plan using radar has been set up.

THE INTERCONNECTED OCEAN
The migration routes of the arctic tern, the humpback whale, and two species of salmon show how the life cycles of sea creatures link all the world's oceans into one interconnected system. These animals regularly travel thousands of miles between seasonal feeding and breeding grounds. The conservation of the global ocean requires countries to share the responsibility for its well-being and work together.

━━━━ Arctic tern migration

◀━━━▶ Humpback whale migration

◀━━▶ Atlantic salmon migration

◀━▶ Pacific salmon migration

Indian Ocean

Antarctic Ocean

Great Barrier Reef

The Antarctic Ocean
is rich in sea life, especially the huge "super-swarms" of krill. Many countries are working together to study the ways in which the different species found in this region, including whales, affect each other in the cold seas of the far south.

The Great Barrier Reef covers 82,800 sq. mi. Mining, oil drilling, and tourism threaten the reef. In 1980 Australia made a 4800 sq. mi. area of the reef a protected marine park.

Protecting Antarctica

Argentina · Australia · Belgium

Chile · France · Japan

New Zealand · Norway · Russia

South Africa · United Kingdom · United States

Twelve countries signed an agreement to protect Antarctica — the Antarctic Treaty — in 1959. The flags of the founder countries are shown above. Since then many other countries have agreed to accept decisions about Antarctica made under the treaty. Seven countries — Argentina, Australia, Chile, France, New Zealand, Norway, and the UK — have claimed part of Antarctica for themselves. The treaty aims to stop countries fighting over Antarctica and to keep it free for peaceful science. The treaty countries agreed in 1991 to ban mining for 50 years, although there are probably large oilfields under the ice.

Antarctica is an important site for study of the Earth. From its deep layers of ice, scientists can tell how the world's climate has changed over thousands of years. In 1985, the British Antarctic scientist Joe Farman first discovered the "hole" in the protective ozone layer of the Earth's atmosphere.

Hope for the future

More than 40 countries have now accepted the Antarctic Treaty — drawn up in originally in 1959 — for the protection of the region. In 1991 these countries also agreed to ban the large-scale mining of resources from Antarctica for 50 years — a hopeful sign that people can put peace and the protection of the environment before exploitation and money making.

4
ENERGY AND ELEMENTS

"I . . . thought how wonderful God has created the Earth. And I looked out over my land, ripped up by human hands and machines. I thought: what will I get out of that dust? . . . . Nothing."

JOYCE HALL,
speaker for the Aboriginal people of Weipa, Australia, describing the mining of her people's land, 1981

Our planet is wonderfully equipped for life: the Sun provides heat and light; we have a constant flow of water; and on the planet's surface and buried underground are huge amounts of useful materials. We have used the power of the Sun — locked up in long-buried fossil fuels — and the Earth's mineral wealth to build modern civilization. But success has also brought failure. Excited by science and technology, we have forgotten the wisdom of not interfering with nature, and have introduced practices that we cannot properly control, with consequences that are not immediately obvious. We need to strike a balance between human achievement and nature's course.

Taking minerals out of the Earth can scar beautiful landscapes. Limestone is quarried in the middle of the Peak District National Park in England.

GLOBAL POWER-HOUSE

People who lived in ancient times worshiped the Sun. They were aware of its great importance in sustaining life on Earth. When, on a winter's night, you come home to a warm house and a cooked supper, you can do so because of forms of energy based on the Sun's power.

Solar energy is used in Nepal to heat domestic water supplies. In countries that have a sunny climate, or a difficult terrain, or that cannot afford coal- or oil-fired power stations, solar energy provides a valuable energy source.

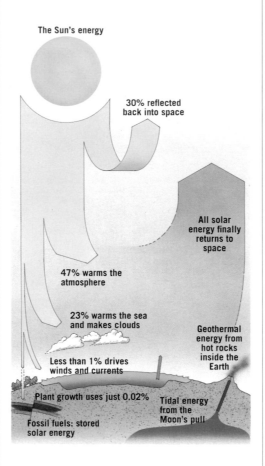

The Sun's energy

30% reflected back into space

All solar energy finally returns to space

47% warms the atmosphere

23% warms the sea and makes clouds

Geothermal energy from hot rocks inside the Earth

Less than 1% drives winds and currents

Plant growth uses just 0.02%

Tidal energy from the Moon's pull

Fossil fuels: stored solar energy

The Sun is the key to life on Earth. Without it our planet would freeze over, and all the animals that rely on its energy for plant growth and food would perish. Most modern comforts and conveniences — heating, lighting, cooked meals, television and radio — and many forms of transport from buses to jet aircraft, depend on our use of coal, gas, and oil. Their connection with the Sun is that they are fossil fuels, formed from decomposed prehistoric plants and animals whose life energy came from . . . the Sun.

Some people benefit much more than others from fossil-fuel energy. The average North American, for example, uses 280 times more than the average Ethiopian. And a lot of cheap electricity and gasoline is wasted in developed countries.

Energy from the Sun

Solar energy warms the Earth's atmosphere, making winds blow and ocean currents flow. It heats seawater, which then evaporates into the air, falling later as rain. The Sun's energy also provides the "fuel" for plants to grow. Fossil fuels represent solar energy stored much earlier in the Earth's history. A little of the energy flow at the Earth's surface comes from other sources: the pull of the Moon powers the tides, and heat from the Earth's interior escapes as "geothermal" energy.

In contrast, millions of people in developing countries do not have enough firewood to cook a meal.

Another problem is that coal, oil, and gas are non-renewable and will not last forever. We are using them up at a worryingly fast rate. And fossil fuels are dirty to use. Air pollution from burning them has created serious environmental problems such as acid rain and global warming.

Fortunately, there are some alternatives to fossil fuels. These are renewable energy sources that use natural flows of energy such as sunlight, wind, rivers, waves, tides, and plant growth. Firewood is a renewable resource that is as old as history itself. Others have been developed recently and as yet are expensive to use widely. Even so, renewable sources promise clean energy and a means by which developing countries can meet their needs.

Some people include nuclear power as an important energy source for the future. Early hopes for nuclear power have faded because of the high costs of building nuclear power plants, fears about nuclear reactor safety after several accidents, and the problems of dealing with radio-active waste materials.

MAKING USE OF ENERGY

The pie chart shows how much of our energy supplies came from each main source in 1990, and how this may change by 2000. (The colors in the pie chart correspond to the base colors of the symbols.) Burning firewood and other plant and animal material was the earliest energy use. Then came sail power, which harnessed the wind, windmills, and waterwheels (using the flow of rivers). People first burned coal about 300 years ago, and oil and gas 200 years after that. Geothermal and nuclear energy have come into use only recently. As fossil fuels run low, we will rely more on renewable resources.

Oil is the world's main fuel source, providing 37 percent of power. Consumption fell in the 1970s after price rises, but the use of oil is increasing again. We could run out in 45–50 years unless we conserve it better or discover new oilfields.

Coal is important in countries such as those of the former Soviet Union and in China. They have huge stocks. Coal provides 23 percent of our energy, but it pollutes more than oil or gas. There is probably enough coal left to last several hundred years.

Natural gas supplies 18 percent of our power. Cleaner than oil or coal, it is fast being developed. Eastern Europe and the former Soviet Union have huge underground gas fields. Yet there may only be 60 years' worth of gas left.

Non-renewable energy sources

 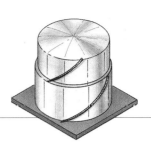

Renewable energy sources

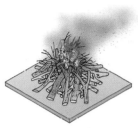

▲ **Firewood and other plant and animal materials,** such as animal dung, were human beings' earliest fuels, and meet about 12 percent of energy needs today. These are still the main fuel supplies for half the world's population, especially in developing countries.

World energy supplies

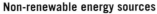

1990

2000

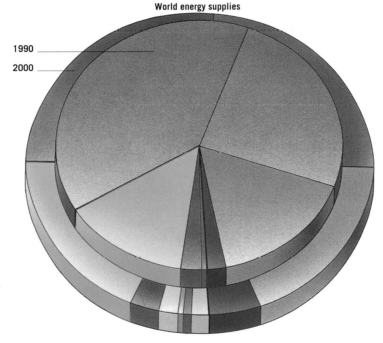

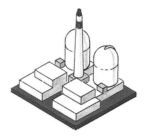

▲ **Nuclear power** is used in about 30 countries and supplies about 4 percent of energy. It once looked as if nuclear power might solve the world's energy problems. But it is expensive, and people worry about health risks from waste disposal and power plant accidents.

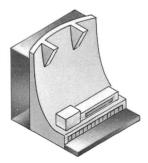 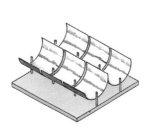 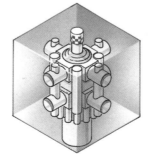  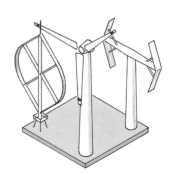

Hydropower provides about 5 percent of our energy. Many rivers in developing countries are suitable for dams. Large-scale projects displace local people and take their land, as well as damaging the environment. Small-scale dams are often more successful.

Solar (the Sun's) power is becoming an important energy source. Good modern buildings are designed to use the Sun's heat. Solar panels heat water, and solar cells convert light into electricity to power equipment and entire buildings.

Power from the sea includes wave power, tidal power, power from sea currents, and "thermal energy conversion," which exploits temperature differences at different depths. Tidal- and wave-power machines exist, but not on a large scale.

Geothermal power uses the Earth's internal heat, by pumping cold water down into hot rock or drawing up naturally heated water. The hot water is used to produce electricity or heat buildings. Several countries have geothermal energy systems.

Wind power could be an important future energy source. Unlike traditional windmills, which ground grain, today's wind machines produce electricity. Wind-blown hills and coastlines are especially suitable for the generation of wind power.

ENERGY STORE

If you live in a centrally heated home, have warm baths or showers, and often travel by car, count yourself lucky. The cheap energy from oil, coal, and gas that we enjoy today became available only 100 years ago and may not last another 100. Hundreds of millions of people now and in the future will never have a share in our "fossil-fuel bonanza."

Differences in underground rock formation and the history of life on Earth have produced a very unequal allocation of fossil-fuel resources — oil, coal, and gas. Some countries have huge energy supplies; others have far fewer resources or none at all.

Owning fossil-fuel resources can be the key to great wealth, as the oil-producing countries of the Middle East discovered in the 1970s. A lack of energy resources is a serious problem for many countries in Africa, South Asia, and Latin America. But Japan has shown that a country can develop well without major fuel stocks.

Oil, gas, and coal will run out one day, even if we find new reserves. It will eventually become too expensive to look for new underground deposits and exploit them (bring them into use). It would be wise to conserve these non-renewable resources carefully and develop new, renewable forms of energy while we still have time.

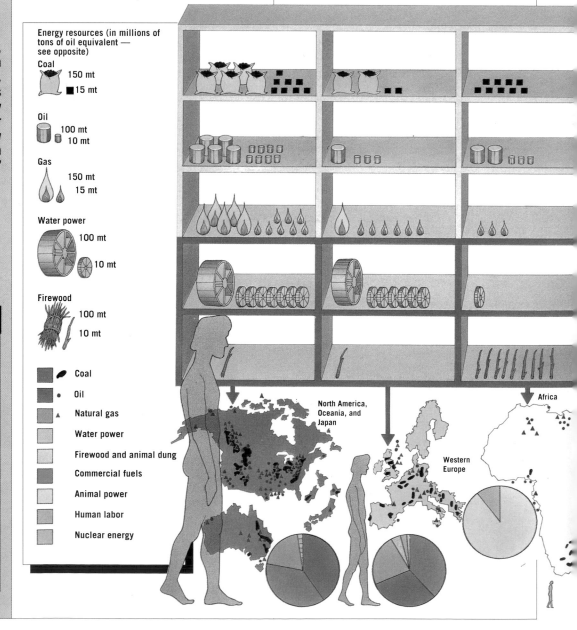

Energy resources (in millions of tons of oil equivalent — see opposite)

Coal
150 mt
15 mt

Oil
100 mt
10 mt

Gas
150 mt
15 mt

Water power
100 mt
10 mt

Firewood
100 mt
10 mt

- Coal
- Oil
- Natural gas
- Water power
- Firewood and animal dung
- Commercial fuels
- Animal power
- Human labor
- Nuclear energy

North America, Oceania, and Japan

Western Europe

Africa

Some regions are energy-rich, others energy-poor. Developed countries own two-thirds of coal, oil, and gas deposits, and use more than their fair share. The industrial revolution of the late 1700s and 1800s was based on coal and iron (another natural resource), and helped cause the split between developed and developing countries.

In North America, Oceania, and Japan the average person uses twice as much energy as the average West European, and 17 times more than the average South Asian. Western Europe relies heavily on oil from abroad, despite North Sea oil deposits, but it has reduced the amount of coal it uses.

Africa is fuel-poor, although Libya and Nigeria have oil, and South Africa has coal. Firewood and animal dung are the main fuels in much of the African countryside.

Eastern Europe and the former Soviet Union have large stocks of coal. The former Soviet countries also produce and sell large amounts of oil and gas.

The Middle East owns more than half of the world's known oil stocks and exports most of the oil it produces.

In Latin America, Mexico and Venezuela have oil, but other countries are fuel-poor. Some are short of firewood.

China mines vast amounts of coal but, despite a large population, relatively little fossil-fuel energy is used. Animals and human labor provide much of the power needed in China.

South Asia has only small fossil-fuel stocks. South Asians use very little energy on average.

THE WORLD'S ENERGY MIX

The top three shelves in the diagram show how much coal, oil, and gas people produce each year in eight world regions. The lower two shelves show the amounts of water power and firewood used. The maps show deposits of underground fossil fuels. The size of each human figure reflects the total amount of energy used by the average person in the region, and the pie charts compare the use of various energy resources.

The amount of energy produced from the various energy resources can be compared by using a measure (usually one million tons) of "oil equivalent." One million tons of oil equivalent produces the same amount of energy as, for example, 1.5 million tons of coal.

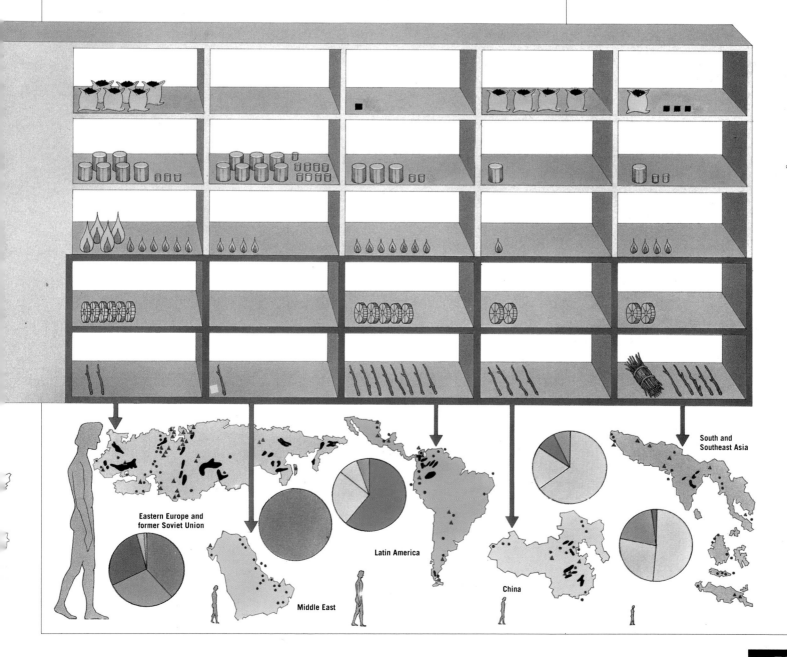

Eastern Europe and former Soviet Union

Middle East

Latin America

China

South and Southeast Asia

MINERAL RESERVES

Do you throw away your empty soda cans? The lightweight aluminum they are made of may seem like garbage. But to produce the millions of cans we drink from each day, parts of the Caribbean, West Africa, and South America have become mining wastelands, and vast amounts of fossil fuels are burned. Recycling cans reduces the need for further mining and fuel burning.

Minerals, ores, reserves, and resources
A mineral is any solid, non-plant, non-animal substance that exists naturally in the Earth's crust. An ore is a metal in its raw state, mixed up with rock, before people process it into a usable form. A mineral resource is the total amount in the ground, while reserves are the quantities of a mineral that we know we can extract by existing methods and use.

MINERAL RESERVES AND TRADE
The map shows which countries or regions of the world own reserves of 20 major minerals, and their share of world stocks. Two kinds of minerals are included: those that are available in large enough amounts to meet today's needs easily, and strategic, or key, minerals. These are defined as those minerals that are essential for modern industry, but that are in relatively short supply.

The map also shows how countries import (buy) and export (sell) mined and processed minerals in the world marketplace, giving as examples the trade in aluminum (bauxite is the raw material) and copper.

 Share of world reserves of minerals

 Share of world reserves of strategic minerals that could run low

 Bauxite (for aluminum) and/or copper ore exported (100,000 tons)

 Bauxite (for aluminum) and/or copper ore imported (100,000 tons)

 Aluminum and/or copper production for own use (100,000 tons)

 Aluminum and/or copper production for export (100,000 tons)

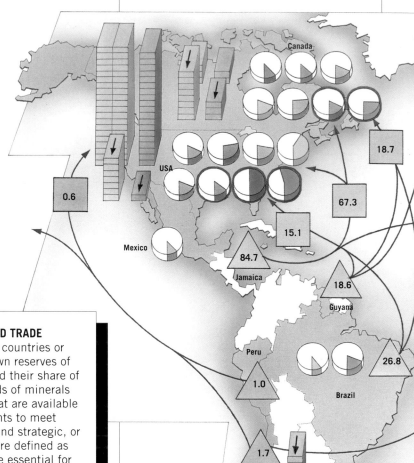

Since humankind first appeared on Earth it has used the planet's mineral wealth. After the Stone Age came the Bronze Age, when people made their tools from bronze, an alloy (a mixture of metals) of copper and tin. Next came the Iron Age, when people learned to work with iron mined from the ground.

Today we rely heavily on about 80 minerals, many of which are still available in large quantities.

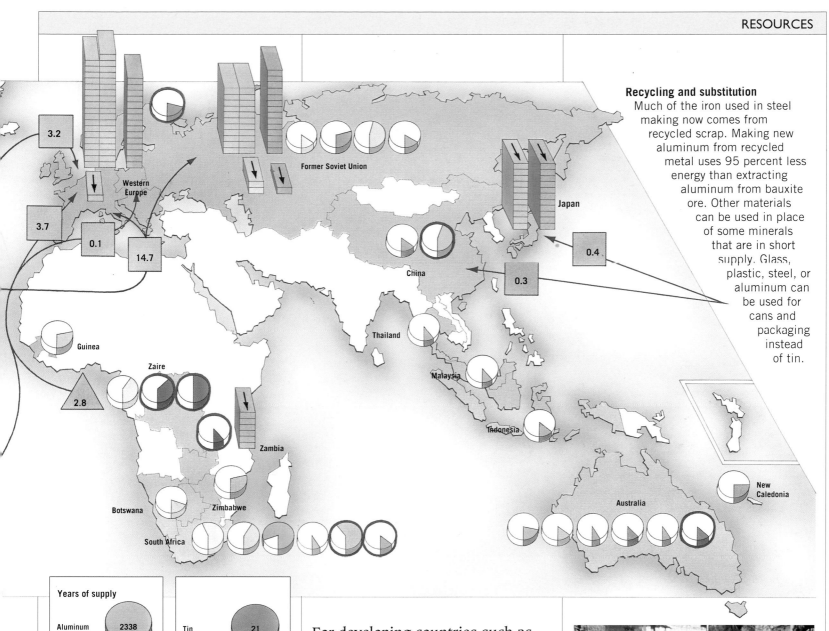

Recycling and substitution
Much of the iron used in steel making now comes from recycled scrap. Making new aluminum from recycled metal uses 95 percent less energy than extracting aluminum from bauxite ore. Other materials can be used in place of some minerals that are in short supply. Glass, plastic, steel, or aluminum can be used for cans and packaging instead of tin.

3.2

Western Europe

3.7

0.1

14.7

Guinea

2.8

Zaire

Zambia

Zimbabwe

Botswana

South Africa

Former Soviet Union

Japan

0.4

China

0.3

Thailand

Malaysia

Indonesia

New Caledonia

Australia

Years of supply

Aluminum (bauxite)	2338
Copper	66
Diamond	20
Gold	30
Iron	236
Lead	37
Manganese	186
Nickel	144
Platinum group	176
Silver	24

Tin	21
Uranium	45+
Zinc	42
Antimony	70
Cadmium	46
Chromium	374
Cobalt	116
Mercury	42
Molybdenum	97
Titanium	138

For developing countries such as Chile, Zambia, and Zaire, exporting minerals is an important way of earning money.

Some important minerals, including lead, tin, and zinc, are getting scarce. Few, if any, will run out, but as reserves get smaller, the costs of getting at them and using them will rise. For this reason, and because of environmental damage and the problems for local people that large-scale mining causes, we need to reduce our use of minerals and recycle more.

We can estimate how many years' supply we have of key minerals (left) by comparing current rates of use with levels of reserves.

Scrap metal that has been salvaged from wrecked or old cars is recycled to make charcoal-burning stoves in Port-au-Prince, the capital of Haiti.

FUEL CRISIS

Are you doing all you can to help avoid a future fuel crisis? How much energy do you waste at home, at school, college or work, or when getting around? If you leave lights on in empty rooms, go by car instead of taking a short walk or bus ride, or cycling, spare a thought for people who have to walk hours to collect firewood each day, and for the Earth's future generations.

North America

South and Central America

OIL STOCKS, RESOURCES, AND TRADE

Oil is the most important energy source for most developed and some developing countries. The map shows where the main oil reserves are, and larger areas where new oilfields might be found. It also shows how much oil each region has produced, how much oil we know each region still has, how long these stocks will last at today's rates of use, and the size and direction of the oil trade worldwide.

Location of known oil reserves

Possible future oilfields

Available oil stocks (1 billion tons)

Oil so far produced and used (1 billion tons)

Years of supply left (full bowl = 100 years)

Size and direction of oil trade

For rich countries in the North, the fuel crisis began in the early 1970s and ended in the mid-1980s. In 1973 oil-producing countries of the Middle East raised the price of oil by three or four times. What had once been a cheap energy source was suddenly very expensive. Developed countries reduced their oil imports, changed to other fuels, and became more efficient in using energy. Many developing countries were not able to switch fuels or reduce energy consumption easily.

They were faced with rising fuel costs and falling prices for their own goods in a world marketplace that was in economic crisis. As a result, people in these countries suffered badly.

The price of oil fell back in 1986. Developed countries lost interest in energy efficiency and increased their use of oil again. Most developing countries have not been able to recover as fast. Supplies of oil will probably run out well before the end of the 21st century.

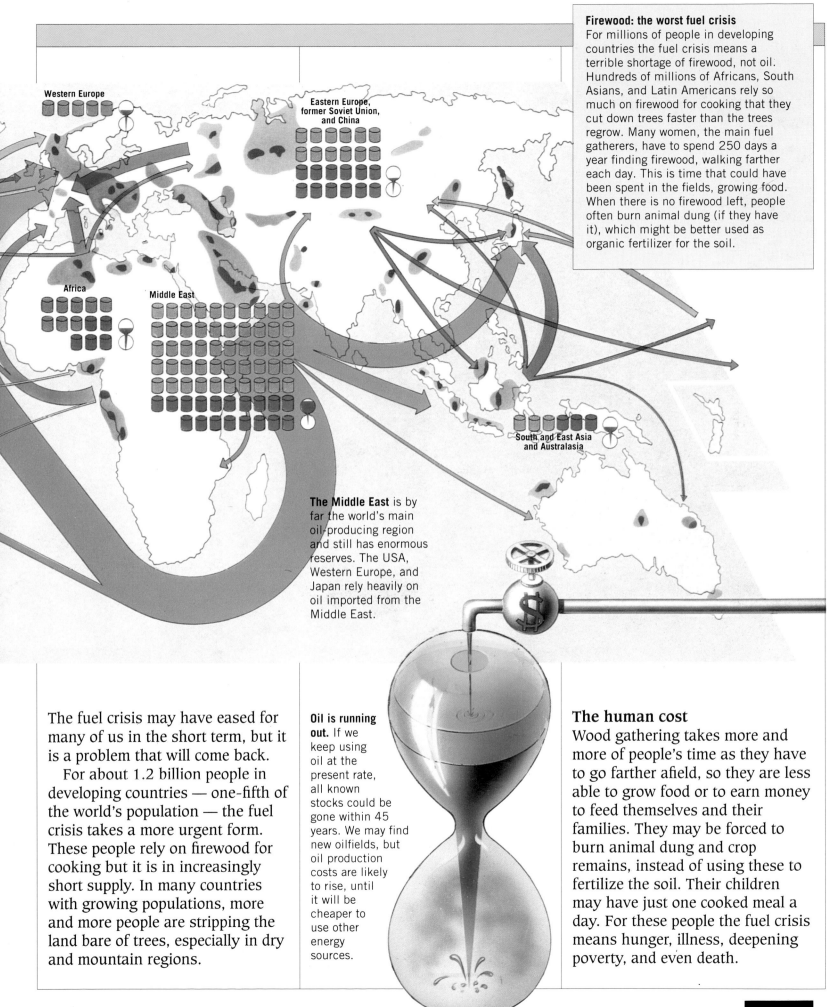

Western Europe

Eastern Europe, former Soviet Union, and China

Africa

Middle East

South and East Asia and Australasia

The Middle East is by far the world's main oil-producing region and still has enormous reserves. The USA, Western Europe, and Japan rely heavily on oil imported from the Middle East.

The fuel crisis may have eased for many of us in the short term, but it is a problem that will come back.

For about 1.2 billion people in developing countries — one-fifth of the world's population — the fuel crisis takes a more urgent form. These people rely on firewood for cooking but it is in increasingly short supply. In many countries with growing populations, more and more people are stripping the land bare of trees, especially in dry and mountain regions.

Oil is running out. If we keep using oil at the present rate, all known stocks could be gone within 45 years. We may find new oilfields, but oil production costs are likely to rise, until it will be cheaper to use other energy sources.

The human cost
Wood gathering takes more and more of people's time as they have to go farther afield, so they are less able to grow food or to earn money to feed themselves and their families. They may be forced to burn animal dung and crop remains, instead of using these to fertilize the soil. Their children may have just one cooked meal a day. For these people the fuel crisis means hunger, illness, deepening poverty, and even death.

GLOBAL WARMING

Have you noticed how, in the last few years, certain parts of the world have had hotter, drier summers, and others have had more frequent tropical storms than usual? Scientists predict that heatwaves and hurricanes will happen more often if the world keeps warming up. Nobody can prove that global warming is a long-term trend, but it looks more and more likely.

Without the natural "greenhouse effect," the Earth would be as cold as the Moon — too cold for life. Carbon dioxide and other gases in the atmosphere trap the Sun's heat after it has reached the planet's surface, preventing its escape. This heat warms the planet.

When people began to burn coal, and later oil and gas, it changed the composition of the atmosphere. As these fuels burn, carbon dioxide goes up in smoke. Cutting down trees, which take in carbon dioxide during photosynthesis (the process by which they make their food), and burning wood also increase carbon dioxide levels.

Activities that warm the world

Other human activities that release the so-called greenhouse gases include farming, coal mining, gas production, garbage disposal, flying aircraft and driving vehicles, using air conditioning and refrigerators, and making insulation and foam packaging. Greenhouse gases include nitrous oxide, methane, chlorofluorocarbons (CFCs), and low-level ozone, plus carbon dioxide. The world has warmed by 33°F on average over the last 100 years. (The 1980s was the hottest 10-year period on record.)

The Earth has warmed and cooled several times during its history, and in warm periods there has always been more carbon dioxide in the atmosphere than during cool periods. So why worry? The difference is that previous warming has always been very gradual. However, at the current rate, the world could become 36.5°F hotter in just 100 years – too fast for many living things to adapt.

Sea levels are already rising as ice melts and as the water warms and expands. They could get 16 or 20 in. higher, flooding islands and low-lying coasts where millions of people live. Mild-climate zones might benefit from sunnier weather, but many food crops would not thrive in hotter, drier conditions. Many forests would be

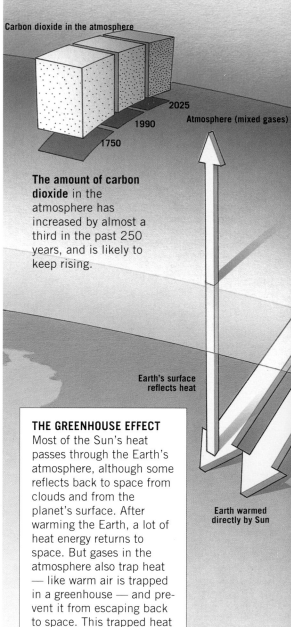

Carbon dioxide in the atmosphere

2025

1990

Atmosphere (mixed gases)

1750

The amount of carbon dioxide in the atmosphere has increased by almost a third in the past 250 years, and is likely to keep rising.

Earth's surface reflects heat

THE GREENHOUSE EFFECT
Most of the Sun's heat passes through the Earth's atmosphere, although some reflects back to space from clouds and from the planet's surface. After warming the Earth, a lot of heat energy returns to space. But gases in the atmosphere also trap heat — like warm air is trapped in a greenhouse — and prevent it from escaping back to space. This trapped heat warms the planet. Human activities add carbon dioxide and other gases to the air, adding to nature's own greenhouse effect.

Earth warmed directly by Sun

reduced to scrubland or desert. Some animals would become extinct; and there might be more violent storms, as well as widespread diseases and pests.

Scientists advise us to reduce the amount of carbon dioxide and other greenhouse gases that we produce. Can we find a way to do this fairly throughout the world?

The Sun is nearly 5 billion years old, halfway through its life as a star. Although the Sun has grown slowly hotter, carbon dioxide in the Earth's atmosphere has decreased since life first began, and this balance kept the Earth's temperature steady until recently.

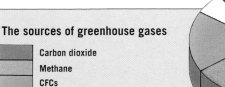

The sources of greenhouse gases

- Carbon dioxide
- Methane
- CFCs
- Nitrous oxide
- Low-altitude ozone

Carbon dioxide is the most important contributor to global warming. Its levels increase as a result of coal, oil, gas, and wood burning, and as we destroy forests. Methane levels are affected by rice cultivation, cattle raising, coal mining, gas leaks, burning garbage, and rotting wastepaper. Refrigerators, aerosols, air conditioning systems, insulation materials, and foam packaging include CFCs. Many countries have reduced the use of CFCs because they damage the important ozone layer in the upper atmosphere. Fuel and wood burning and the use of fertilizers release nitrous oxide. In strong sunlight, air pollution from cars, power stations, and factories produces harmful low-level ozone.

The effects of global warming
We cannot be sure how global warming will affect us in the future. Scientists on the Intergovernmental Panel on Climatic Change (IPCC) agree that the Earth could be 36.5°F warmer 100 years from now due to the presence of more greenhouse gases, especially carbon dioxide, in the atmosphere. This could cause sea levels to rise by 16 in. or more as the water warms and expands, and as polar ice and glaciers melt into the sea. Low-lying islands and coastal areas — such as parts of southeast England and Holland, where millions of people live — may be flooded permanently. Millions of people would lose their homes and farmland, and their supplies of drinking water. Changing temperatures and rainfall patterns could also mean that tree and grass species, including wheat and other basic food crops, no longer grow as well as before, so there would be food shortages and even widespread famine. Animals that cannot adjust to a quickly changing climate would die out. With warmer air currents in the atmosphere, storms will probably be more frequent and more violent. Tropical insects and diseases such as malaria and yellow fever may spread to temperate regions of the world.

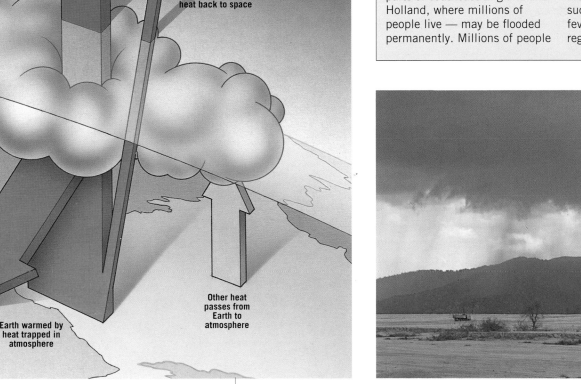

Heat from Sun

Clouds reflect heat

Heat warms atmosphere and clouds

Earth, atmosphere, and clouds radiate heat back to space

Atmosphere traps "greenhouse" heat close to Earth

Earth warmed by heat trapped in atmosphere

Other heat passes from Earth to atmosphere

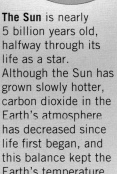

Mount Pinatubo, a volcano in the Philippines, erupted in 1991 and released masses of tiny chemical particles into the air. Scientists think these particles helped screen out sunlight, which could explain why global warming was less noticeable in the early 1990s.

OZONE LOSS

Human-made chemicals called chlorofluorocarbons (ÇFCs) have damaged the ozone layer, 9 to 30 miles high in the Earth's atmosphere. This is the layer that protects the planet against high-energy ultraviolet (UV) rays from the Sun. Any damage to the ozone layer results in these harmful rays reaching the Earth's surface.

CFCs are used in refrigerators, air conditioning systems, spray cans, insulation materials, plastic packaging, and as cleaning fluids. The use of these machines and materials results in the release of CFC gas into the air, where it lingers for between 60 and 400 years. Other chemicals also act as ozone-destroying gases.

It is an alarming thought that a familiar household item such as a refrigerator can damage the environment and ultimately your health. Its cooling liquid may be one of the CFCs or HCFCs that in gas form damage the Earth's ozone layer, resulting in more cases of skin cancer and eye trouble. If we replace old machines with ozone-friendly ones, we can help stop the damage to the ozone layer.

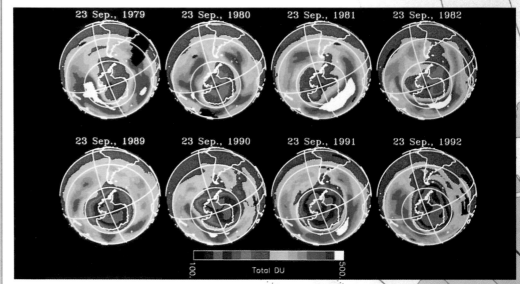

Damage to the ozone layer over Antarctica is visible in this series of satellite images. Red indicates the least ozone loss; yellow, medium loss; while blue, red-brown, and black indicate the worst depletion. By 1992 the ozone "hole" was as big as Antarctica (outlined in white). DU stands for Dobson units, in which ozone levels are measured.

OZONE LOSS
The ozone layer has thinned during the last ten years. Thinning is worst at the poles during early spring, but the layer partly recovers in summer and autumn.

Ozone loss over 10 years

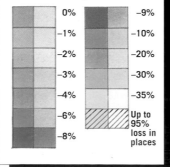

0%	−9%
−1%	−10%
−2%	−20%
−3%	−30%
−4%	−35%
−6%	Up to 95% loss in places
−8%	

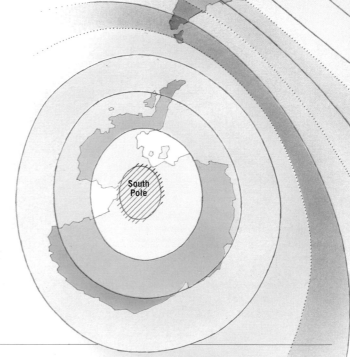

South Pole

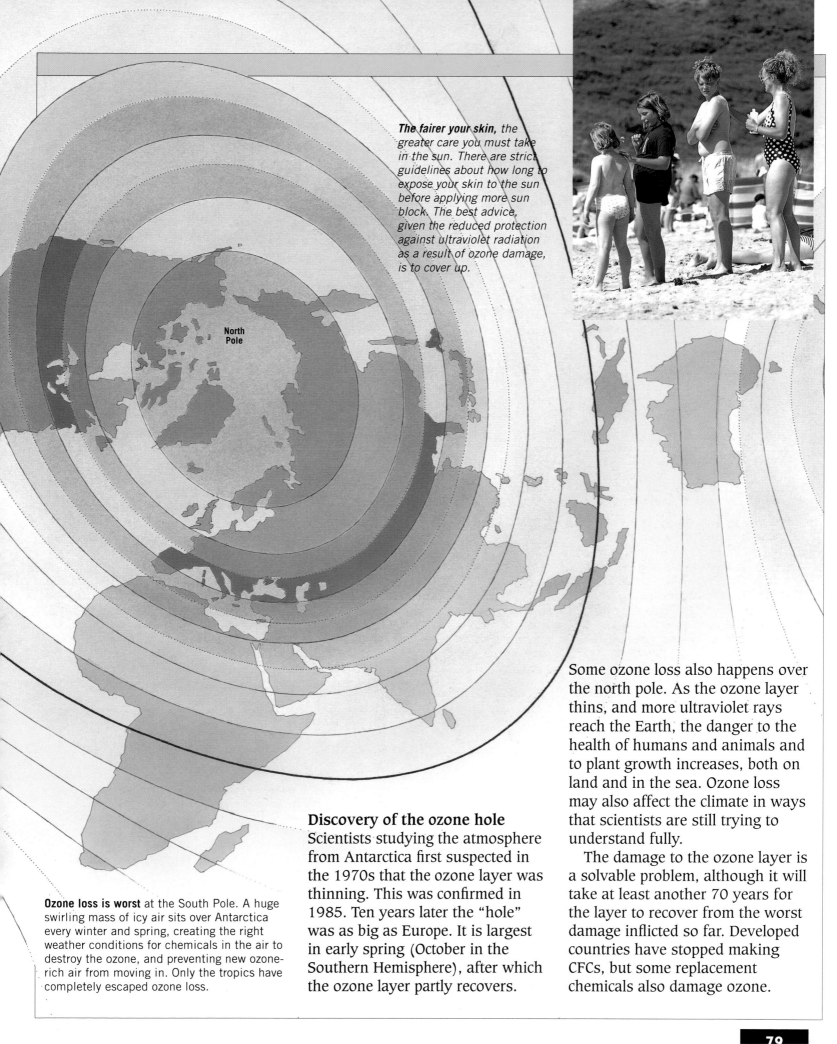

The fairer your skin, the greater care you must take in the sun. There are strict guidelines about how long to expose your skin to the sun before applying more sun block. The best advice, given the reduced protection against ultraviolet radiation as a result of ozone damage, is to cover up.

North Pole

Ozone loss is worst at the South Pole. A huge swirling mass of icy air sits over Antarctica every winter and spring, creating the right weather conditions for chemicals in the air to destroy the ozone, and preventing new ozone-rich air from moving in. Only the tropics have completely escaped ozone loss.

Discovery of the ozone hole

Scientists studying the atmosphere from Antarctica first suspected in the 1970s that the ozone layer was thinning. This was confirmed in 1985. Ten years later the "hole" was as big as Europe. It is largest in early spring (October in the Southern Hemisphere), after which the ozone layer partly recovers.

Some ozone loss also happens over the north pole. As the ozone layer thins, and more ultraviolet rays reach the Earth, the danger to the health of humans and animals and to plant growth increases, both on land and in the sea. Ozone loss may also affect the climate in ways that scientists are still trying to understand fully.

The damage to the ozone layer is a solvable problem, although it will take at least another 70 years for the layer to recover from the worst damage inflicted so far. Developed countries have stopped making CFCs, but some replacement chemicals also damage ozone.

AIR POLLUTION

In the laboratory we treat acid with extreme care because of the damage it can do. On a large scale, the effect of acid, even in a weak form, on trees, water, soils, animals, and buildings, and on human health, can be very damaging. Add to this all the other poisons that modern society pumps into the air, and we have a serious air pollution problem.

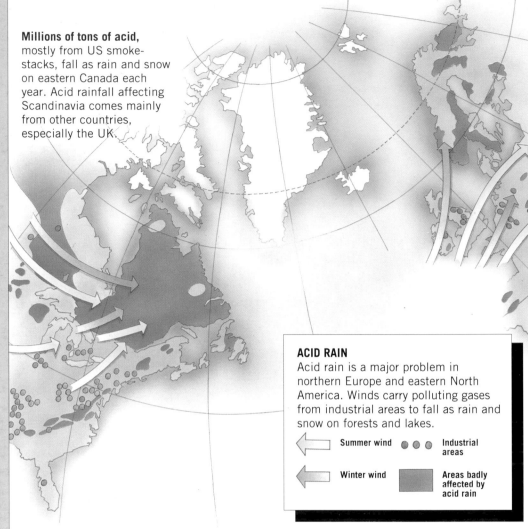

Millions of tons of acid, mostly from US smoke-stacks, fall as rain and snow on eastern Canada each year. Acid rainfall affecting Scandinavia comes mainly from other countries, especially the UK.

ACID RAIN
Acid rain is a major problem in northern Europe and eastern North America. Winds carry polluting gases from industrial areas to fall as rain and snow on forests and lakes.

⬅ Summer wind   ● ● ●   Industrial areas

⬅ Winter wind   ▮   Areas badly affected by acid rain

The air we breathe can be dirty and dangerous because of the pollution it contains. Power stations, factories, motor vehicles, and fuel burning in homes are the main causes of air pollution, which the wind can spread far and wide.

Acid rain

What we call acid rain is the pollution that forms when chemicals in waste gases from motor traffic and chimneys combine with water in the air. The acidic mixture falls as rain, sleet, mist, or snow, or as solid flakes. Northeast North America and parts of Europe suffer most, but the problem is growing worldwide.

Many Scandinavian lakes are lifeless. Their water is too acidic for snails, insects, birds, fish, or plants: only a few mosses, algae, and eels survive. Acid rain has damaged and killed millions of trees in North America, central Europe, Scandinavia, the former Soviet Union, the UK, and else-where. It also harms food crops.

Acid rain also eats away at the stonework of famous monuments such as the Sphinx in Egypt, the Taj Mahal in India, and St. Paul's Cathedral in London, as well as the concrete of modern buildings.

Human health is at risk from all forms of air pollution. Heart and lung disease, asthma, cancer, and

Acid rain: causes and effects

Strong winds carry away sulfur dioxide and nitrogen dioxide that are produced as waste gases in the smoke from the chimneys of power stations and other industrial sites. The gases mix with water in the air to form sulfuric and nitric acid, which then falls as acid rain, sleet, and snow. Acid rain harms trees, other plants, soils, rivers, lakes, fish, and other forms of water life.

Polluting waste gases

Power stations and factories

Acid snow on mountains

Waste gases mixed with water fall as acid rain

Melting acid snow damages soil and trees

Fish die in lakes

Lake-floor mosses survive but other water plants die

reduced brain growth in children may result from it. Poisoned air in some industrial areas of Eastern Europe has caused deformities in thousands of children and many cases of early death.

Waste gases from vehicles and factories often combine in strong sunlight to make a dangerous mixture of ozone and other chemicals that poisons the air.

Big-city smog

Cities suffer from smog (smoke plus fog) when polluted air, caused mainly by motor traffic, is made worse by strong sunlight and cannot escape. Most famously, in Los Angeles, in summer, a layer of warm air lying

over cool air and the surrounding mountains trap a mass of polluted air at ground level. The orange-brown smog damages people's health and plants in particular. Many other cities and industrial areas worldwide are affected by smog.

Strong sunlight

Layer of warm air over cooler air traps smog

City of Los Angeles

San Gabriel Mountains

Smog alerts

These are now a fact of life during the summer in many large cities. In Mexico City the problem is so bad that people have considered using giant fans to clear the air. Air pollution in developing countries includes fumes from high-lead gasoline burned in old, inefficient vehicles, and sooty smoke from coal and charcoal burning.

Some countries have begun to take action. In developed countries power stations have reduced waste gases, and cars use catalytic converters to clean exhaust fumes. Some cities have banned cars or factories; others run their buses on cleaner, plant-based fuels. These solutions are often too expensive for developing countries. We need a wide range of measures, from fuel efficiency to international agreements, to solve the problem.

SPREAD OF POISONS

Is there any plywood, hardboard, or chipboard in your home? Products made from these cheap, handy materials often use glue containing formaldehyde. We now know that this chemical gives off poisonous fumes. Yet we still use it. Isn't it time we stopped adding poisons like formaldehyde to our environment?

HOME ACTION

Help reduce the spread of poisons and pollution.

- Use natural materials at home; wear natural-fiber clothes; do not use harmful chemicals.
- Use rechargeable batteries and fewer battery-powered items; non-rechargeable batteries leak poisonous chemicals after disposal.
- Buy pesticide-free organic food; grow plants organically in your garden, without weedkiller.
- Recycle your refuse and buy recycled goods; with less waste to handle, we can deal with dangerous waste better.
- Reuse plastic bags and other human-made items as many times as possible before replacing them.
- Report illegal waste dumping to the municipal authorities.

POISONS IN THE ENVIRONMENT
Modern industry, including high-tech farming that uses many fertilizers and pesticides, has poisoned rivers and seas, soils and food crops, and animal and human food chains with chemicals that do not naturally break down or disappear. We dump vast amounts of dangerous waste in the ground, where some of it leaks into the soil and groundwater. Developed countries sell developing countries chemicals that they consider too deadly to use at home. Our bodies carry more and more traces of cancer-causing substances.

1 Modern industry produces ever-larger quantities and an ever-greater variety of dangerous chemicals. Many more metals are now known to cause cancer than was thought 50 years ago. PCBs, human-made chemicals used in the plastics and electrical industries, are very damaging to important organs in the body.

2 Dangerous wastes may leak from storage containers and poison the soil and water supplies. People living above an old underground waste dump at Love Canal, in New York State, suffered high levels of cancer and birth defects in the 1970s and 1980s. The national government declared the site a disaster area, and nobody can live there now.

3 Factory wastes pollute many rivers worldwide. But the situation is worst in developing countries where pollution controls are weak and people use the rivers as open sewers. Communities downstream often depend directly on river water for washing, drinking, and watering crops. People whose water is poisoned and polluted in this way suffer illnesses such as gastro-enteritis and more serious problems such as greater numbers of infant deaths.

4 Waste disposal is often cheap in developing countries and not as strictly controlled by governments. Companies in developed countries may try to gain from these low costs and lax controls by shipping dangerous wastes abroad, where dumping sites also tend to be badly managed. Companies in developing countries sometimes accept containers of deadly waste without knowing what the contents are.

Poisons in the food chain
River and coastal waters contain many human-made poisons. Filter-feeding shellfish and plant-feeding fish absorb metals, pesticides, and other deadly substances as they feed. The poisons stay in their body fat. When larger fish, seabirds, and sea mammals feed on the smaller species, the poison enters the larger creature's body. Human beings become part of the chain when they eat the larger fish.

8 Food crops that developed countries buy from developing countries can contain heavy traces of poisonous pesticides. African, Asian, and Latin American coffee, beef, fruit, and vegetables, for example, may be contaminated.

5 Pesticide spraying is often careless, damaging the environment and doing little to help the growth of crops. Pests can get used to a spray so it is no longer effective. When pesticides kill weaker pests — as well as creatures that kill them — stronger ones may increase in number, or new pests may move in. Farmers then need to use even more poisonous chemicals next time, which kill small mammals, birds, and other helpful animals.

6 Companies from developed countries often take advantage of weaker pollution laws and controls in developing countries to set up their more dangerous chemical factories abroad. They also continue to sell to developing countries pesticides such as DDT and other products that they themselves have stopped using because of the dangers to health.

7 Pesticide poisoning harms or kills up to two million people each year — mainly in developing countries, where crop sprayers use the most dangerous chemicals, lack protective clothing, and often either cannot read or do not have instructions in their own language. The effects of poisoning include vomiting, diarrhea, coma, blindness, brain damage, and death.

Dangerous chemicals from modern industry are poisoning our air, water, soil, and food, affecting animal populations and human health. Developed countries were the first to create chemical pollution, but developing countries, building up their industries and modernizing farming methods, are rapidly adding to the problem.

Some of the poisons entering the environment do not exist naturally at all: most are long lasting and almost impossible to dispose of safely. Many of them enter the food chains of plants and animals after factories release them with waste water into rivers and seas. Others leak into underground water supplies, or into the soil, after burial in containers and pits.

Chemicals in the body

Once these chemicals enter the body they threaten its health. "Heavy metals" such as nickel damage the nervous system, lungs, heart, and kidneys. PCB-type chemicals, used in electrical work, and many pesticides are linked with cancer, blood disease, and birth defects. Dioxins — products of paper bleaching, pesticide production, and burning plastic — also cause cancer; traces have been found in disposable diapers.

Most people living in developed countries have small quantities of these chemicals in their bodies. In Germany doctors have told women to breastfeed less because of dioxins in breast milk. The worst poisoning, bringing illness and death to thousands of people, has resulted from factory explosions such as those at Seveso in Italy in 1976 and Bhopal in India in 1984.

NUCLEAR DEBATE

There are beaches in Cumbria, UK, where some people think it is dangerous for children to play, although the danger is invisible. Near these beaches the Sellafield nuclear plant releases radioactive waste water into the sea. Some people argue that having nuclear-powered electricity is worth a few closed-off beaches, while still others believe there is no danger at all. What do you think?

DID YOU KNOW?

How to meet energy needs
Some people say that the further development of nuclear power would help reduce global warming. To meet today's energy needs we would have to build a new nuclear plant every five days for 30 years. US energy companies have found it far cheaper to reduce electricity needs through energy conservation than by building a nuclear power station.

NUCLEAR ENERGY WORLDWIDE
The map compares the number of nuclear reactors each country had at the start of the 1990s with the number they had ten years earlier. It also shows the relative importance of nuclear power as an electricity source in each country, and where the world's major nuclear accidents have taken place.

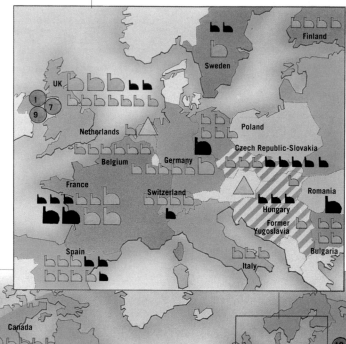

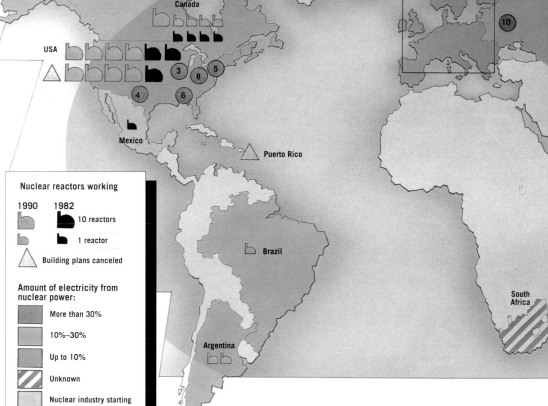

Nuclear reactors working

1990	1982	
		10 reactors
		1 reactor
△		Building plans canceled

Amount of electricity from nuclear power:

More than 30%

10%–30%

Up to 10%

Unknown

Nuclear industry starting

① Nuclear accident sites

NUCLEAR ACCIDENTS
1 In 1957 at Windscale, UK, a reactor fire polluted 320 sq. mi. 20 people subsequently died from cancer.
2 In 1958 in the Urals, in the Soviet Union, a nuclear waste explosion probably killed hundreds of people.
3 In 1968 in Detroit, a reactor overheated and its core began to melt.

4 In 1969 in Colorado, a nuclear waste pile caught fire, leaking radioactive dust.
5 In 1972 in New York, an explosion at a plutonium factory led to its closure.
6 In 1975 at Browns Ferry, Athens, AL, fire damaged emergency

systems and almost destroyed a nuclear reactor.
7 In 1976 at Windscale, UK, 520,000 gal. of radioactive water leaked from a reactor.
8 In 1979 at Three Mile Island, PA, a reactor overheated and began to melt;

How long does radiation last?

The "half-life" of a radioactive material is the time needed for half its radioactivity to die away. The nuclear fuel plutonium has a half-life of 24,000 years. After 50,000 years it will still be deadly.

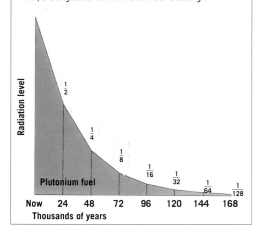

Radiation level

$\frac{1}{2}$ $\frac{1}{4}$ $\frac{1}{8}$ $\frac{1}{16}$ $\frac{1}{32}$ $\frac{1}{64}$ $\frac{1}{128}$

Plutonium fuel

Now 24 48 72 96 120 144 168
Thousands of years

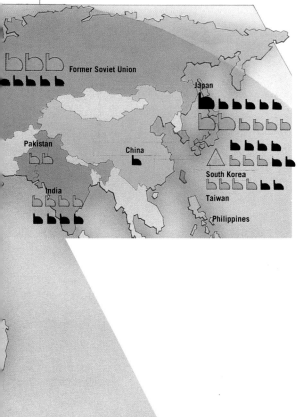

Former Soviet Union

Japan

Pakistan

China

South Korea

India

Taiwan

Philippines

Thirty years ago many people thought nuclear power would supply most of our energy needs. It seemed to promise cheap, clean, safe energy that would not pollute the air or use up fossil fuels. In the 1960s and 1970s France, Japan, the Soviet Union, the UK, the USA, and other countries built nuclear power stations. By the 1990s more than 400 nuclear plants running in 27 countries supplied more than a sixth of the world's electricity.

We now know that nuclear power will never produce low-cost or problem-free electricity. It has proved complicated and expensive to develop, with many technical difficulties. We cannot be sure about the health risks to workers in nuclear power stations and to people living nearby. Whether we can safely handle and dispose of radioactive waste that will be deadly for thousands of years, or safely dismantle nuclear plants when they are too old for use, is even more doubtful.

Then there is the fear of a nuclear disaster. The explosion at Chernobyl in the Soviet Union in 1986 killed thousands of people, ruined the health of very many more, and made huge areas of land unusable. Many nuclear plants in the countries of Eastern Europe need repair.

Some people also fear that terrorist groups will get hold of dangerous radioactive materials from the nuclear industry: both the generation of nuclear power and the manufacture of nuclear weapons use plutonium.

The nuclear industry still has its supporters, and some countries, such as China, still want to develop nuclear power. Yet, after years of pouring vast sums of money into the industry, most countries have stopped building new power plants. Sweden even plans to close down its nuclear industry completely over the next 15 years. Has nuclear power reached the end of the road?

France has 55 nuclear reactors, more than any other country except the USA, and produces three-quarters of its electricty using nuclear power. The Tricastin plant is in the Rhône valley.

radioactive gas leaked, possibly causing thousands of deaths among local people in later years.
9 In 1981 at Windscale, UK, leaking radioactive gas poisoned local dairy herds' milk.
10 In 1986 at Chernobyl, in the

Soviet Union, a reactor explosion caused the world's worst nuclear disaster. Radioactive clouds spread across Europe. Thousands of people in the area surrounding the plant have died from radiation sickness and related cancers.

GAIA WATCH

PLANET-FRIENDLY ENERGY

Everything we do uses energy. At home we need energy for warmth and cooking. Outside we need it for transport, industry, farming, shopping, and at school.

Every household in the world uses energy, but they don't all use electricity or gas. Many use wood, charcoal, paraffin, twigs, leaves, crop remains, or animal dung. Homes in developing countries use much less energy than homes in developed countries. The average person in Ethiopia uses 280 kWh (kilowatt hours) each day, and in Pakistan, 2800 kWh. This contrasts sharply with 47,000 in the UK, and 128,000 in the USA.

In developing countries, people use many forms of energy, including people-power for pulling rickshaws and small carts or carrying loads, and animal-power for pulling plows, carrying loads, or turning waterwheels.

▲ **Animal-power** makes plowing more efficient (main picture) and means farmers do not have to buy expensive machinery. Donkeys also pull carts to market, and animal manure is used as fertilizer.

◀ **Strange-looking objects are appearing** in many villages in India, often next to latrines. They are tanks for collecting waste from latrines and other waste, such as animal dung and leaves, which is mixed with water and added to the tanks. As the waste rots it gives off gas. The gas is collected in a second tank, and fed through pipes to where it is wanted. In this village, near Balgaum, families use the gas for cooking. The rotted waste is used as fertilizer.

We think of wind, water, and solar power as new technologies, but people have been using them for thousands of years. The Sun dries clothes, wood, and pottery, and is used to dry foods to preserve them; the wind powers boats and windmills; and water turns waterwheels and transports timber. New uses are being found for traditional forms of energy.

Hydropower in Vietnam

Na Lang hamlet looks much like any other settlement in the Lao Cai district of Vietnam. It is high up in the mountains, surrounded by terraces of rice and vegetables. The houses have woven bamboo walls and roofs thatched with banana leaves. But there is a difference: the eight families living in Na Lang are using water to make electricity.

Near the hamlet is a small stream and in the bed of the stream are eight small turbines. As the stream flows down the mountain, some of the water is directed into a channel. This makes the water flow fast enough to spin the turbines that generate electricity. The turbines produce enough electricity for every household to have an electric light.

▲ **Fast-flowing mountain streams** are used to drive turbines — here being checked to make sure they are in working order — in this small-scale hydroelectric operation in Vietnam.

◄ **In the Turkana District of Kenya**, windmills are used for drawing groundwater up to the surface. Rainfall is sparse, and the windmills provide a reliable source of water for people and livestock. Families from the surrounding area come here to collect water, to wash, and to water their herds of goats, sheep, and camels.

REUSE, REPAIR, RECYCLE

What happens to garbage thrown on the ground? Metal cans take the rest of your lifetime to break down and disappear. Glass breaks into tiny pieces and then stays that way. Plastic will survive whole or in pieces for hundreds, perhaps thousands, of years. Shouldn't we dispose of these materials in a responsible way?

HOME ACTION

We can all help reduce waste.
- Reject goods in stores that are heavily packaged; try to buy items loose and unpackaged.
- Use refillable containers, for example for milk, and return them.
- Repair things instead of throwing them away: get your broken bike fixed rather than buy a new one.
- Look for recycled products and choose materials that can be recycled easily.
- Give old furniture and other goods to a local charity store or repair workshop.
- Recycle all your paper, cardboard, glass, metal, plastic, and textiles.
- Compost garden and kitchen wastes.
- Campaign for better local recycling facilities in your area, including doorstep collection.

Like all plants and animals, we use energy and produce waste. But the energy, once used, is mostly gone forever, and most human waste is of no use to other living things.

In developed countries people usually consume more resources and produce more waste than those in developing countries, where poorer people make use of as much waste material as possible. Whole families collect, sort, and recycle garbage for a living, often living on the dumps.

In the developed world we have become more aware of waste, and industries are recycling more materials. Car manufacturers now design vehicles with recyclable parts. Community recycling programs have increased, and more businesses use recycled materials. Yet we still live in a "throw-away" society, buying new goods rather than secondhand ones, or rather than repairing old items.

The benefits of waste saving

Reducing waste will help solve problems of energy, pollution, garbage disposal, and jobs. If all US beverage containers were returnable, we would save half a million tons of glass and 50 million tons of oil a year. Of the third of a ton of garbage that the average Western European creates each year, most is buried underground (some is burned, giving off poisonous fumes). Yet recycling creates more jobs than dumping.

Working together, we can do more as customers and householders. Industries should make products longer lasting and easily recyclable; governments can do more to encourage waste saving.

Recycling paper saves forests and energy and reduces the amount of greenhouse gases given off into the atmosphere. The world recycles only a quarter of its paper today: by doubling this amount we would free millions of acres of forest from paper production. Some countries, such as Mexico, Japan, and the Netherlands, already recycle about half their paper.

Recycling iron and steel saves energy and water, cuts out mining wastes, reduces pollution by three-quarters, and creates thousands of jobs. The world makes a quarter of its steel, and the USA more than a third of its steel, from recycled scrap metal. Metal can be used many times, so in the future we should be able to use recycled scrap for almost all our steel needs.

Recycling aluminum saves about 95 percent of the energy needed to make a new soda can, so it saves money too. Today we recycle less than a third of the aluminum we use, but it should be possible to recycle more than three-quarters. If all states charged a deposit on soda and juice cans, aluminum recycling would increase enormously.

Sorting is the key to recycling. Recycling programs in North America, Western Europe, Japan, and elsewhere rely on people sorting their household refuse at recycling centers or for collection. Machines can help: for example, magnets remove scrap iron and steel. In developing countries many people depend on refuse sorting and recycling for a living, although this is unhealthy, low-paid work.

Job creation is an important benefit of recycling. Repair and recycling are cheaper and provide more work than dumping or burning refuse. In the USA more people work in recycling than in metal mining, and the recycling industry is creating more jobs worldwide. Millions of people in developing countries already earn their living by repairing and recycling, which is useful work that should be fairly rewarded.

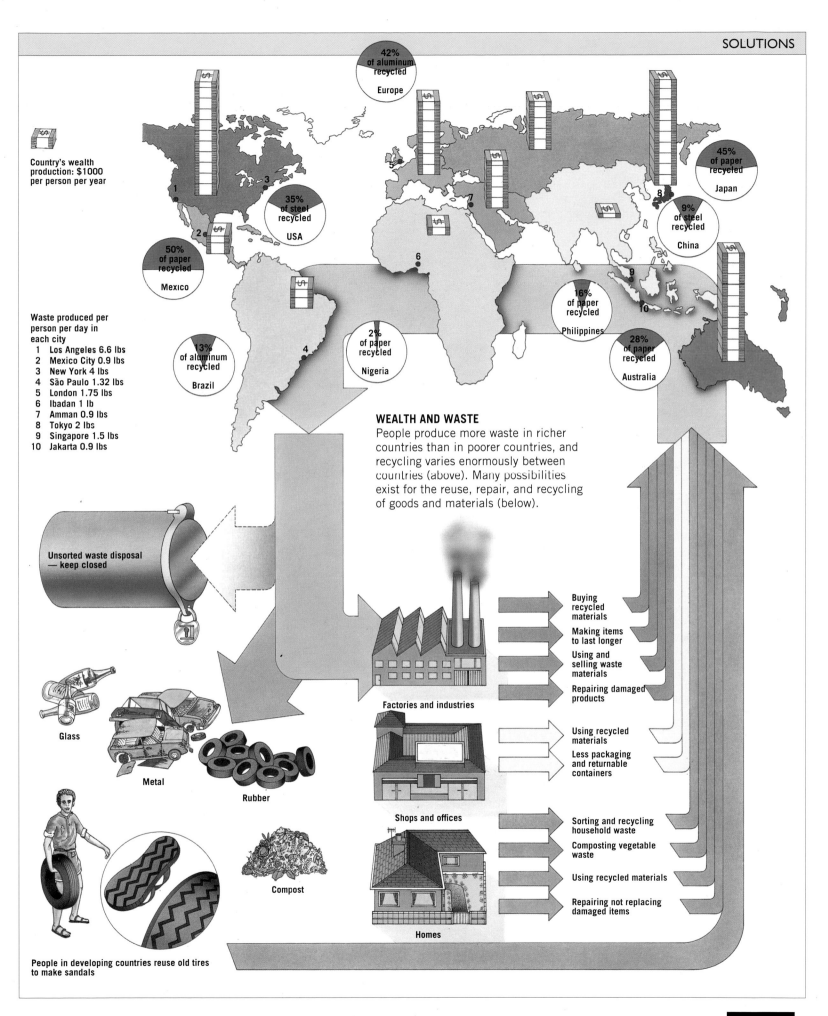

Country's wealth
production: $1000
per person per year

42%
of aluminum
recycled
Europe

45%
of paper
recycled
Japan

35%
of steel
recycled
USA

9%
of steel
recycled
China

50%
of paper
recycled
Mexico

Waste produced per
person per day in
each city
1   Los Angeles 6.6 lbs
2   Mexico City 0.9 lbs
3   New York 4 lbs
4   São Paulo 1.32 lbs
5   London 1.75 lbs
6   Ibadan 1 lb
7   Amman 0.9 lbs
8   Tokyo 2 lbs
9   Singapore 1.5 lbs
10 Jakarta 0.9 lbs

13%
of aluminum
recycled
Brazil

2%
of paper
recycled
Nigeria

16%
of paper
recycled
Philippines

28%
of paper
recycled
Australia

WEALTH AND WASTE
People produce more waste in richer
countries than in poorer countries, and
recycling varies enormously between
countries (above). Many possibilities
exist for the reuse, repair, and recycling
of goods and materials (below).

Unsorted waste disposal
— keep closed

Glass

Metal

Rubber

Compost

People in developing countries reuse old tires
to make sandals

Factories and industries

Buying
recycled
materials

Making items
to last longer

Using and
selling waste
materials

Repairing damaged
products

Shops and offices

Using recycled
materials

Less packaging
and returnable
containers

Homes

Sorting and recycling
household waste

Composting vegetable
waste

Using recycled materials

Repairing not replacing
damaged items

NEW ENERGY PATHS

Do you use a solar-powered calculator or battery charger? Such simple everyday items that make the most of pollution-free natural resources — in this case sunlight — show modern science and technology at their best. If only providing almost 6 billion people with the energy they need for living were equally simple!

The Earth cannot support increasing numbers of people burning more and more fuel. But people will always need energy for heating, lighting, cooking, and transport. Changing the nature and distribution of that energy use, and ensuring a fairer sharing of wealth so that people in the developing world can improve their living standards, could be humankind's biggest challenge yet. We need to switch from fossil fuels and nuclear power to renewable sources, while saving energy whenever we can. Where fossil fuels are in use, we need more efficient methods such as those that recycle waste heat, reducing the amount of fuel used.

Renewable energy sources, such as water power, wood, charcoal, and animal dung, provide nearly a fifth of the world's energy today. To increase this share, solar power, which works even on cloudy days, has to be further developed and its use extended. Millions of homes worldwide now have solar water heaters, and solar electric cells can effectively provide a power source for entire buildings.

From high-energy past to lower-energy future
We have used energy carelessly, building giant power stations and drilling new oil wells whenever we wanted more fuel or power. The challenge is to use far less energy, produced by means of the least polluting methods, to meet our needs.

The old way of providing energy (below, left) in developed countries and in some parts of the developing world depends on large power stations using fossil fuels, nuclear power, and hydroelectricity. We waste much of this energy, and create masses of pollution and "throw-away" goods.

The new energy path (below, right) will provide modern comforts but by means of energy-efficient and less polluting methods. Fossil fuels and large-scale power sources can be replaced by local, small-scale energy sources based on solar, wind, and water power operations, and biogas.

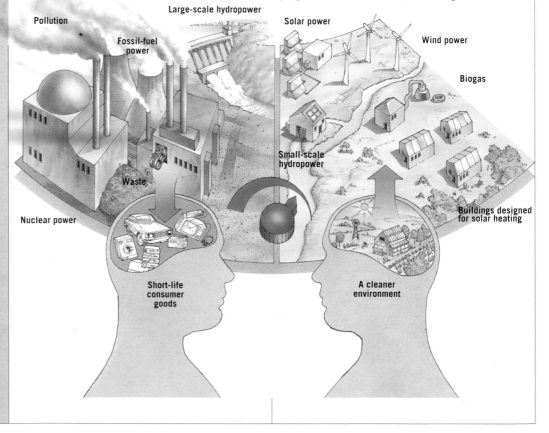

Pollution

Large-scale hydropower

Solar power

Wind power

Fossil-fuel power

Biogas

Nuclear power

Waste

Small-scale hydropower

Short-life consumer goods

A cleaner environment

Buildings designed for solar heating

Factories, offices, and other work-places are now investing in ways of saving energy. Combined heating and power-generation systems recycle waste heat, saving fuel.

WORLD OF WORK

IN THE HOME

TRANSPORT

Fuel-efficient cars, carpooling and park-and-ride plans

Carefully planned transport systems

More buses, trolleys, and light railways

Towns and cities encourage walking and cycling

Tomorrow's transport systems will make better use of efficient train, trolley, and bus networks. Town planning will reduce people's need to travel long distances for work, shopping, and entertainment.

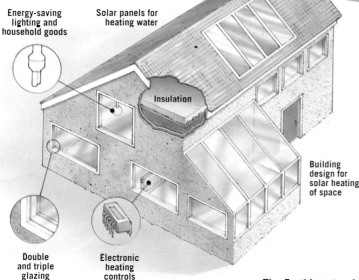

Energy-saving lighting and household goods

Solar panels for heating water

Insulation

Building design for solar heating of space

Double and triple glazing

Electronic heating controls

In the home we can quite easily halve the amount of energy we use for heating, lighting, hot water, and food storage. Energy-efficient lightbulbs use 75 percent less energy than others, and well-designed modern buildings require less heating or cooling. The best refrigerators use only a quarter of the electricity other models need.

The Earth's natural heat can be used as a source of energy — geothermal energy. Hot springs occur where water heated deep in the Earth's crust comes to the surface. In some places the springs are close to towns and cities. In Lyon, France, geothermally heated water is used to heat homes directly, an energy-efficient system.

Making the most of alternatives
Businesses now know that energy efficiency saves money as well as reducing pollution. A low-energy lightbulb saves $30 a year. Car manufacturers can build vehicles four times more fuel-efficient than the worst gas-guzzlers. Transporting goods by rail or canal, rather than by road, can bring huge savings.

In developing countries many people depend on firewood and need millions of new trees. Local people are best at protecting the forest: successes include village tree planting in Kenya, and a program in South Korea that has reforested a third of the country.

Biogas is another major source of energy in the developing world.

Made from animal dung and human waste, it is widely used for lighting, cooking, and powering machinery. Other systems include small-scale hydropower supplies and fuel from sugarcane and other crops. Renewable energy relies more on people than on costly equipment, creating jobs and suiting poor countries in particular.

5
FRESH WATER

"Of all our natural resources, water has become the most precious."

RACHEL CARSON,
US scientist and author
of *Silent Spring*

"Water, water, everywhere, nor any drop to drink" runs *The Rime of the Ancient Mariner* by Samuel Taylor Coleridge, reminding us that, despite all the saltwater in the oceans, we cannot survive without fresh water. Thirst is one of the most terrible ways to suffer and die. *Silent Spring*, a book published in 1962, first alerted us to the dangers posed to our water supplies by damage inflicted on the environment. Why is it, when we can explore the farthest reaches of the Solar System and link all the world's cities by immensely complicated computer systems, that we can't ensure that every man, woman, and child on Earth has the safe water that they need for health and survival?

The magnificent Iguaçu Falls — on the border of Argentina and Brazil — demonstrates in 275 separate falls, divided by forested, rocky outcrops, the power and drama of the natural flow of fresh water.

CLIMATE & RAIN

Some people complain a lot about the weather, especially if it rains heavily on a day when they want sunshine. But regular rainfall is one of the best things that the climate can bring us — as anybody who has lived in drought conditions can tell you. If it rained a lot less, we might soon experience serious food shortages.

Temperature and winds vary around the world. The hottest regions are where the Sun is directly overhead, at and near the equator. Warm damp air at the equator rises and moves toward the poles, carrying heat and warming colder lands. Below this, cooler air moves toward the equator from the tropics. The direction of the resulting winds curves because the Earth spins.

Ocean currents are the result of winds, the Earth's rotation, and the position of the continents. Carrying huge amounts of water, currents affect climate. The Labrador Current flowing from the arctic brings lower temperatures to northeast Canada. The Gulf Stream flowing from the Gulf of Mexico raises temperatures in Northwest Europe.

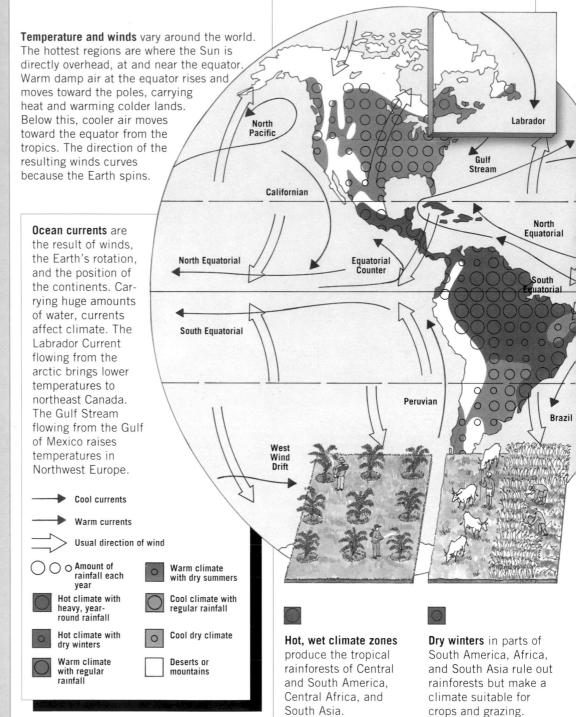

→ Cool currents

→ Warm currents

⇨ Usual direction of wind

○○○ Amount of rainfall each year

◉ Hot climate with heavy, year-round rainfall

◉ Hot climate with dry winters

◉ Warm climate with regular rainfall

◘ Warm climate with dry summers

◉ Cool climate with regular rainfall

◌ Cool dry climate

☐ Deserts or mountains

Hot, wet climate zones produce the tropical rainforests of Central and South America, Central Africa, and South Asia.

Dry winters in parts of South America, Africa, and South Asia rule out rainforests but make a climate suitable for crops and grazing.

Weather can change from one day to the next: climate describes weather patterns over a longer period. Climates vary around the world as the Sun's heat, winds, sea currents, and the frequency of rainfall affect each region differently. Climates have changed throughout the planet's history.

During the last ice age, 10,500 years ago, average temperatures on Earth were 36.5°F cooler than today — a lot in climatic terms.

The strength of the Sun varies according to latitude, or distance from the equator. The Earth is warmest at the equator, where the Sun is most directly overhead.

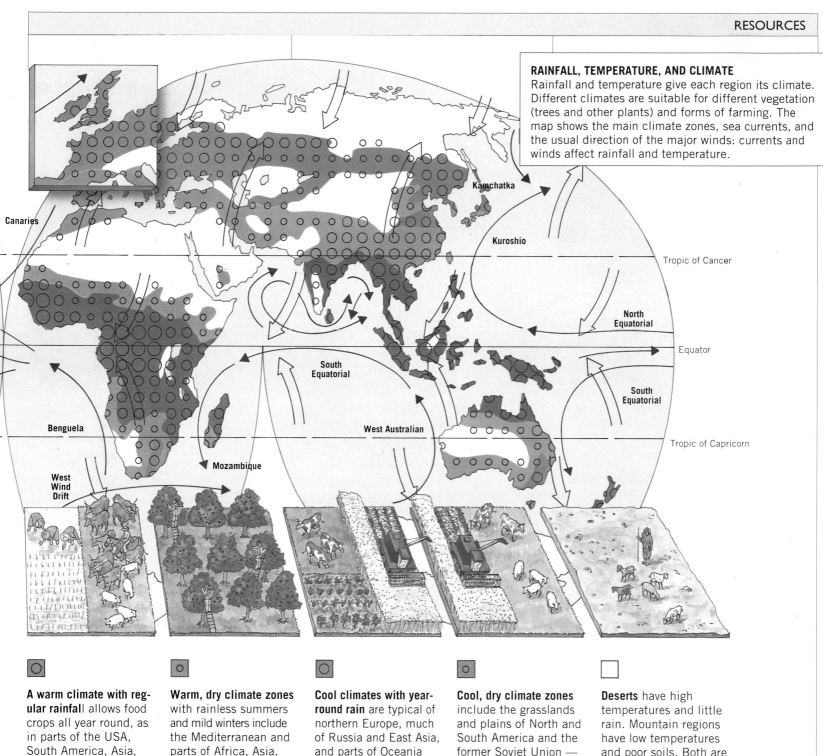

RAINFALL, TEMPERATURE, AND CLIMATE
Rainfall and temperature give each region its climate. Different climates are suitable for different vegetation (trees and other plants) and forms of farming. The map shows the main climate zones, sea currents, and the usual direction of the major winds: currents and winds affect rainfall and temperature.

Canaries

Kamchatka

Kuroshio

Tropic of Cancer

North Equatorial

Equator

South Equatorial

South Equatorial

Benguela

West Australian

Tropic of Capricorn

Mozambique

West Wind Drift

A warm climate with regular rainfall allows food crops all year round, as in parts of the USA, South America, Asia, and eastern Australia.

Warm, dry climate zones with rainless summers and mild winters include the Mediterranean and parts of Africa, Asia, and Australia.

Cool climates with year-round rain are typical of northern Europe, much of Russia and East Asia, and parts of Oceania and North America.

Cool, dry climate zones include the grasslands and plains of North and South America and the former Soviet Union — lands of grain and cows.

Deserts have high temperatures and little rain. Mountain regions have low temperatures and poor soils. Both are unsuitable for crops.

At the poles, the Sun's rays reach the planet at a low sloping angle, giving less heat. Winds — flows of warm or cool air — help to even out temperatures worldwide, as do ocean currents.

Water evaporates (rises in tiny droplets) into the air from warm seas and later falls as rain or snow.

The shape of the land affects rainfall. Warm winds carrying water rise and cool when they reach mountains, releasing rain (which eventually feeds rivers). The winds continue as dry winds on the other side of the mountains.

Each climate zone has plants that are typical of that region.

They range from steamy rainforest trees to the small, sparse shrubs and mosses of the far north. Climate limits food production. Too much or too little warmth or water destroys crops and harms livestock. Low rainfall in the Sahel in Africa, combined with the effects of war, has led to terrible famines.

WATER RESERVES

Imagine a flood that covered all the continents on Earth with 32 inches of water. That's how much rain and snow fall on land every year. With so much fresh water coming our way, it seems impossible that we could ever be short of it. Yet because of uneven distribution and as a result of a variety of human activities, serious water shortages occur.

It is amazing how little of all the water on our planet we can use. Only a small fraction is fresh — the rest, seawater, is too salty for our needs — and much of the fresh water is permanently frozen or deep underground. Although about 40,000 cubic kilometres of fresh water (more than a quadrillion gallons) flow from rivers and lakes each year, two-thirds of this disappears in floods or enters swamps and the soil before we can collect or save it.

There should still be more than enough for all the world's people. The trouble is that water is not always available in large enough quantities where it is needed. Canada and China, for example, receive similar amounts of rainfall each year, but China has 40 times more people. So each Chinese man, woman, or child has roughly 40 times less water than the average Canadian.

City inhabitants in developed countries use up to 50 times more water than villagers in developing countries. Most modern toilets, for example, use at least a gallon of what is usually drinking-quality water each time they flush — as much as some people in developing countries have for all their daily needs. Millions of women and children have to walk for hours every day to fetch the few quarts of water they need.

It is easy to take a steady supply of water for granted: but without it our health would suffer and our way of life could come to a halt. Farmland irrigation and industries that make plastics and paper consume huge quantities of water.

The main uses of fresh water are for irrigating farmland, for industry — as a cooling liquid, for cleaning purposes, and to water down pollution, for example — and for household needs such as drinking, cooking, keeping clean, laundry, dishwashing, and, in developed countries, toilet flushing, garden watering, and car washing.

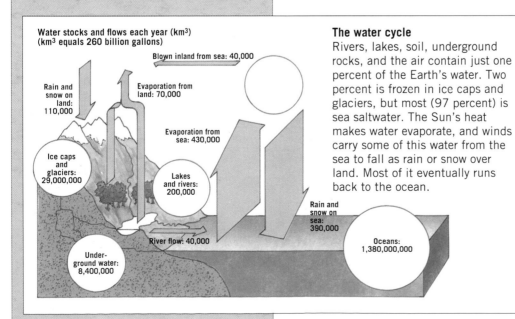

Water stocks and flows each year (km³)
(km³ equals 260 billion gallons)

Blown inland from sea: 40,000

Rain and snow on land: 110,000

Evaporation from land: 70,000

Evaporation from sea: 430,000

Ice caps and glaciers: 29,000,000

Lakes and rivers: 200,000

Rain and snow on sea: 390,000

River flow: 40,000

Oceans: 1,380,000,000

Underground water: 8,400,000

The water cycle
Rivers, lakes, soil, underground rocks, and the air contain just one percent of the Earth's water. Two percent is frozen in ice caps and glaciers, but most (97 percent) is sea saltwater. The Sun's heat makes water evaporate, and winds carry some of this water from the sea to fall as rain or snow over land. Most of it eventually runs back to the ocean.

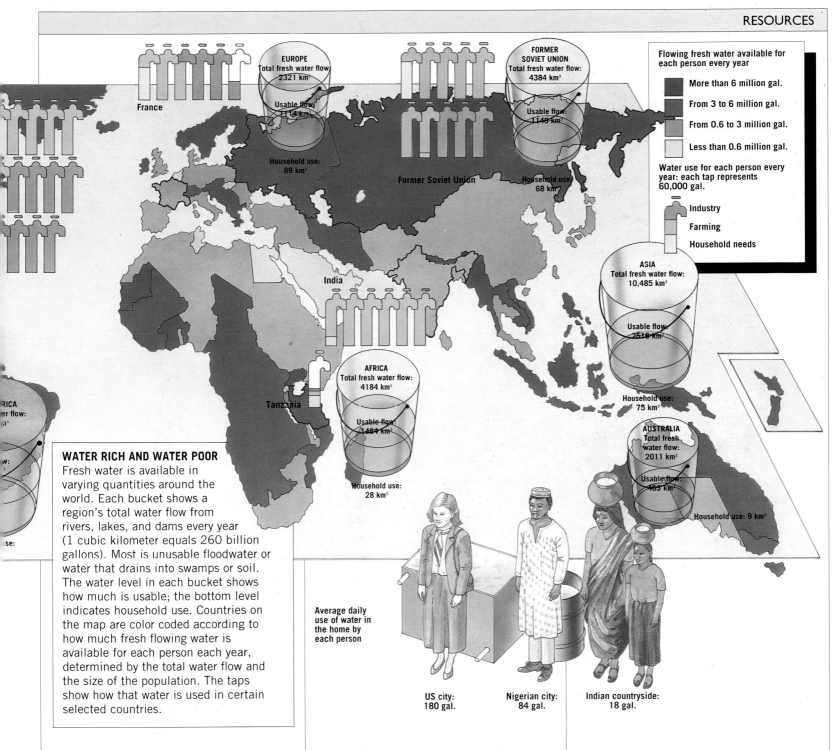

Flowing fresh water available for each person every year

- More than 6 million gal.
- From 3 to 6 million gal.
- From 0.6 to 3 million gal.
- Less than 0.6 million gal.

Water use for each person every year: each tap represents 60,000 gal.

- Industry
- Farming
- Household needs

EUROPE
Total fresh water flow: 2321 km³
Usable flow: 1114 km³
Household use: 89 km³

France

FORMER SOVIET UNION
Total fresh water flow: 4384 km³
Usable flow: 1140 km³
Household use: 68 km³

Former Soviet Union

India

ASIA
Total fresh water flow: 10,485 km³
Usable flow: 2518 km³
Household use: 75 km³

AFRICA
Total fresh water flow: 4184 km³
Usable flow: 1484 km³
Household use: 28 km³

Tanzania

AUSTRALIA
Total fresh water flow: 2011 km³
Usable flow: 465 km³
Household use: 9 km³

RICA
er flow:
w:
se:

WATER RICH AND WATER POOR

Fresh water is available in varying quantities around the world. Each bucket shows a region's total water flow from rivers, lakes, and dams every year (1 cubic kilometer equals 260 billion gallons). Most is unusable floodwater or water that drains into swamps or soil. The water level in each bucket shows how much is usable; the bottom level indicates household use. Countries on the map are color coded according to how much fresh flowing water is available for each person each year, determined by the total water flow and the size of the population. The taps show how that water is used in certain selected countries.

Average daily use of water in the home by each person

US city: 180 gal.

Nigerian city: 84 gal.

Indian countryside: 18 gal.

Developed countries do, however, recycle a surprisingly large amount of water. More than three-quarters of the water that runs in our homes and factories may go back into rivers, from where we take it again, purify it, and reuse it.

The demand for water is increasing everywhere, and human activities are overstretching the available supplies in many regions.

People add to the amount of surface water by bringing up more from underground, some using traditional wells, others by means of modern pumping stations. However, "mining" water can be expensive and people often consume supplies faster than they can be replaced. Such sources may have taken hundreds or thousands of years to collect.

About 48 gallons of water a day are — or perhaps should be — enough for the needs of the average person. But levels of water use vary enormously from region to region worldwide. In the USA average daily consumption in the home is 180 gallons or more, whereas people in Madagascar use less than a fiftieth of this amount. Irrigation is by far the world's biggest water user, although the manufacture of plastics and other industries are also very "thirsty." Much of the water that we use in homes and factories flows back into rivers, from where it is taken again and reused: most irrigation water is never recovered.

WATER THAT KILLS

Do you drink tap water? Some people in developed countries worry about water quality and drink only bottled water or use a water filter. That may be wise. But let's not forget that in developing countries many people drink, cook with, and wash in water dirtier than that used in developed countries for flushing toilets.

DID YOU KNOW?

Where water is not on tap
In developing countries millions of village women and children have to walk for hours each day to fetch water from the nearest pond or stream. Poor people in cities are also badly off, standing in line for hours in the street at public taps or buying water from private sellers at very high prices. In many cities in the developing world, richer people usually live upstream where water is relatively clean, while the poor live downstream and receive only dirty supplies for their daily needs.

Many developing countries worked hard to provide safe water and toilet facilities for all in the 1980s, with support from the UN. But they could not keep pace with rising populations: by 1990 there were more people without clean water than 10 years earlier.

Hundreds of millions of people in developing countries do not have clean water and proper sanitation (facilities to protect public health). With no drinkable water near their homes, they use ponds, streams, rivers, and lakes for their water supply and as toilet sites, often using the same water over and over again, risking their health every day.

Unsafe water is the world's main carrier of disease. People who drink, cook, wash, and bathe using dirty water become ill with malaria, river blindness, cholera, leprosy, hepatitis, yellow fever, and a host of other serious infections. Insects, snails, and worms that breed in water spread many of these illnesses, which kill at least 25 million people throughout the world — including 15 million children — each year. Diarrhea is the biggest water-linked killer, especially of young children, often through repeated attacks on the same person.

The countries of the world agreed at the United Nations in 1981 to make major new efforts over the next ten years to bring safe, clean water supplies and proper toilet facilities to all their people. Many countries, such as

Malawi in Africa and Bangladesh and India in Asia, made good progress. Yet, because of increasing human numbers, there were more people without water and sanitation in 1990 than there had been a decade earlier.

The problem is worst in the countryside, where many villagers live a long walk away from the nearest supply of often unclean water. But large numbers of town and city dwellers in developing countries are also badly off. In Cairo in Egypt, for example, 11 million people make do with water supply and sewage systems that were designed for a population of just two million. Many rivers in cities in developing countries are used as that city's main sewer.

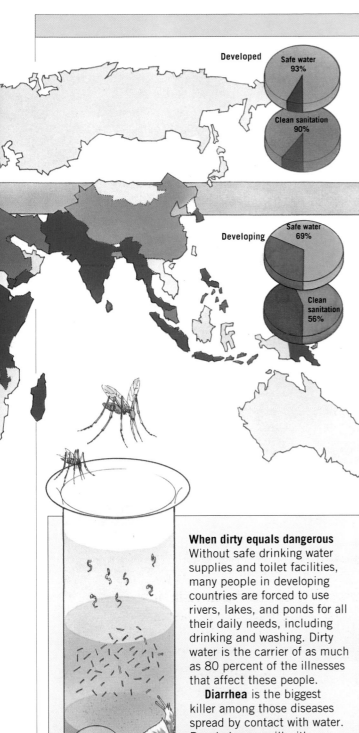

Developed

Safe water
93%

Clean sanitation
90%

Developing

Safe water
69%

Clean sanitation
56%

WHO HAS SAFE WATER? — THE NORTH–SOUTH DIVIDE

Percentage of the population who have safe water available

- 0%–40%
- 81%–100%
- 41%–80%
- No information

The map shows those populations that do not have adequate access to safe water supplies. The availability of clean water varies greatly across the world. Almost everyone living in developed countries, which are mainly in the North, has both clean water and reasonable sanitation facilities. In developing countries of the South nearly one person in three lacks safe water, and more than two out of five lack sanitation facilities.

Counting taps, not beds
Experts often count the number of hospital beds for every 1000 people to compare countries' health services. But the number of taps and toilets per 1000 people is probably a better indicator of the health of the population.

When dirty equals dangerous
Without safe drinking water supplies and toilet facilities, many people in developing countries are forced to use rivers, lakes, and ponds for all their daily needs, including drinking and washing. Dirty water is the carrier of as much as 80 percent of the illnesses that affect these people.

Diarrhea is the biggest killer among those diseases spread by contact with water. People become ill with diarrhea through drinking or washing in infected water. They then lack the clean water that would help them recover. About 10 million people — almost half of them children aged under 5 — die each year from some form of this disease, which is not a killer in the developed world.

Malaria is also a water-related killer. It affects many millions of people and results in more than 1 million deaths every year. Insects that breed in water, such as mosquitoes, spread malaria, yellow fever, and other diseases.

Contact with snails and worms that carry parasites and breed in unsafe water can cause infections in adults and children, killing 1 million people each year.

Hookworms enter the human body when the eggs are swallowed or when the young burrow through the soles of people's feet. The disease of the same name occurs where there are inadequate toilet facilities. Every year thousands of children in developing countries die from it.

Other illnesses that result from a lack of clean water include leprosy, cholera, river blindness, and scabies. These diseases, most of which affect the skin and eyes, do not usually kill but they harm the health of hundreds of millions of people.

The costs of unsafe water
Besides the great human suffering inflicted, a high rate of illness and death makes poor countries even poorer. India, for example, loses 73 million work days every year to illnesses caused by unsafe water, with the cost of medical treatment and lost production reaching close to $1 billion.

The deaths of many children in developing countries from water-related diseases encourages people to have more children than they really want, because of the fear that some of their children will die. This keeps families poor, harms women's health, and, if all their children do survive, adds to the problem of fast-growing populations in the developing world. This, in turn, prevents these countries from improving their living standards.

WATER SUPPLIES IN SUDAN

Sheikh Issa Wintuk lives in Omeim, a Beja settlement in a valley in North Tokar, Sudan. The village is encircled by rocky mountains, jagged peaks, dry earth, and sand dunes. Acacia trees, shaped by the wind, are scattered through the valley.

In the past, wells were dug by hand. The walls often fell in, the wells dried up, and people then had to travel a long way to find water. Even when the wells were full, the water was rarely clean. People often fell ill.

Sheikh Issa Wintuk is helping to build a new well in his community. "We heard that Oxfam supported people in making wells for agriculture and domestic use, and we started a well, which you see us working on now.

"I attended a hygiene workshop in Tokar, and learned that many diseases are caused by tiny creatures present in dirty water. When I got home, I told people what I had learned. It was clear that we must have a proper well and clean water."

▲ *This dry, wind-blown landscape,* with its sand dunes and scattered pockets of hardy vegetation, is typical of North Tokar in Sudan.

▶ *New wells* are being dug in several villages in the region. All new wells are lined with clay bricks to stop the walls from caving in.

The people of another village, Dolabiay, have built a well too. They are using water from the well for irrigation to grow food. They needed a pump, and someone to keep it running. Mohammed Ahmed El Haj was chosen to attend a course: "I have been trained to maintain the water pump. I know how to take apart and reassemble a pump, as well as maintaining it."

Not so long ago, the Beja were pastoralists, dependent on cattle, camels, sheep, and goats. They were nomads, traveling great distances from their settlements in search of pasture and water. Now, some families still have animals, but only the men travel with them; women and children stay in the villages. Many people have decided that there are advantages in living in a settled community: better water supplies, health care, schools, and training for adults. But, in other countries, pastoralists have been forced by governments to give up their traditional way of life without such community support.

▼ **The establishment of a supply of water** encourages permanent settlement. Hadlul Ahmed Adam is in his family vegetable garden in Khor Baraka. The family grows melon, okra, and millet.

▼ **Women and children** from Belgigio settlement gather at the new communal well to wash clothes.

WISE USE OF WATER

Do you let the tap run all the time when you brush your teeth, or only as you need water? Turning it off may not make much difference to the total amount of water you use each day, but if everybody did the same, it would reduce water consumption significantly. It is also a way to remember how important water is and the wisdom of using it more carefully.

Water is piped from spring to village in bamboo tubes in Java, Indonesia. When villagers have taken all they need, they put a stopper in the end of the pipe so no water is wasted.

Water shortages and wastage, and the lack of clean supplies in developing countries, are serious and sometimes connected problems. People without enough clean water may live near large farms that use water wastefully when irrigating land. Governments of developing countries could help to manage supplies better by preventing big water users — farms and factories — from taking more than their fair share, as well as helping to provide villages with the safe water supplies and sanitation they need.

MANAGING WATER BETTER

Our use of water is likely to increase. Careful water management will help us meet tomorrow's needs. New dams, computerized monitoring of supplies, less wasteful crop irrigation, more water recycling, the replacement of leaking supply systems, and the use of water-efficient equipment will all be important. We will also need to use water less wastefully in our daily lives.

River dams (1) help control flooding and store water. But large dams can bring large problems, including increases in water-related diseases around the lake and irrigation channels. Small dams are often better.

Computerized monitoring (2), linked to satellite systems, can provide up-to-date information on floods and water pollution.

"Drip-feed" irrigation (3) is a low-waste method of keeping food crops well watered by the release of small amounts of water directly to parts of the plant that need it. Other irrigation systems waste up to 70 percent of water used. Farmers can irrigate crops less wastefully by employing more people to work on the land.

Health education helps people make the best use of clean water supplies and toilet facilities once these are working.

Involving local people in setting up and running water and sanitation programs gives them the best chance of success.

Money in the hands of local people often solves sanitation problems better than money controlled by government.

Better health results from clean water and sanitation programs, which reduce both the risks and the costs of disease.

Fewer children become ill and die where there is clean water and good sanitation. We could save millions more young lives.

Populations grow more slowly if more children survive. People do not need to have more children in case some die.

Clean water for health

It would cost less than the world spends on weapons every two months to give everybody on the planet clean water and sanitation. The diagram shows three important conditions needed for successful water and sanitation programs, and three major results of programs such as these in developing countries.

Old, leaking supply systems in cities **(4)** waste a lot of water, and need replacing. Also, we need more systems such as those in Hong Kong, Italy, and Japan that use wastewater and seawater when pure water is not needed.

These programs can do more to improve people's health than building new hospitals.

Villagers often need health education as well as clean water. Programs usually work best when local people play a role in deciding where to set up wells and pumps, help to build and keep them in working order, as well as controlling the money involved.

Tomorrow's water-consuming equipment (5), such as washing machines, will waste much less water. Many such machines could run perfectly well on partly treated wastewater instead of water of drinking quality.

Low-cost toilets, including composting ones that turn human waste into clean, useful fertilizer, often work better and are easier to repair than expensive piped sewage systems. The main results of improvements in water supply and sanitation include better health, fewer child deaths, and ultimately slower population growth.

Farming — the biggest consumer of water — and industry both need to apply less wasteful methods of using water. These include better irrigation control in farming, and in industry more recycling of waste materials — which often saves water — and of waste water itself.

Today we pump a lot of water from pure underground sources, or purify other supplies, before using it for activities that do not need the cleanest water, including toilet flushing, clothes washing, crop irrigation, and many purposes in factories. Tomorrow's towns and cities could have systems — already developed on a small scale — that save the purest water for important uses such as in kitchens and hospitals, while meeting other needs with less pure, "recycled" water, or even seawater. Without such changes we could all face major water shortages in the not-too-distant future.

Warm wastewater from factories **(6)** could be piped to greenhouses or fish ponds, reducing river pollution.

103

6
PLANTS AND ANIMALS

"Our special responsibility . . . is more than is expected of the elephants and butterflies. In making sure that they and their future generations survive, we shall be ensuring the survival of our own species."

WANGARI MAATHAI,
leader of Kenya's Green Belt
movement, which has planted
millions of new trees

The natural world is filled with wonders and surprises, from the complicated chemistry that takes place inside the tiniest life-forms to the ways in which different species of plants and animals interact with each other. Human beings are very much part of the world of plants and animals, not outside it, and we can be proud of many of our achievements in understanding the workings of the rest of nature. Yet we are unique in our ability to affect what happens on our planet. No other species is as powerful. Often too clever for our own good, we have badly interfered with the natural environment. Now is the time to repair the damage done.

African elephants stride out across their native savanna. These intelligent, social animals were put at risk of extinction by hunters who killed them for their tusks. A worldwide ban in 1989, however, has led to a steady reduction in the ivory trade.

WEB OF LIFE

Most of us have tiny, spider-like mites living on our skin. You can scrape them off your forehead and see them under a microscope. These creatures are just one example of the way life forms exist everywhere, often where we least expect them. Perhaps equally as surprising are the many and complex connections between all living things that are as important as the differences between them.

LIFE FORMS AND THEIR LINKS

All plants and animals have developed by means of evolution over tens or hundreds of millions of years. They all share the same "building blocks" of life — tiny living cells that contain substances such as nucleic acids. One of these, DNA, is the basis of the genetic "information" passed from one generation to the next. Different species depend on each other in many ways, especially through food webs, in which flows of energy, nutrients (nourishing substances), and minerals link plants and animals together.

Life began on Earth 3.7 billion years ago, about 800 million years after a whirling mass of matter surrounding the young Sun had cooled and become solid, forming our planet and the rest of the Sun's planetary system. From life's beginnings in chemical reactions — powered by the Sun's energy — in the Earth's shallow seas, it has developed continuously and slowly. This process of evolution has produced the huge variety of plant and animal life-forms, or species, that we have on our planet today.

Species evolve through very gradual changes in their physical form and behavior. Plants and animals reproduce (breed) when they find a place in their surroundings that gives them the food and protection they need. As time goes on, new generations become more closely linked to that environment, finding new ways to survive or adapt to their surroundings. The ways in which they do this allow many species to share the same living space, as when several bird species in one tree feed off different kinds of insect.

The four main kinds of species are vertebrates (animals with a backbone); invertebrates (animals without a backbone); fungi, algae, and bacteria; and plants.

Mammals
Birds
Reptiles
Amphibians
Fish
Lampreys
Sea squirts
Echinoderms

Insects

Centipedes
Millipedes

Crustaceans

Spiders,
scorpions

Ringed
worms

Squid,
octopus

Bivalve
(two-shell)
molluscs

One-shell
molluscs

Brachiopods
(lamp shells)

Flat worms

Jellyfish, corals

Sponges

One-celled animals

Each species group started to evolve (develop) at a different time, as the time-lines show. Mammals were "late developers," beginning just over 195 million years ago, long after most other groups. Flowering plants came even later. The thickness of the time-lines reflects the number of species in each group.

Fungi,
algae,
bacteria,
lichens

Mosses

Cycads

Horsetails   Club mosses   Ferns

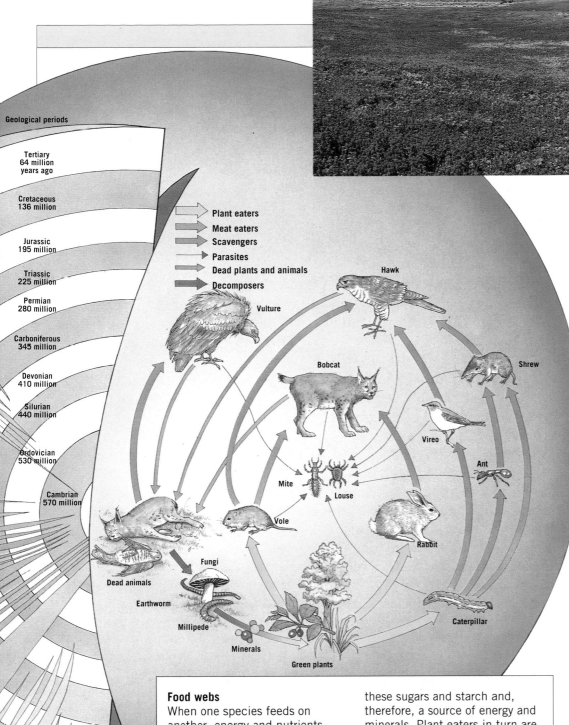

Geological periods

Tertiary
64 million
years ago

Cretaceous
136 million

Jurassic
195 million

Triassic
225 million

Permian
280 million

Carboniferous
345 million

Devonian
410 million

Silurian
440 million

Ordovician
530 million

Cambrian
570 million

Plant eaters
Meat eaters
Scavengers
Parasites
Dead plants and animals
Decomposers

Hawk

Vulture

Bobcat

Shrew

Vireo

Ant

Mite

Louse

Vole

Rabbit

Fungi

Dead animals

Earthworm

Millipede

Minerals

Green plants

Caterpillar

Conifers

Flowering plants

Flowers burst into life when the California desert receives a few precious drops of rain. The varieties include California poppies and owl clover.

How many species?

We know of about 1.8 million species. Of these, 350,000 are types of plant, 45,000 are vertebrates (animals with backbones, including human beings), and well over a million are invertebrates (animals without backbones), including 750,000 insects. Between 4 million and 30 million species may exist in all, most of them as yet undiscovered types of insect.

Many species have come and gone through history. Scientists believe that species usually survive for "only" about 5 million years before dying out, with new ones replacing them, because they did not adapt successfully to changing conditions. Different groups of creatures have been dominant on Earth at different times. Now it is the turn of the mammals, but in an earlier age certain reptiles — including the dinosaurs — were dominant.

Food webs

When one species feeds on another, energy and nutrients pass from the food to the feeder. These feeding links are called "food chains." Species higher up on the food chain have less energy available to them because energy is lost as it passes up the chain. Chains linked together make a "food web."

The energy in a food web comes from the Sun. Plants use this energy to convert carbon dioxide from the air, and water and minerals from the soil into sugars and starch (the process called photosynthesis). Animals that eat plants (herbivores) obtain these sugars and starch and, therefore, a source of energy and minerals. Plant eaters in turn are food for meat eaters (carnivores). There are carnivorous plants, which eat insects. Parasites are living things that feed off larger ones without killing them.

Dead animals are eaten by scavengers (carnivores that do not hunt to kill). Decomposers — fungi, bacteria (one-celled life forms), earthworms, and other creatures in the soil — break down whatever is left into minerals that plants can once again take from the soil.

There are similar food webs in the ocean.

DID YOU KNOW?

The difference between a species and a variety

A species is any group of animals or plants that can breed together and produce offspring. Lions, tigers, and cheetahs are different species of cat. Within a species there may be different varieties: a domestic cat, for example, may be a Persian or a Siamese.

STRATEGY FOR LIFE

Alligators in Florida help birds raise their young. How? The alligators build up nest mounds in the swamps, gradually forming small islands where trees can grow. Herons and other birds nest and raise young in the trees, more safely than they would elsewhere. Nature is often co-operative, but not always.

Climates and communities
Climates and land formations vary from region to region. Different conditions suit different communities of plants and animals, but all depend on the local environment and

on each other. Northern forests **(1)**, 11 percent of the Earth's land surface, have fewer species than many other regions. Moose feed on spruce and birch trees, and provide food for wolves. Mild-climate forests **(2)** cover nine

Different life forms relate to each other in fascinating ways. People once thought of the natural world as a battlefield where species struggled with each other to survive. Many plants and animals probably have become extinct because another species took over their living space or food source. But many species co-operate too.

Some forms of co-operation — such as bees gathering pollen from flowers to feed their larvae (young) and at the same time helping plants reproduce — are well known. But a host of other relationships exist. In the human body, for example, the intestines provide a warm, safe place for tiny life forms — microbes — that help the human body break down food and absorb essential nutrients.

The basic chemical processes of life were developed by bacteria thousands of millions of years ago. They transformed the earth, air, and oceans into an environment in which other life forms could evolve. Today plants and animals live together in communities that make good use of local conditions and each other. Tropical rainforests are famous for their enormous range of species that take advantage of every possible living space, from treetops to forest floor, and food source, from leaves and fruits to ants and worms. By contrast, communities in cold, northern forests and dry, hot deserts, where there are fewer sources of food and fewer adequate living spaces to choose from, are far smaller.

Bacteria develop into early plant and animal forms

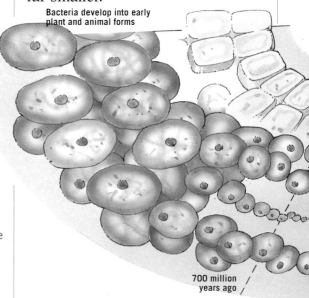

700 million years ago

▶ **Evolution and extinction**
For the first 2 billion years, life on Earth consisted only of bacteria. These simple, tiny "germs," or microbes, are still with us. Every plant and animal species has developed from these primitive ancestors. Many groups of species, such as the dinosaurs, have evolved and then disappeared: other species, such as the deep-sea coelacanth and the rhinoceros, have survived for many millions of years. Nobody can be sure why some species became extinct in the past while others lived on.

percent of the land. Their mixture of trees and other plants provides living space and food for a rich variety of animals. Savanna **(3)**, or tropical grassland — 11 percent of the land surface — feeds millions of grass eaters

such as zebra and wildebeest. Lions, cheetahs, and hyenas feed on the grazers. Deserts and semi-deserts **(4)** cover almost a quarter of the land. With few plants apart from cacti providing food, only a small number of

scattered animals can survive. Tropical forests **(5)**, making up about 14 percent of the land surface, are especially rich in plants and animals. Up to half the world's species may live in such forests.

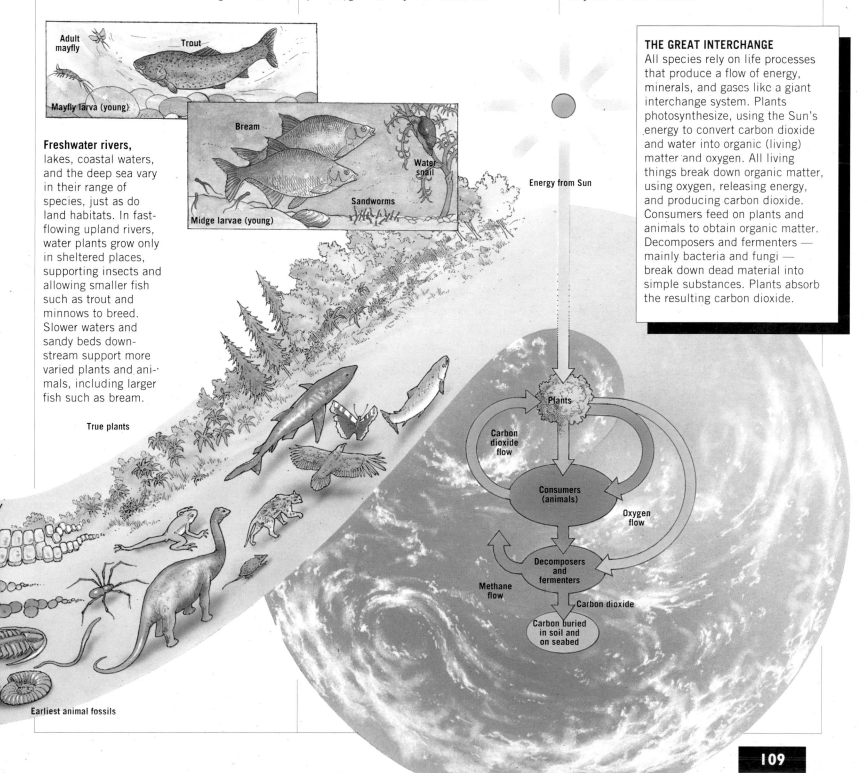

Freshwater rivers, lakes, coastal waters, and the deep sea vary in their range of species, just as do land habitats. In fast-flowing upland rivers, water plants grow only in sheltered places, supporting insects and allowing smaller fish such as trout and minnows to breed. Slower waters and sandy beds down-stream support more varied plants and animals, including larger fish such as bream.

THE GREAT INTERCHANGE
All species rely on life processes that produce a flow of energy, minerals, and gases like a giant interchange system. Plants photosynthesize, using the Sun's energy to convert carbon dioxide and water into organic (living) matter and oxygen. All living things break down organic matter, using oxygen, releasing energy, and producing carbon dioxide. Consumers feed on plants and animals to obtain organic matter. Decomposers and fermenters — mainly bacteria and fungi — break down dead material into simple substances. Plants absorb the resulting carbon dioxide.

Adult mayfly

Trout

Mayfly larva (young)

Bream

Water snail

Sandworms

Midge larvae (young)

True plants

Earliest animal fossils

Energy from Sun

Plants

Carbon dioxide flow

Consumers (animals)

Oxygen flow

Decomposers and fermenters

Methane flow

Carbon dioxide

Carbon buried in soil and on seabed

PARTNERS IN EVOLUTION

The earliest humans lived by hunting and gathering, using as food any available wild animal or edible plant. Then, about 10,000 years ago, people started to control and manage plants and animals for food. Farming had begun.

Farmers sow seeds, harvest crops, and raise animals: they choose which specimens and varieties to breed from. With each selection and each new generation, crops and farmed animals change a little more from their ancestors. This is a form of evolution in which human beings are partners, and modern science allows us to produce completely new varieties by crossbreeding. Using fungi and bacteria, people have also learned to make cheese from milk, wine from grape juice, and so on.

Farming has transformed wild grasses into succulent cereal crops.

Wild sheep, pigs, and cattle have evolved into today's range of domesticated breeds. The process began at a similar time in different parts of the world, but each region had its own climate and native species. People in East Africa were the earliest coffee growers, for example, while Southeast Asia was the first rice-farming region. Migrations of people helped spread crops and animals to new regions. Today, many farmers all over the world produce similar food crops, although there are still considerable local differences.

Strangely, our ancestors mainly chose to farm fewer than 50 plant and animal species, out of the many hundreds that earlier hunter-gatherers had used, and out of some 80,000 edible plants. Today 95 per cent of our food comes from 30 crops and a few animal species.

Your bread or breakfast cereal is partly the result of decisions made by generations of farmers over thousands of years. Wild grasses were the forerunners of all our cereals, and were gradually developed into today's nourishing varieties.

Early farming developed in several main regions. The most important native crops and animals are listed for each region. Explorers, traders, and invaders often took animals and plants with them on their travels, spreading maize, for example, from Central America to Europe, Africa, Asia, and Australia.

Early centers of farming

Spread of corn cultivation

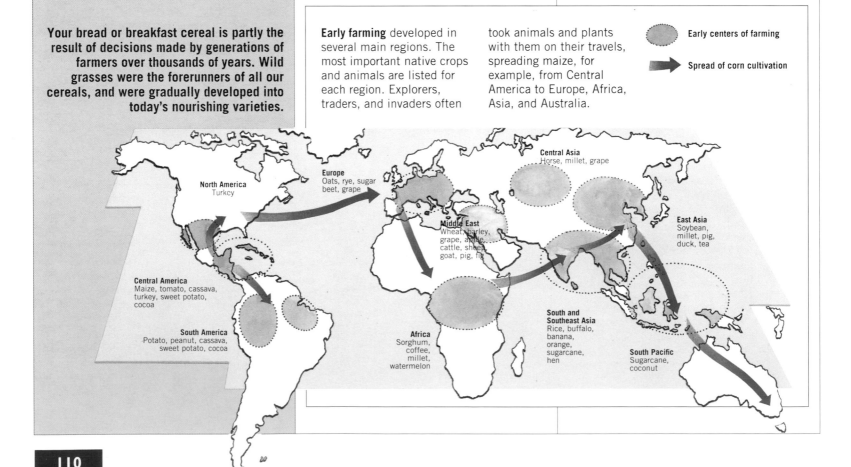

Central Asia
Horse, millet, grape

Europe
Oats, rye, sugar beet, grape

North America
Turkey

Middle East
Wheat, barley, grape, apple, cattle, sheep, goat, pig, fig

East Asia
Soybean, millet, pig, duck, tea

Central America
Maize, tomato, cassava, turkey, sweet potato, cocoa

South America
Potato, peanut, cassava, sweet potato, cocoa

Africa
Sorghum, coffee, millet, watermelon

South and Southeast Asia
Rice, buffalo, banana, orange, sugarcane, hen

South Pacific
Sugarcane, coconut

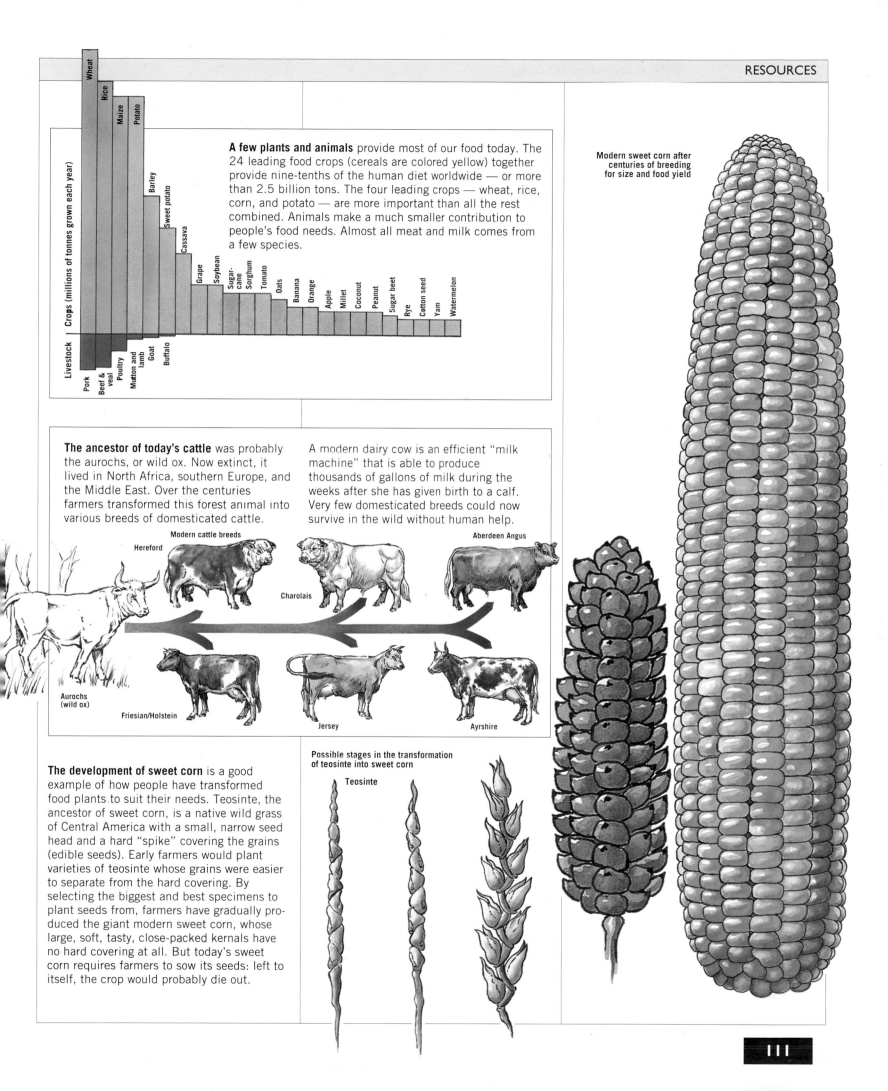

A few plants and animals provide most of our food today. The 24 leading food crops (cereals are colored yellow) together provide nine-tenths of the human diet worldwide — or more than 2.5 billion tons. The four leading crops — wheat, rice, corn, and potato — are more important than all the rest combined. Animals make a much smaller contribution to people's food needs. Almost all meat and milk comes from a few species.

Crops (millions of tonnes grown each year)

Wheat, Rice, Maize, Potato, Barley, Sweet potato, Cassava, Grape, Soybean, Sugar-cane, Sorghum, Tomato, Oats, Banana, Orange, Apple, Millet, Coconut, Peanut, Sugar beet, Rye, Cotton seed, Yam, Watermelon

Livestock

Pork, Beef & veal, Poultry, Mutton and lamb, Goat, Buffalo

Modern sweet corn after centuries of breeding for size and food yield

The ancestor of today's cattle was probably the aurochs, or wild ox. Now extinct, it lived in North Africa, southern Europe, and the Middle East. Over the centuries farmers transformed this forest animal into various breeds of domesticated cattle.

A modern dairy cow is an efficient "milk machine" that is able to produce thousands of gallons of milk during the weeks after she has given birth to a calf. Very few domesticated breeds could now survive in the wild without human help.

Modern cattle breeds

Hereford

Charolais

Aberdeen Angus

Aurochs (wild ox)

Friesian/Holstein

Jersey

Ayrshire

The development of sweet corn is a good example of how people have transformed food plants to suit their needs. Teosinte, the ancestor of sweet corn, is a native wild grass of Central America with a small, narrow seed head and a hard "spike" covering the grains (edible seeds). Early farmers would plant varieties of teosinte whose grains were easier to separate from the hard covering. By selecting the biggest and best specimens to plant seeds from, farmers have gradually produced the giant modern sweet corn, whose large, soft, tasty, close-packed kernals have no hard covering at all. But today's sweet corn requires farmers to sow its seeds: left to itself, the crop would probably die out.

Possible stages in the transformation of teosinte into sweet corn

Teosinte

THREAT TO DIVERSITY

The Earth's natural diversity has been compared to a giant library, with each species representing a book. We are familiar with many of the "books," but there are whole "shelves" that we have never looked at. Millions of species are awaiting our investigation.

Species generally develop better together than apart. We benefit from natural diversity in a number of ways. All our foods, most medicines, and countless other products — from furniture polish to the soles of shoes — come from wild plants and animals. Without the willow we would have no aspirin, for example; and the Pacific yew has recently provided a promising new anti-cancer drug. Diversity is also important for our happiness: imagine a world without the variety of wildlife and habitats that we have on Earth.

We are, however, losing species and habitats at a frightening rate. Rainforests, coral reefs, wetlands,

Many shells, corals, and other exotic sea-life "trophies," such as sharks' jaws, are sold all over the world as souvenirs.

and other species-rich zones are fast disappearing. They are being replaced by species-poor deserts and totally unnatural, human-made environments.

Sometimes poverty drives people to cause habitat damage, for example when they have nowhere to grow food, so they clear forests.

The dodo looked like a clumsy, waddling bird and it could not fly. It died out about 300 years ago, soon after European sailors landed on the island of Mauritius and killed the bird for food. Named after the Portuguese word meaning "stupid," the dodo became a figure of fun. But the loss of animal and plant species is no laughing matter.

The Sumatran rhinoceros — the smallest rhinoceros — is in great danger of extinction. Rhino horn is believed by many people in East and Southeast Asia to have medicinal qualities and is therefore highly prized.

Some bauxite mines in Jamaica are so big they can be seen from space. Large diggers gouge out the land surface, destroying all vegetation, and any wildlife within it, in their path.

The Madagascan rosy periwinkle is a wild forest plant that provides ingredients for two types of anti-cancer drug, helping to save the lives of children with leukemia.

More often, environmental damage results from the demands of the rich for the items that maintain their lifestyles. The activities that provide what these wealthy people want — luxury foods, hardwood furniture, and a whole range of other "consumer" goods — all lead to habitat damage or destruction.

The history of extinction

Throughout the history of life on Earth, species have become extinct and new species have evolved in a slow, continuous process. Over the last 2000 years or so, a few species were lost each year, mainly because human beings hunted them into extinction or damaged their habitats to the extent that they were unable to survive there. The rate of species loss has dramatically increased, however, during the 20th century, especially since 1950. Human numbers have increased in a similarly dramatic way, inflicting more and more damage on the environment as communities have grown.

Scientists have calculated that up to nine-tenths of all the species that have ever lived on Earth are probably now extinct. They fear that we may be losing between 50 and 100 species every day — more in a day than we used to lose in a century. This alarming rate of loss could get worse unless we stop cutting down rainforests, reduce the pollution of air and oceans, and prevent the loss of and damage to wild spaces as a result of farming, mining, other industrial activities, and the spread of towns, cities, and roads.

Species at risk today

More than half a million species, mainly animals, could be at risk of extinction today. They range from the tiger, giant panda, mountain gorilla, and white and black rhinoceros to 6000 types of European insect. With the loss of just a few plant species may go valuable sources of food or medicines not yet discovered. If most or all of the species under threat become extinct, it will be the greatest loss of diversity since the dinosaurs died out 65 million years ago.

HOME ACTION

Here are some ideas for helping to save habitats and species.

- Create a pond or wild area in your garden to encourage birds and other animals and wildflowers.
- Respect the countryside, don't pick wildflowers or grasses.
- Make fewer car trips: less car use means less demand for new roads, and therefore a reduction in the habitat destruction and pollution caused by road construction and use.

- Do not keep exotic animals as pets.
- Do not buy animal skins, furs, ivory goods, coral, or souvenir shells.
- Do not buy goods made out of tropical hardwoods, the demand for which increases the threat to the world's rainforests.
- Join a nature conservation group or wildlife campaign.
- Volunteer at a local zoo, city farm, ecology park, or rare-breeds center.

HIGH-RISK OUTPUT

When greenflies or blackflies attack a bush or small tree, they can reduce its leaves to tatters. Insect pests damage farmers' crops in the same way. Sometimes in the past pests and diseases have destroyed so much of the harvest that people have starved to death. How safe from that threat is food production today?

DID YOU KNOW?

The problems for India's cattle
Different cattle breeds evolved in different places around the world in order to adapt to local conditions. Traditional Indian cattle, for example, have light-colored skin to help them stay cool in the heat, long ears and tails to flick insects away, and a hump to store fat for times of food shortage. To increase milk and meat output many farmers in India now raise cattle cross-bred with animals from other regions. This has led to widespread outbreaks of cattle illnesses that are new to India.

Farming is a success story that shows how well we can work with other species. But too much human interference with nature can lead to a dangerous loss of diversity. Many food crops and domesticated animals have little natural resistance to pests and diseases.

Western-style farming aims to produce the largest possible harvests and yields for the lowest cost. So we have bred crops and animals that produce the maximum edible grain, fruit, meat, milk, and so on. As more and more farmers use similar high-output varieties and breeds, local variations disappear. In Greece, for example, 95 percent of native wheat varieties have gone since 1925; throughout Europe 118 cattle breeds are now few in number and uncertain to survive; and in India farmers are giving up many traditional rice types in favor of modern high-yield varieties.

Diversity is desirable
The more we rely on only a few varieties, the greater the risks. An insect pest that attacks only one of several different wheat varieties in a field will damage just part of the crop. If there is only one variety in the field the pest may destroy it all. Imagine the scale of the disaster if all the farms in one country grew the same variety. In fact, the average lifetime of most modern wheat varieties is 5–15 years, after which farmers need to switch to a new variety to prevent diseases and pests from becoming established. Diversity in the varieties used is the best defense against crop failure and animal disease. Variety encourages resistance.

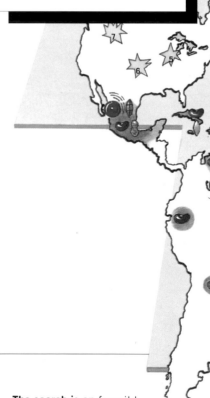

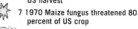

The search is on for wild relatives that will help strengthen today's food crops against pests and diseases. Scientists crossbreed tougher wild varieties with high-output farmed crops to produce the next generation of plants.

Changing landscapes
The traditional farming landscape (above) consisted of a varied patchwork of fields, in which were grown a wide variety of crops, interspersed with areas of woodland. In many countries today, however, farmland (below) consists of much larger fields resembling prairies (extensive, treeless grasslands) where farmers grow almost identical high-output crops. Much, if not all, of the woodland has gone.

Mixing old and new

Crossbreeding allows us to draw on the useful qualities of wild relatives of crops and of traditional animal breeds. Little-known or half-forgotten varieties and breeds often come to the rescue when problems affect modern strains. The Cornish chicken was much reduced in numbers when poultry breeders found they needed it to breed with farmed hens to improve their growth rate. And researchers have found just 2000 surviving specimens of a disease-resistant Mexican wild maize that may protect the world's sweet corn crop.

Crop failure threatens more than our food. If disease struck down the world's maize crops, it would threaten the manufacture of products that involve the use of maize, including medicines such as aspirin and penicillin, and the varnish on the pages of printed books.

Crops threatened by disease
- Maize
- Wheat
- Rice
- Common bean
  Groundnut (peanut)
- Sugarcane

Areas where useful wild relatives of food plants grow

Wheat

Soyabean

Potato

Coffee

Many important crops are at risk. Canada relies on just four wheat varieties; the US soybean is a blend of only six plants from one part of Asia; most of Brazil's coffee trees are very close relatives; and only four varieties of potato produce nearly three-quarters of the US crop.

WILDLIFE SANCTUARY IN SIERRA LEONE

In 1979, Dr. John Oates, a professor of anthropology at the City University of New York, set out to establish a research station and wildlife sanctuary on Tiwai Island in the middle of the Moa River in Sierra Leone, West Africa. "I was looking for a new research area where my postgraduate students could study the social behavior of monkeys," he explains.

"Tiwai Island is a 12-square-kilometer area of rainforest owned by the local Mende community. People did not live on the island but in villages along the river-

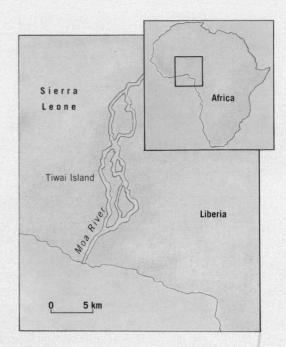

▶ *A Mende fisherman* (main picture) at work on the Moa River. Tiwai Island is on the right.

▼ *Mende women* work alongside research students growing new trees to restock the forest.

banks and within the surrounding Gola Forest. There was some farming but no large-scale felling or removal of trees. On Tiwai there were thriving populations of chimpanzees, colobus monkeys, and other primates. Given help from the Sierra Leone government, I thought a reserve could be set up where my students and local people could study and work side by side. The reserve would attract tourists, providing income to make the project self-financing."

► **Among the inhabitants of Tiwai Island** are at least 200 species of birds, including hornbills (**1**), as well as chimpanzees (**2**), Diana monkeys (**3**), colobus monkeys (**4**), pygmy hippos (**5**), which are endangered, and royal antelope (**6**).

▲ **Sanctuary areas** have been set up where biologists can study the behavior of monkeys such as this olive colobus. Local people used to hunt the monkeys for their meat.

▼ **Research huts** are built from small trees growing outside the fully protected parts of the sanctuary. Neither large-scale logging nor mining (for diamonds) is allowed.

With support from the City University of New York, the US Wildlife Conservation Society, the University of Sierra Leone, and the Sierra Leone Ministry of Agriculture, Forestry, and Natural Resources, Dr. Oates and his colleagues began in 1982 to build up a detailed knowledge of the ecosystem. Then, after discussions with the Mende about their needs for resources, plans were made for the management of the forest. A wildlife sanctuary was created by the government in January, 1987. The management plan was agreed by all the people and organizations working at Tiwai in 1989.

The project has been a success. More than 20 students have completed wildlife research projects at Tiwai, and local people are more active in managing their local environment. In the last four years, however, civil war has raged in Sierra Leone. Rebels have taken over the area around Tiwai. The fate of the sanctuary is unknown.

PARTNERS IN CONSERVATION

It will need a huge effort to halt the loss of diversity of plant and animal species in farming and the destruction of habitats and species worldwide. In the future we will want new crops to withstand pest attack without heavy doses of chemicals, or to grow well in a changing climate, and we will always be on the lookout for new substances for medicines. Only wild plant and animal species include the genetic diversity — the variety of life forms and their qualities — that we will need.

Thousands of new plant species *may await discovery in the lush growth of the rainforest.*

WORKING WITH NATURE, SURVIVING TOGETHER

There is a saying in Surinam: "In the jungle, the Indian knows everything." Traditional peoples are in danger of being brushed to the side of the path of modern "progress," yet their deep understanding of nature can help us make the best use of the Earth's rich resources. A sharing of skills and knowledge between traditional and Western cultures will be to the benefit of all of us.

Kayapo farmers in the Amazon rainforest plant banana-tree hedges for wasps to nest in around their fields. The wasps keep out the ants that would otherwise eat the crops. Forest peoples have a great many natural answers to everyday problems, and this kind of knowledge could be crucial to reducing the risks to the planet.

DID YOU KNOW?

Plants waiting to be "discovered"
We now grow only a few of the hundred varieties of potato that early South Americans farmed, and perhaps not the best ones. Two West African plants produce edible substances many times sweeter than sugar cane and sugar beet. The Amazonian babassu palm is the most productive known source of vegetable oil, yet few people have heard of it. The tamarugo tree thrives in dry, salty soil and could help reclaim salt-damaged land.

Many wild species are already of help to us in this way, yet researchers have investigated only a fraction of the Earth's plant and animal potential. We have much to learn from people who belong to traditional cultures and rely on untamed environments to support themselves. They know how to make good use of nature without damaging it. Many countries now encourage traditional medicine, and researchers are cataloging the useful properties of species in rainforests and elsewhere.

Another form of conservation partnership involves people using plants and animals instead of pesticides to control pests and diseases. In China, for example, citrus ants help protect mandarin oranges from caterpillars, and farmers use herds of ducklings to control rice-eating grasshoppers.

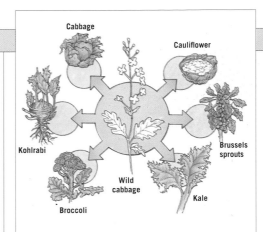

Farmers have developed a whole range of food plants — from cauliflower to broccoli — from a single ancestor, the wild cabbage. Who knows how many new food crops we will need to develop in the future? The evolution of new species depends on the unique "genetic library" of plants growing in the wild.

Rainforest people in Guyana (1) use a substance that scientists hope will be the basis of a drug to allow doctors to stop a person's heart safely during surgery. The heart can be restarted afterwards with another drug, also from a plant.

A tree in Tanzania (2) that local people use to cure toothache belongs to a species that Western scientists did not know existed until recently. Other medicines used by forest peoples include a muscle-relaxant made from the pareira plant.

Traditional local healers (3) are today sharing their knowledge of plants and animals with researchers. In Amazonia a study team has listed hundreds of plants that forest people use for food and medicines.

Native Americans discovered the healing properties of the mayapple **(4)** centuries ago, using it to treat warts, deafness, and parasitic worms. Chemists **(5)** have already produced a successful new drug from the plant, which may also provide treatments for cancer, measles, and influenza in the future.

SAVING SPECIES & HABITATS

ACTION FOR THREATENED SPECIES

Where it is not possible to conserve species in the wild, we can store plant seeds, cultivate specimens, and breed animals in captivity, away from their natural habitats. Animal species that are kept in captivity are moved from zoo to zoo for breeding purposes to maintain genetic diversity.

Gene and seed banks can store the seeds of many thousands of plants in cool, dry conditions for long periods.

Botanical gardens, such as those at Kew, England, both store seeds and cultivate specimens of rare plant species.

Zoos have bred endangered species successfully and then returned them to the wild.

If you were given a colorful, talkative pet parrot, or a tank of beautiful tropical fish, would you refuse the gift? The trade in exotic species is reducing their numbers close to extinction. In protecting habitats and species worldwide we face some difficult choices.

Rare-breeds centers are living museums of farm animal breeds that we no longer use but that could be important in the future.

Safeguarding a wide variety of habitats and species is an awesome task. Worldwide more than 3500 reserves and national parks cover 1 billion acres, an area the size of Western Europe. But there is still little protection for some important habitats.

The first nature reserves tried to keep people out. Now we know that tropical forests, for example, are most likely to survive if local people continue to live in them, use their resources, and work toward their conservation.

Gene and seed banks, botanical gardens, and zoos are another way to protect species. Yet they can never contain more than a small percentage of the total number of species. Many seeds will not survive undamaged in seed banks, and animal populations in zoos are often too small to guarantee their survival. Nature reserves and species collections are costly to run. A tax on biotechnology companies could help pay for them.

World action

Countries have signed many conservation agreements. The Convention on International Trade in Endangered Species (CITES) has been one of the most important, banning or controlling trade in thousands of rare plant and animal species and products. Yet illegal trade still threatens many species. Under the Biodiversity Treaty, signed in 1992 at the Earth Summit in Rio de Janeiro, Brazil, developed countries promised to help developing countries pay for the protection of species-rich areas. But have we done enough to protect the Earth's biodiversity?

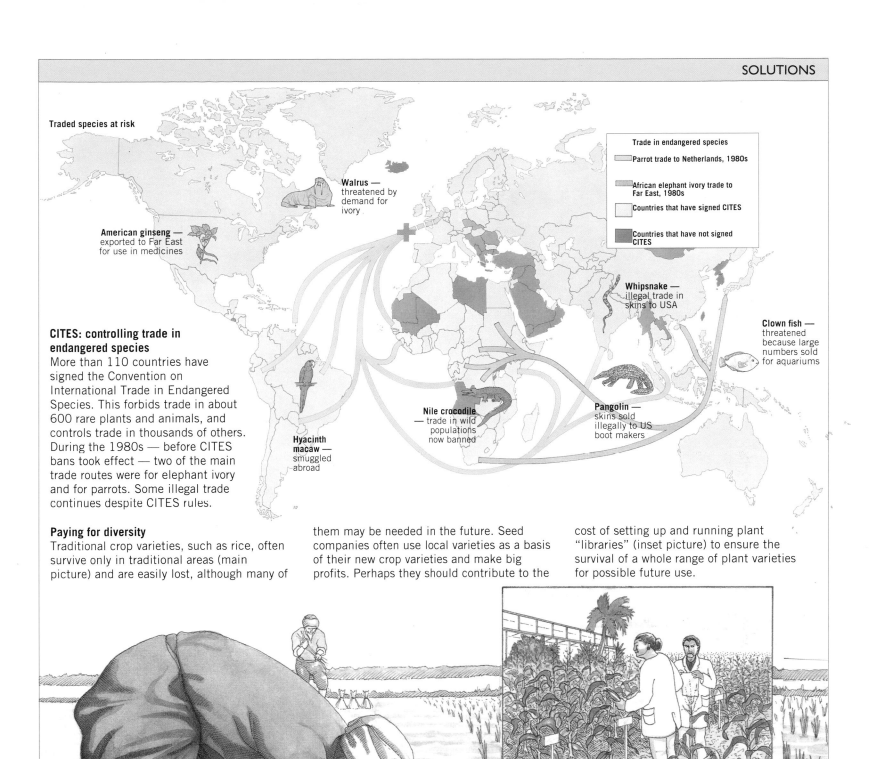

Traded species at risk

Trade in endangered species

Parrot trade to Netherlands, 1980s

African elephant ivory trade to Far East, 1980s

Countries that have signed CITES

Countries that have not signed CITES

Walrus — threatened by demand for ivory

American ginseng — exported to Far East for use in medicines

Whipsnake — illegal trade in skins to USA

Clown fish — threatened because large numbers sold for aquariums

CITES: controlling trade in endangered species

More than 110 countries have signed the Convention on International Trade in Endangered Species. This forbids trade in about 600 rare plants and animals, and controls trade in thousands of others. During the 1980s — before CITES bans took effect — two of the main trade routes were for elephant ivory and for parrots. Some illegal trade continues despite CITES rules.

Nile crocodile — trade in wild populations now banned

Hyacinth macaw — smuggled abroad

Pangolin — skins sold illegally to US boot makers

Paying for diversity

Traditional crop varieties, such as rice, often survive only in traditional areas (main picture) and are easily lost, although many of them may be needed in the future. Seed companies often use local varieties as a basis of their new crop varieties and make big profits. Perhaps they should contribute to the cost of setting up and running plant "libraries" (inset picture) to ensure the survival of a whole range of plant varieties for possible future use.

7 HUMANKIND

"Local groups are now demanding a halt to the destructiveness of modern society. It is through such groups . . . that change will come about . . . not imposed from above but created from below by ordinary people."

EDITORS OF *THE ECOLOGIST*, a leading UK environmental magazine

People are the greatest resource the Earth has — and its biggest problem. Clever, adaptable, skillful, and strong, we spend much of our time ignoring the needs of our fellow human beings, and our shared environment, and thinking of our own private wishes instead. We take advantage of each other's difficulties and sometimes act with cruelty and violence toward each other. It often seems as if we will never be able to control the increase in human numbers, or stop damaging our natural surroundings and harming others. But hope is at hand. We can and do learn from our mistakes, and this fact offers everybody a real opportunity to make the world a better place.

Zulu boys at work with oxen and plow in South Africa. In many traditional communities, learning to work the land is an important part of a child's family upbringing.

NEEDS & RIGHTS

If you are reading this book you are literate; you probably have a comfortable home and attend school; and you can look forward as an adult to a choice of occupation and a say in decisions that affect your life. Potentially, you are one of tomorrow's problem-solvers rather than a part of one of its problems.

DID YOU KNOW?

Richest doesn't always mean best
While richer, developed countries are usually in a stronger position than poorer, developing countries to meet their people's needs and respect their rights, some countries do far better or worse than we might expect. The USA, for example, which has the world's largest industrial economy, has 100,000 homeless and 500,000 badly fed children; while Cuba, a poor country, has achieved impressive standards of health care – especially in primary (basic) and maternal and child health.

About 5.7 billion people live on Earth today. Among us, we surely have the knowledge and skills to make the world a fit place for all to live in; a world in which humankind is at peace with the rest of nature. For this to happen, every human being needs the chance to develop his or her full potential.

The world is full of active, able people, young and old, in every country, who are making positive contributions to society. But, sadly, millions of others cannot develop fully, because they are denied one or more of their needs and rights — the things you believe you are entitled to as a member of society.

Since the dawn of history some human beings have suffered hunger, poverty, slavery, cruelty, and death at the hands of others. Yet, it can be argued, some groups of people, such as the African San (Bushmen), have avoided war and developed fair ways of living together that harm nobody.

Putting the wrongs right

We have a broad range of tools with which to solve our problems: laws, which set rules for human behavior; technology, which helps get jobs done; and democratic politics, with which we can make decisions together. A great belief in humanity's problem-solving abilities led the United Nations to proclaim the Universal Declaration of Human Rights in 1948, with the words "all members of the human family . . . are born free and equal in dignity and rights . . . and should act towards each other in a spirit of brotherhood."

Despite any progress we may have made in improving the way

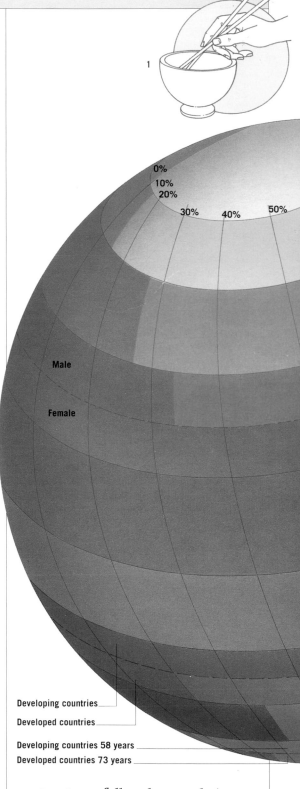

1

0%
10%
20%
30% 40% 50% 60%

Male

Female

Developing countries
Developed countries

Developing countries 58 years
Developed countries 73 years

we treat our fellow human beings, more people across the globe suffer serious deprivation today than ever before. Only when the needs and rights of these people have been properly satisfied will we be able to meet with confidence the other challenges facing the world.

1 Enough food to eat is essential for all living things. Yet 800 million people do not eat enough to stay healthy.

2 Infant death in the developing world is such that seven out of every 100 babies die before their first birthday, compared with one in 100 in developed countries.

3 Primary schooling is every child's right. More than 90 percent of all children start school, but 40 percent don't finish primary education.

4 Literacy has improved worldwide since the 1960s. Even so, half the world's females and a third of its males cannot read or write.

5 Adequate housing includes access to clean water and a proper toilet. Only a quarter of humanity has these facilities.

6 Government welfare helps people who cannot work or earn. Millions have no such protection.

7 Basic freedoms include being able to express your opinion and vote in elections. Many people lack these freedoms.

8 Work is another human right, a source of self-respect as well as income. More than a third of people of working age are unemployed or lack enough work.

9 Life expectancy varies widely. People in some parts of the world die, on average, in their 40s; elsewhere they can expect to live 30 years longer.

Needs and rights in selected countries
Below are three examples of how different countries provide for the needs and rights of their citizens. The nine disks in each diagram match the numbered needs and rights in the main illustration (left).

China, a poor country with a population of 1.22 billion, has improved the lives of most of its people since 1950. The availability of food, education, employment, and life expectancy are all better than before. But many citizens, especially girls and orphans, suffer cruelly, and there is little democracy or freedom.

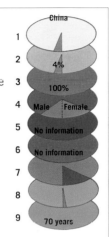

China
1
2 4%
3 100%
4 Male Female
5 No information
6 No information
7
8
9 70 years

Costa Rica, in Central America, disbanded its army 40 years ago and has enjoyed peace and prosperity since, unlike its neighbors. All Costa Ricans attend primary school and most are literate. They have political freedom and good life expectancy. Welfare is limited, but unemployment is low. Costa Rica's environmental record is good.

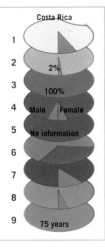

Costa Rica
1
2 2%
3 100%
4 Male Female
5 No information
6
7
8
9 75 years

Denmark is highly successful at providing for its citizens. It has high literacy, low infant mortality, and high life expectancy. Some Danes are unemployed, or do not receive adequate welfare protection. But Denmark sets a good example in areas such as energy efficiency and donations of aid to developing countries.

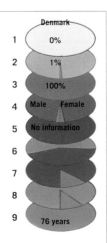

Denmark
1 0%
2 1%
3 100%
4 Male Female
5 No information
6
7
8
9 76 years

HAVES AND HAVE-NOTS: HUMAN NEEDS AND HUMAN RIGHTS
Millions of people suffer a lack of one or more of the essential requirements for a decent life, most of which are interconnected. Clean water, a safe environment, protection from violence, and equality of opportunity are everyone's right. The numbered bands on the globe represent other key human needs or rights. The lighter shaded area at the right-hand side of each band shows the percentage of the world's population whose needs are met and who enjoy adequate rights. The darker shaded area at the left-hand side shows the proportion of people whose needs or rights are unfulfilled.

WORLD AT WORK

What job would you like to have when you are older? Like most people, you probably hope to combine reasonably good earnings with doing something worthwhile and useful. Worldwide, however, few people can be sure of a satisfying and well-paid job for life. Advances in technology and changes of government policy mean that the employment market is changing fast.

THE HUMAN RESOURCE
The ways in which human skills and energy are used are affected by the numbers of people in the work force and how quickly they increase, the proportions of men and women in the work force, the changing nature of work, and how we value work — whether it is paid or unpaid, for example. There are great differences between regions of the developed world (right) and those of the developing world (far right). Work forces are expanding much more slowly in developed countries, and women make up a larger proportion of paid workers. Every region of the world, however, is being affected by major changes in work practices.

Work was once simply what people did to survive: hunting, gathering, farming; making tools and shelter; learning, teaching, and practicing skills. Even after trade and money first developed, most work was based on farming.

With the rise of modern industry, work moved from fields to factories and offices — although millions of people, mainly in developing countries, still live by farming and fishing. Work has come more and more to mean having a paid job. We sometimes forget there are many people who work but are not in paid jobs.

Changes in technology affect employment. The spread of labor-saving technologies results in job losses in traditional industries. On the plus side, electronics, wholesale and retail selling, services such as leisure, and other industries have created new white-collar (non-manual, office-type) jobs.

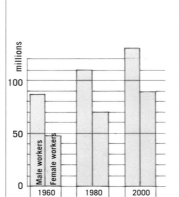

In North America, Japan, and Oceania more and more women are entering a steadily expanding work force.

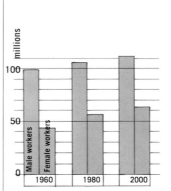

Western Europe has a slow-growing work force. Women's share of paid work is increasing, but only gradually.

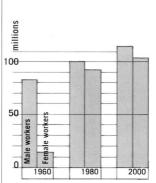

Eastern Europe and the former USSR now have almost as many women as men at work, a huge change since 1960.

The United States has seen a loss of farm-based work, especially on smaller farms, and blue-collar jobs (manual jobs in industry). White-collar (office-type) employment in services such as finance and in government has expanded.

Germany has the strongest economy in Europe, despite problems caused by uniting with poorer East Germany in 1990. Like the USA, Germany has lost jobs in agriculture and heavy industry and gained them in services.

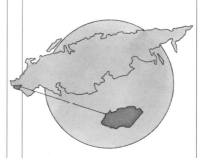

Hungary has one of the more successful economies of the former Communist countries of Eastern Europe. Many new industrial jobs have developed, although farm work has declined. Women make up almost half the work force.

At the same time, more women have gone out to work — although many of them part-time, and often as cheap labor. In developing countries fast-rising populations are perhaps the main factor affecting the employment market.

The global work force is growing by about 50 million people a year. The challenge for the future is to ensure that the work most worth doing gets done, while every adult has a decent job and a fair income.

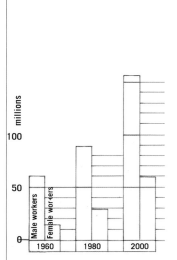

In Latin America and the Caribbean the paid work force has always contained more than twice as many men as women.

Brazil is the economic giant of South America, with employment growing in industry and services. But rising poverty has led to a huge increase in the numbers of city slum dwellers doing very low-paid casual work.

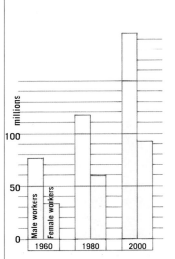

Africa's ratio of paid female to male workers has stayed steady since 1960. Yet millions of unpaid women farmers support their families.

Mali is poor but has little unemployment because most Malians support themselves as small-scale farmers. Modernization of agriculture could help the country's industry to develop but may lead to serious unemployment.

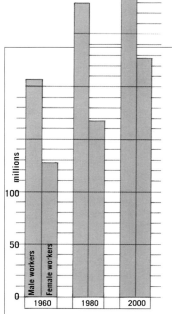

East Asia, including China, has a large and rapidly growing work force. About 40 percent of East Asian workers are women.

China has an enormous population that is still based mainly in peasant farming communities. Job opportunities are in towns and cities, where factory work is increasing and industries producing goods for export are expanding.

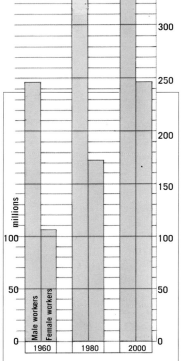

South and Southeast Asia have a fast-rising population and the world's largest work force. Men far outnumber women in the employment market.

India has a larger population than any country except China. More than two-thirds of its people depend on the land, many of them as self-employed farmers. Its work force looks set to be the world's largest by the year 2040.

CLEVER OR WISE?

Being clever is not the same as being intelligent. A cunning thief who climbs through a window and steals a camera, for example, may realize later that his actions were not wise. We have put much of our human cleverness to good use, and we call ourselves *Homo sapiens* — "wise man" — but there is still room for improvement.

Children in Simiatug, in the highlands of Ecuador, learn to read in Quechua, the traditional language of the Andean peoples.

Unlike other animal species, we can transform our environment. The history of human development is one of impressive achievement based on knowledge and skill: towns and cities, farms and factories, mighty machines and beautiful buildings, and great art.

With knowledge comes the need to learn. More people can read and write than ever before, and almost three-quarters of the world's children are in school. We build more universities and publish more books than ever, while newspapers, radio, and television reach their largest-ever audiences. We spend more money than ever on developing new technologies, although many of these are for military purposes.

Even so, millions of people worldwide still lack schooling and access to modern information channels. A decent life is possible without literacy or schooling but difficult to achieve. Illiterate people are more likely to suffer poverty and ill-health, for example.

But more does not always mean better. Modern Western science and learning are sometimes too highly specialized to affect human well-being. Education does not always lead to an understanding of the best way to solve real-life problems. And we have neglected the wisdom of traditional communities such as rainforest peoples.

Many people believe we need to close the gaps that separate science from art, modern knowledge from old-fashioned intelligence, high technology from everyday usefulness, and information-rich people in developed countries from their information-poor cousins in the developing world.

The information gap

We rely on information media and technology to tell us about the modern world. Most people who use these live in the developed world, but developing countries need them just as much.

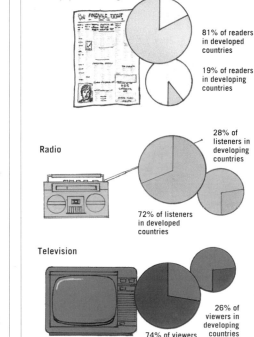

Newspapers and magazines

81% of readers in developed countries

19% of readers in developing countries

Radio

28% of listeners in developing countries

72% of listeners in developed countries

Television

26% of viewers in developing countries

74% of viewers in developed countries

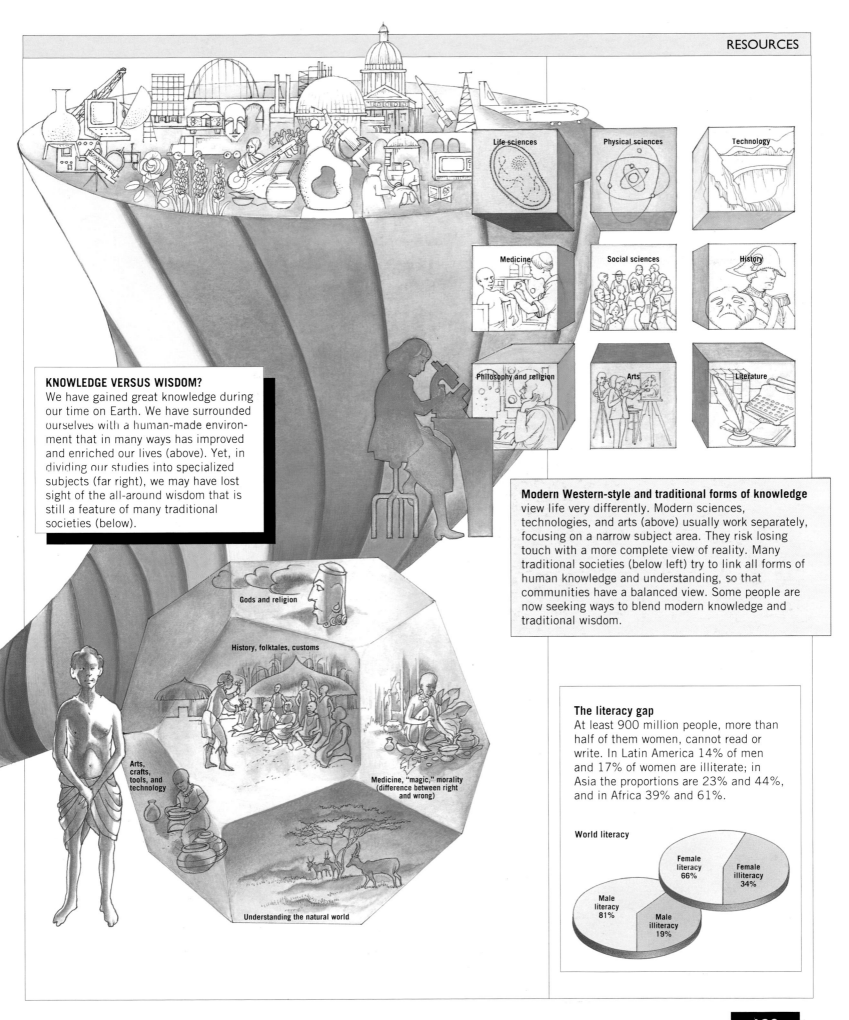

Life sciences

Physical sciences

Technology

Medicine

Social sciences

History

Philosophy and religion

Arts

Literature

KNOWLEDGE VERSUS WISDOM?

We have gained great knowledge during our time on Earth. We have surrounded ourselves with a human-made environment that in many ways has improved and enriched our lives (above). Yet, in dividing our studies into specialized subjects (far right), we may have lost sight of the all-around wisdom that is still a feature of many traditional societies (below).

Modern Western-style and traditional forms of knowledge view life very differently. Modern sciences, technologies, and arts (above) usually work separately, focusing on a narrow subject area. They risk losing touch with a more complete view of reality. Many traditional societies (below left) try to link all forms of human knowledge and understanding, so that communities have a balanced view. Some people are now seeking ways to blend modern knowledge and traditional wisdom.

Gods and religion

History, folktales, customs

Arts, crafts, tools, and technology

Medicine, "magic," morality (difference between right and wrong)

Understanding the natural world

The literacy gap

At least 900 million people, more than half of them women, cannot read or write. In Latin America 14% of men and 17% of women are illiterate; in Asia the proportions are 23% and 44%, and in Africa 39% and 61%.

World literacy

Female literacy 66%

Female illiteracy 34%

Male literacy 81%

Male illiteracy 19%

129

PEOPLE & HEALTH

In the time it takes to count from 1 to 60, 180 babies are born, and 25 children aged five or under die. Most of these births and deaths take place in developing countries. The birth of a baby and growth of a child should bring great joy, but hunger, sickness, poverty, and death dominate the lives of many parents in the developing world. Are we doing enough to correct this?

The world population is increasing by 90–100 million a year. Africa has the fastest growth rate and will double its population in 23 years.

Why are numbers rising so fast? Modern health care has reduced death rates, so more people live longer. Birth rates have risen in many developing countries as industrialization changes traditional communities. Women often lack adequate birth control, and poor people see children as useful workers and have more in the hope that at least some of them will survive.

Developed countries take more than their fair share of resources. Rich countries import much of their food from hungry Africa, Asia, and Latin America.

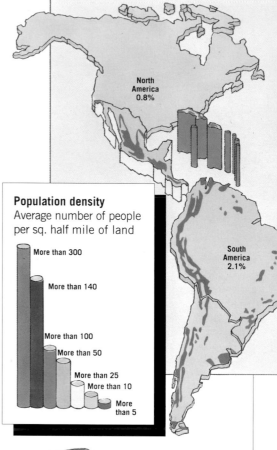

North America 0.8%

South America 2.1%

Population density
Average number of people per sq. half mile of land

More than 300
More than 140
More than 100
More than 50
More than 25
More than 10
More than 5

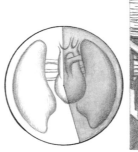

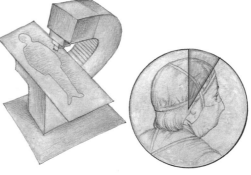

New illnesses, some of them the result of people having wealthier lifestyles, include cancer, heart disease, and AIDS, which is spreading at a rate of a million new cases a year.

Mental and emotional illness affects more than 40 million people worldwide. We spend a lot of money on treatments to relieve stress, but many of them bring their own problems, such as addiction.

High-technology medicine is costly and cures only a few known diseases. In developing countries especially, money spent on simpler ways of preventing illness benefits many more people.

Health-care budgets vary enormously. Developed countries, which have smaller populations and fewer health problems, spend ten times more on health overall than developing countries.

6000 BC   5000 BC   4000 BC   3000 BC

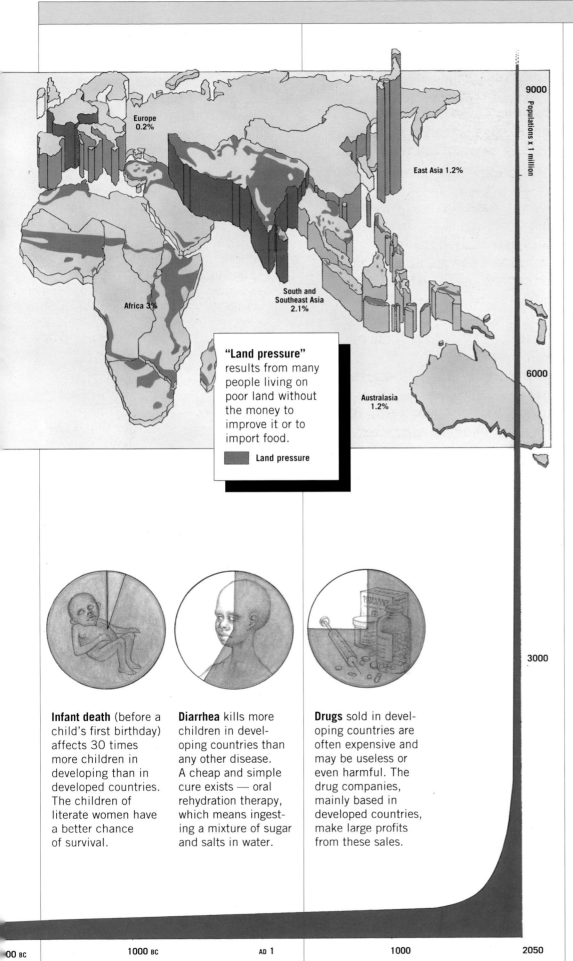

Europe
0.2%

East Asia 1.2%

South and
Southeast Asia
2.1%

Africa 3%

"Land pressure" results from many people living on poor land without the money to improve it or to import food.

◼ Land pressure

Australasia
1.2%

Populations x 1 million

9000

6000

3000

Infant death (before a child's first birthday) affects 30 times more children in developing than in developed countries. The children of literate women have a better chance of survival.

Diarrhea kills more children in developing countries than any other disease. A cheap and simple cure exists — oral rehydration therapy, which means ingesting a mixture of sugar and salts in water.

Drugs sold in developing countries are often expensive and may be useless or even harmful. The drug companies, mainly based in developed countries, make large profits from these sales.

00 BC   1000 BC   AD 1   1000   2050

High- and low-population regions and population growth
The map shows regional rates of population growth, population density, and areas where large numbers of people, poor land, and low incomes threaten hunger, ill-health, and worsening poverty.

Better health care
Millions of people die each year from malnutrition (poor diet) and preventable infections. About 900 million people in developing countries have few medical services, and many millions lack education in basic hygiene.

Poisoned environments are an increasing cause of illness, especially in the countries of the former Soviet Union and Eastern Europe, where industrial development has been badly managed. Much of the water in these countries is unfit to drink, and millions are at risk from cancer, asthma, birth defects, and mental illness.

We spend much more money coping with illness than preventing it. Larger budgets for health education and other forms of prevention in developed countries could reduce heart disease, stress, alcoholism, drug addiction, and cancer deaths from smoking. More spending on health care for women and children and on birth control in developing countries could also bring about major improvements.

Population explosion?
Human numbers increased slowly for thousands of years, but then that increase accelerated dramatically. There were 1 billion people alive by the year 1800, 2 billion by 1935, 3 billion by 1960, 4 billion by 1974, 5 billion by 1987. An end-of-century total of more than 6 billion is certain, rising to perhaps 9 billion or more by the year 2050.

131

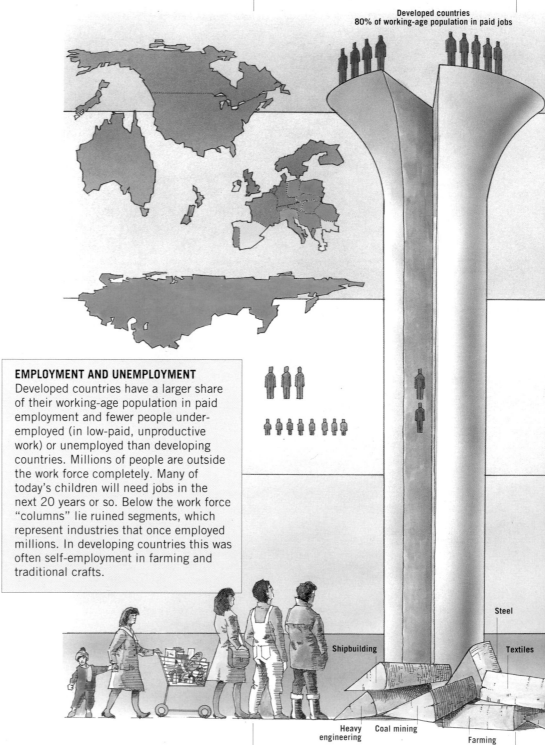

OUT OF WORK

Millions of adults who are willing to work cannot find useful jobs. Unemployment has badly hit developed countries since the mid-1970s, despite some new job opportunities. Governments could create many more jobs by taxing pollution and the use of resources.

Developed countries saw their unemployment rates double between 1973 and 1988. During periods of economic difficulty, industries reduced their work forces, closed down altogether, or moved to developing countries where labor was cheaper.

Being out of work means more than not earning money, as any adult who has lost a job will tell you. It can make a person feel frustrated or a complete failure. Worse than this, in poor countries where there are few welfare provisions, people who lose their livelihood and cannot support themselves or their families risk losing everything, perhaps even life itself.

Entire families live and work on Aroma, the main garbage dump for the sprawling city of Manila in the Philippines. They collect anything that can be recycled — glass, plastic, fabric, or scrap metal — and sell it to survive.

Developed countries
80% of working-age population in paid jobs

EMPLOYMENT AND UNEMPLOYMENT
Developed countries have a larger share of their working-age population in paid employment and fewer people under-employed (in low-paid, unproductive work) or unemployed than developing countries. Millions of people are outside the work force completely. Many of today's children will need jobs in the next 20 years or so. Below the work force "columns" lie ruined segments, which represent industries that once employed millions. In developing countries this was often self-employment in farming and traditional crafts.

Steel

Shipbuilding

Textiles

Heavy engineering

Coal mining

Farming

In developing countries most people were once farmers, fishers, craft workers, or traders. Paid work has always been in short supply. But age-old ways of life are under threat, often because big business has taken over the land. Fast-rising populations worsen the problem. The result has been a massive movement of people from countryside to city.

Not enough new jobs are to be found in the expanding cities of developing countries, however. In desperation, many people join the "informal" economy of casual and sometimes illegal work, where nobody keeps records or pays tax, and income is uncertain. Such work might be in street trading, garbage recycling, or other, often unhealthy, areas of unofficial employment. Tragically, some people take advantage of children, employing them in factories or as prostitutes.

People seeking work also travel to developed countries. The USA and Western Europe used to welcome unskilled migrants as low-paid workers — such as Turkish workers in Germany in the 1960s — but no longer do so.

Some groups are less successful than others in the job market. Many women and members of ethnic minorities find it hard to enter some better-paid occupations or achieve senior levels in others.

Yet there is more to work than paid jobs. Women still grow a huge share of the world's food for home and village consumption, and do most of the housework, including the collection of water and firewood in developing countries. They receive no payment for this work.

Developed countries have lost many jobs in traditional industries such as shipbuilding since the 1970s. Fewer jobs in services and other areas have been created.

Developing countries have many more low-paid or unpaid jobs than well-paid ones, for example in farming; few welfare programs; and millions of people who eke out a living.

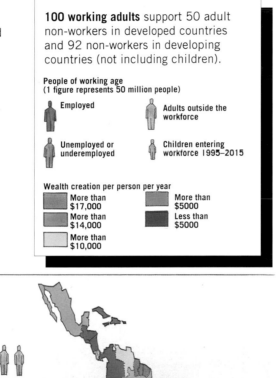

100 working adults support 50 adult non-workers in developed countries and 92 non-workers in developing countries (not including children).

People of working age
(1 figure represents 50 million people)

Employed

Adults outside the workforce

Unemployed or underemployed

Children entering workforce 1995–2015

Wealth creation per person per year

More than $17,000

More than $5000

More than $14,000

Less than $5000

More than $10,000

Developing countries
64% of working-age population in paid jobs

Traditional crafts

Farming   Sugar   Jute

RIGHTS IN CRISIS

Children often say "It's not fair," and their protest may well be about a silly, unimportant issue. But unfairness can be serious, as when a bigger child harms a smaller one. Bullying goes on among adults too: stronger groups of people mistreat weaker ones, sometimes with great cruelty. Is there anything we can do to help make the world a fairer place?

Rwandan refugees live in camps in the Karagwe district of Tanzania. Aid agencies help provide food and health care. Up to ten people live in a brende, *a wooden-framed shelter with walls made from reeds or mud and a plastic sheet for a roof.*

The 1948 United Nations Declaration of Human Rights aims to guarantee people everywhere a decent standard of living, the right to education and equality in law, the freedom to hold opinions and speak without fear, and freedom from violence and oppression. But for millions of people — including women, children, minority groups, and those with unjust rulers — these rights and freedoms mean little. In many developing countries women have fewer rights than men. Some societies prevent women from owning land, for example, or think it natural to treat boys better than girls and for men to control and mistreat women. Violence against women is a problem almost everywhere.

Children suffer when poverty denies them education or forces them into work, sometimes as slaves. In many countries homeless youngsters live on city streets, begging, stealing, or taking drugs: many die young. Others are the victims of war, made to fight (as young as ten), or killed by adults.

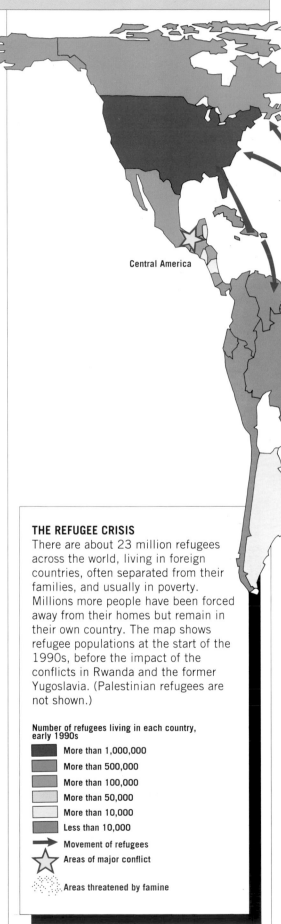

Central America

THE REFUGEE CRISIS
There are about 23 million refugees across the world, living in foreign countries, often separated from their families, and usually in poverty. Millions more people have been forced away from their homes but remain in their own country. The map shows refugee populations at the start of the 1990s, before the impact of the conflicts in Rwanda and the former Yugoslavia. (Palestinian refugees are not shown.)

Number of refugees living in each country, early 1990s

■	More than 1,000,000
■	More than 500,000
■	More than 100,000
■	More than 50,000
■	More than 10,000
■	Less than 10,000
→	Movement of refugees
☆	Areas of major conflict
⋯	Areas threatened by famine

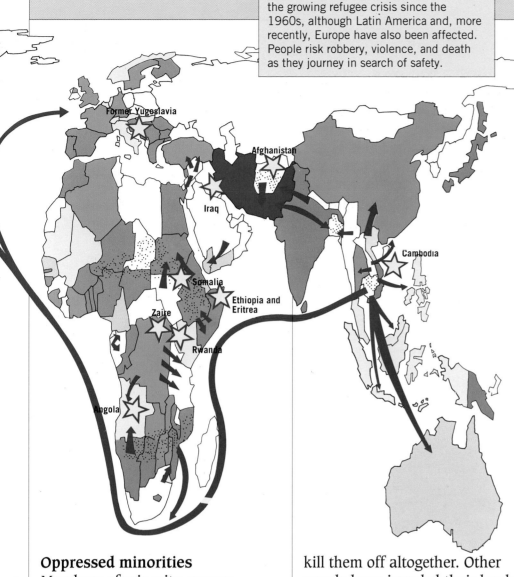

Africa and Asia have suffered most from the growing refugee crisis since the 1960s, although Latin America and, more recently, Europe have also been affected. People risk robbery, violence, and death as they journey in search of safety.

Oppressed minorities

Members of minority groups — people who are different from the majority of the population in their religion, language, culture, or ethnic background — often do not enjoy the full range of freedoms and rights that the majority do. Some minorities cannot practice their religion openly or at all, are trapped in poverty because they are discriminated against throughout society, or they lose control over their traditional lands.

The world's 250 million indigenous people (the original inhabitants of a region), including the rainforest tribes, have suffered terrible injustice and cruelty. Some settlers and governments have tried to destroy their way of life or kill them off altogether. Other people have invaded their lands, often bringing "development" in the shape of logging, big-business farming, dams, and mines. Many indigenous peoples have organized themselves to demand their rights.

The rule of tyrants

A lack of democracy in some developing countries, such as China, means that rulers mistreat their citizens, imposing unjust laws. Human rights groups have thousands of files listing the wrongful arrest, torture, imprisonment, disappearance, and killing of innocent people.

Developed countries are also involved in the human rights crisis. They have established and benefit from a world system of trade and communication that makes some people rich and powerful and others poor and weak. Their governments sometimes support violent rulers if it suits them, for the sake of trade agreements for example, or else they may not deal adequately with the poor treatment of their own minority groups.

Millions of people whose human rights are denied become refugees, leaving their countries in search of a better chance of survival elsewhere. Most refugees, half of whom are children, live in developing countries, often in unhealthy and overcrowded camps or slums. Sudden movements of refugees can cause environmental crises when lots of people overwhelm local facilities. Others, unable to escape, suffer poverty and persecution in their own countries.

But the picture is not hopeless. With the end of apartheid in South Africa in 1993–94, for example, the black population emerged from decades of suffering to face a hopeful future.

HOME ACTION

Help improve human rights worldwide.
- Treat people fairly, whatever their background or origins.
- Complain when somebody is mistreated.
- Support calls for better rights for people with disabilities.
- Support women's organizations, such as those working for equal opportunities.
- Buy fair-traded goods.
- Write to newspapers, magazines, and your representative in government about human rights problems.
- Join a human rights organization such as Amnesty International, the Minority Rights Group, or Survival International.

135

GAIA WATCH

THE MACUXI OF BRAZIL

"There used to be a lot of game here: deer, armadillos, anteaters, capybara, ducks. We used to hunt them with bows and arrows and with rifles. I was a good shot with a bow and arrow . . . but now it's all gone, and nowadays even fish are difficult to find. Everything got bad when the ranchers came in. The river used to be very clear in the summer: now it's just as muddy as it is in the winter, in the rainy season."

Ricardo Nascimento remembers how life used to be for the Macuxi people, who live near the River Mau, a tributary of the Branco, in northern Brazil. For many years their way of life has been under threat. Cattle ranchers are buying up what was traditionally Macuxi land, and gold miners are polluting the rivers with mercury. But politicians tell the Macuxi that they have to change to be part of the new Brazil.

▲ **The River Mau** lies on Brazil's northwestern border with Guyana. Mining for gold and diamonds began here on a small scale in the 1930s, but by the early 1990s hundreds of miners were extracting gold from the river-bed. The local community of Macuxi Indians, who have lived here for generations, resented the miners' invasion. They organized a campaign to evict them from the land. Although the gold miners have now gone, "scars" remain along the riverbanks.

▶ **The activities of the gold miners** polluted the river, killing fish, and drove away some of the wildlife of a region originally rich in plant and animal life.

Lindalva Nascimento, whose daughter is a health worker, says: "In the past, our children were not taught at school about our Macuxi customs — the herbs we used for medicines, the prayers of the *pajes* (doctor-priests) — and they were lost. Now we want to go back to them: it's not easy, but we have begun. Now my daughter and the other health workers are learning how to make potions and creams, and how to prescribe traditional herbal treatments for things like toothache and earache."

Geronimo de Oliviera teaches math at Siminyo school, the largest school in the Macuxi territory. "The school is important because our children learn to read and write in their own language. It is vital for rescuing our culture. It all began when the *tuaxas* (community leaders) decided it was wrong to be ashamed of our culture, to have no more dancing and singing. Of course there were problems — there were no books. We had to write all the materials: we have even written books of Macuxi legends.

"The politicians say we want to return to the past," says Geronimo, "that we aren't Indian any more; that we are standing in the way of progress. But we are not. We just want our rights to be respected. We want to be seen as human beings, of a different culture."

▼ **Health workers** are learning how to make tinctures (medicinal preparations), creams, and herbal remedies so they can treat people according to traditional Macuxi methods. The most common complaints are diarrhea, influenza, and toothache. There has been malaria too since the miners came.

▼ **Macuxi students** can now learn their own language, and about their culture and history, as part of their formal education. Knowledge and stories from the past were not being passed on from generation to generation, but now efforts are being made to keep that knowledge alive within the Macuxi community.

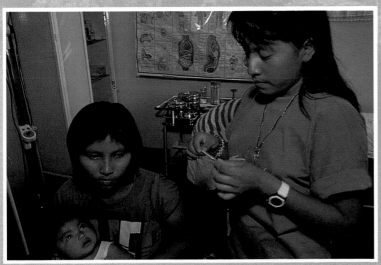

BETTER HEALTH

Your parents may have often told you to wash your hands before meals and to brush your teeth afterward. These chores can be a nuisance when you're in a hurry. But if you got food poisoning or a raging toothache you would realize that prevention is better than cure. And that's the message of family planning and primary health care too.

Managing human numbers is essential if health is to improve. To reduce birthrates women need access to well-run family planning services, more opportunities for education (literate women have fewer, healthier children), and better welfare services. Greater equality between rich and poor, and between women and men, usually results in smaller families.

China, Colombia, Cuba, Kerala state in India, Singapore, Sri Lanka, and Tunisia all reduced birthrates in the 1960s and 1970s by promoting birth control, and improving child health and the social position of women. Government policies encouraged small families with tax relief, pensions, and other programs.

An international effort could bring the projected world population figure of 9–10 billion by 2050 down to 8.5 billion.

▶ **Community health workers** bridge the gap between government services and the people. They can help identify sickness early and advise people on healthier ways of living.

▶ **Regular check-ups** not only improve personal health but save money by detecting illness at the start, when treatment is often less expensive than at a later stage.

Primary health care for all
Primary health care services use links between health workers and the community to prevent illness or treat it as early as possible. Mother and child health is a key aspect of this. People in both developed and developing countries benefit from primary health care. The defense of health is symbolized by the snakes and rod of the Roman god of healing, Aesculapius.

Developed countries have successful primary health care programs. These programs have helped reduce infant deaths and hospital admissions. Public education campaigns in Scandinavia promoting healthier lifestyles have led to lower rates of tooth decay, cancer, and deaths from heart disease.

Developed country

Community hospital/
health center

Community health workers

Self-help groups

Early detection of
health problems

▲ **Self-help groups** allow women to plan their families better, and help people overcome health problems such as alcoholism, drug addiction, depression, and physical disability.

◀ **"Alternative" medicine,** based on traditional treatments such as acupuncture, yoga, and herbal remedies, is growing in popularity in developed countries. "Complementary" medicine, drawing on both conventional and alternative treatments, is also receiving more attention from medical professionals.

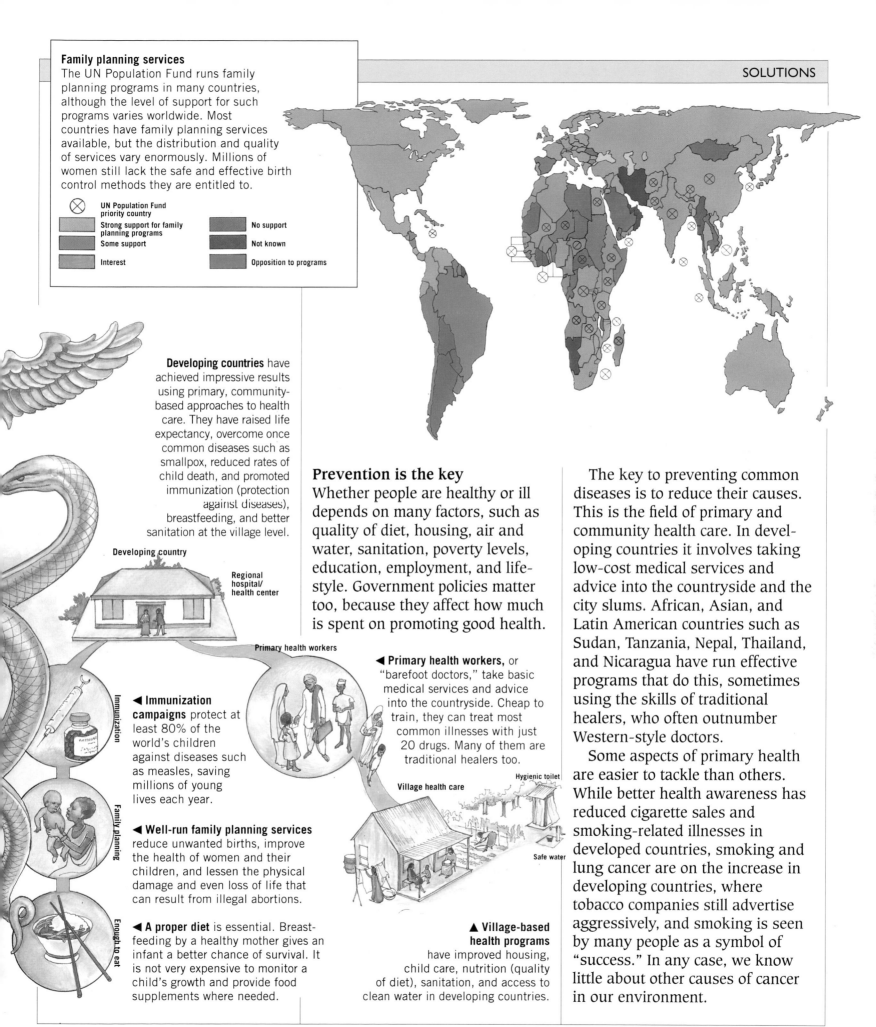

Family planning services
The UN Population Fund runs family planning programs in many countries, although the level of support for such programs varies worldwide. Most countries have family planning services available, but the distribution and quality of services vary enormously. Millions of women still lack the safe and effective birth control methods they are entitled to.

⊗ UN Population Fund priority country

Strong support for family planning programs

Some support

Interest

No support

Not known

Opposition to programs

Developing countries have achieved impressive results using primary, community-based approaches to health care. They have raised life expectancy, overcome once common diseases such as smallpox, reduced rates of child death, and promoted immunization (protection against diseases), breastfeeding, and better sanitation at the village level.

Developing country

Regional hospital/ health center

Primary health workers

◄ **Immunization campaigns** protect at least 80% of the world's children against diseases such as measles, saving millions of young lives each year.

◄ **Well-run family planning services** reduce unwanted births, improve the health of women and their children, and lessen the physical damage and even loss of life that can result from illegal abortions.

◄ **A proper diet** is essential. Breastfeeding by a healthy mother gives an infant a better chance of survival. It is not very expensive to monitor a child's growth and provide food supplements where needed.

◄ **Primary health workers,** or "barefoot doctors," take basic medical services and advice into the countryside. Cheap to train, they can treat most common illnesses with just 20 drugs. Many of them are traditional healers too.

Hygienic toilet

Village health care

Safe water

▲ **Village-based health programs** have improved housing, child care, nutrition (quality of diet), sanitation, and access to clean water in developing countries.

Prevention is the key

Whether people are healthy or ill depends on many factors, such as quality of diet, housing, air and water, sanitation, poverty levels, education, employment, and lifestyle. Government policies matter too, because they affect how much is spent on promoting good health.

The key to preventing common diseases is to reduce their causes. This is the field of primary and community health care. In developing countries it involves taking low-cost medical services and advice into the countryside and the city slums. African, Asian, and Latin American countries such as Sudan, Tanzania, Nepal, Thailand, and Nicaragua have run effective programs that do this, sometimes using the skills of traditional healers, who often outnumber Western-style doctors.

Some aspects of primary health are easier to tackle than others. While better health awareness has reduced cigarette sales and smoking-related illnesses in developed countries, smoking and lung cancer are on the increase in developing countries, where tobacco companies still advertise aggressively, and smoking is seen by many people as a symbol of "success." In any case, we know little about other causes of cancer in our environment.

SHARING SKILLS

The problems we face need community-wide solutions. While millions of people lack paid work, an enormous range of worthwhile tasks need doing. These include cleaning up polluted sites; planting trees; producing food and energy in an environmentally friendly way; building low-cost housing; repairing and recycling; bringing health and education services to villages and slums in developing countries; and caring for older people and those with disabilities. All over the world people are working together in communities to improve the quality of life for everyone. Government policies often help but sometimes hinder this work.

Suppose that each of us has a broken bicycle. You know how to fix a bike but don't have any tools; I am no good at mending things but I have a box of wrenches and spare parts. If we won't talk to each other we're stuck. But by sharing our skills and resources, working as a team, or community, we might end up with two working bikes.

DID YOU KNOW?

Trade without money
Local Exchange Trading Systems, or LETS, are a new and popular form of community action. Members of a LETS system use each other's skills and services — from babysitting to house building — but pay in "local currency," that is, each other's services, not cash. A central computer prints a monthly statement showing what each person has "bought" and "sold." People using LETS find that their quality of life improves, while their cash spending decreases. Hundreds of groups are now running in Western Europe, North America, and Australasia.

Community education means using schools and colleges for the whole community — not just for training for jobs. People of all ages welcome the opportunity to learn new skills, extend their knowledge, and find new ways to manage their lives.

WORKING AS A COMMUNITY: THE KEY TO PROGRESS
All around the world people are working together locally and globally to solve problems. Community groups are not perfect, and there are sometimes problems between members. But successful "grass-roots" efforts show that it is possible to overcome poverty, unemployment, physical health problems, and lack of education, to protect and improve local environments, and to make societies more fair and equal through peaceful social and political change.

Low-cost technologies and good communications are important in developing countries. Organizations such as Intermediate Technology help local people set up small-scale community businesses (below). Satellites are used to bring much-needed information to the poor in the countryside (right).

Fair-trade organizations help producer cooperatives in developing countries sell their produce in the developed world for decent prices. A growing network of non-governmental organizations (NGOs) and human rights groups is working to make cooperation the basis of the way human beings go about their business.

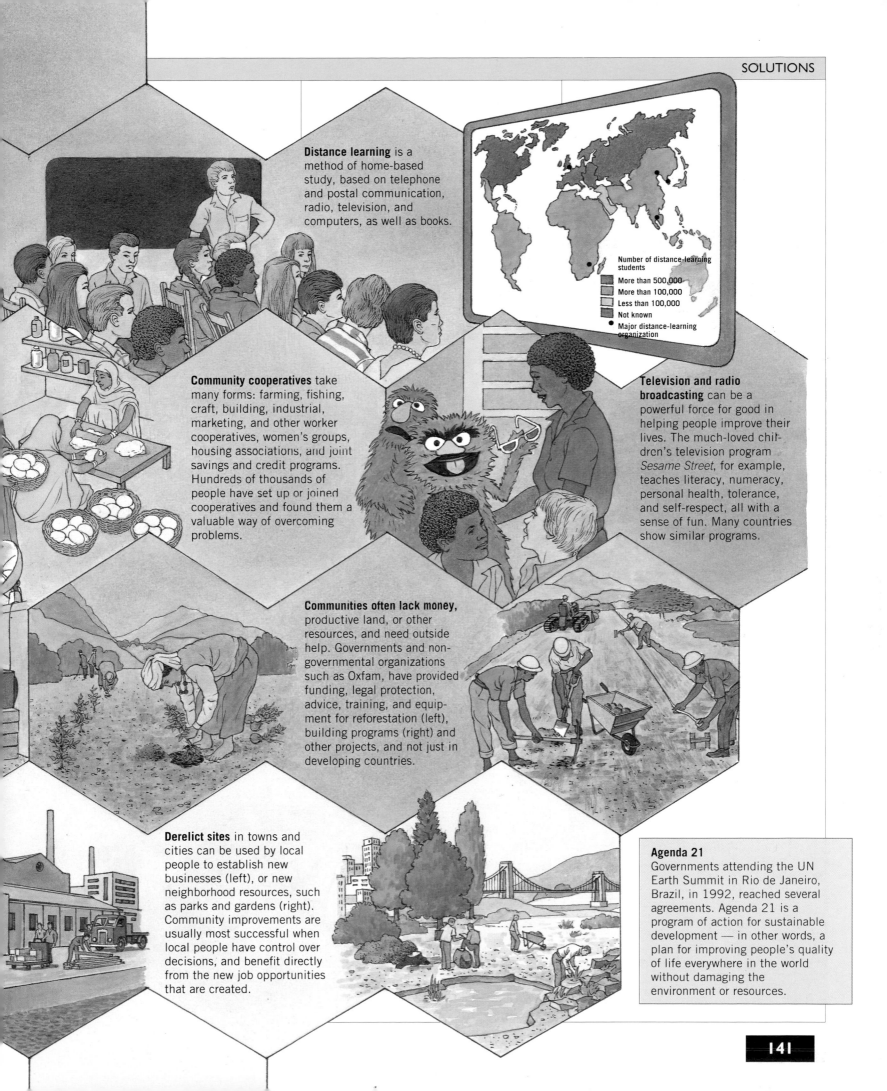

Distance learning is a method of home-based study, based on telephone and postal communication, radio, television, and computers, as well as books.

Number of distance-learning students
More than 500,000
More than 100,000
Less than 100,000
Not known
● Major distance-learning organization

Community cooperatives take many forms: farming, fishing, craft, building, industrial, marketing, and other worker cooperatives, women's groups, housing associations, and joint savings and credit programs. Hundreds of thousands of people have set up or joined cooperatives and found them a valuable way of overcoming problems.

Television and radio broadcasting can be a powerful force for good in helping people improve their lives. The much-loved children's television program *Sesame Street*, for example, teaches literacy, numeracy, personal health, tolerance, and self-respect, all with a sense of fun. Many countries show similar programs.

Communities often lack money, productive land, or other resources, and need outside help. Governments and non-governmental organizations such as Oxfam, have provided funding, legal protection, advice, training, and equipment for reforestation (left), building programs (right) and other projects, and not just in developing countries.

Derelict sites in towns and cities can be used by local people to establish new businesses (left), or new neighborhood resources, such as parks and gardens (right). Community improvements are usually most successful when local people have control over decisions, and benefit directly from the new job opportunities that are created.

Agenda 21
Governments attending the UN Earth Summit in Rio de Janeiro, Brazil, in 1992, reached several agreements. Agenda 21 is a program of action for sustainable development — in other words, a plan for improving people's quality of life everywhere in the world without damaging the environment or resources.

8 CIVILIZATION

"The only war we seek should be . . . against humankind's ancient enemies — poverty, hunger, illiteracy, and preventable disease. . . . Poor people, women, youth, the disabled, older people . . . we are all in this together."

PETRA KELLY,
leader of Germany's Green
movement, who died in 1992

Civilization: what a splendid word! It sums up everything that human beings can be proud of. We can boast of many magnificent achievements in the past and more recently; and there will be more in the future. But let's be honest. We have built a lot more slums than palaces and cathedrals; at least as many people have died in poverty around the world as have lived in comfort; and we spend vast sums of money arming for war. So just how civilized are we? If we succeed in building a fairer and more peaceful world in the future, we may look back and find that 20th-century humanity was not very civilized after all.

The traditions of ancient civilizations live on today. Here crowds assemble for the Q'Collor-Riti festival in the Peruvian Andes, honoring the snow-capped mountain Auzangate. This is one of several peaks believed to have been the protectors of Cuzco, the capital of the ancient Inca Empire.

LIVING IN CITIES

Bright lights, big city! Cities can be exciting places, with their busy streets, crowded markets, inviting shops, cinemas and theatres, interesting museums, and much more. Many people think that cities represent what modern life is all about. Some people love them, and others say they hate them. How important are cities in our world today?

Dhaka, capital city of Bangladesh, has severe traffic congestion in the rush-hour, like big cities everywhere. Many people use cycle rickshaws to get around: they are cheap and reliable, and do not pollute the environment.

The first civilizations had small settlements of only a few thousand people. In the Middle Ages the world's larger cities had 40,000 or more inhabitants. By the mid-1800s several cities, including London, Paris, New York, Tokyo, and Shanghai, had populations of more than one million. Today's largest cities, such as Mexico City and Tokyo-Yokohama, have more than 20 million inhabitants.

What cities have to offer

The inhabitants of cities have achieved great things. The Roman Empire, for example, with its architecture, engineering, law, literature, and system of government, was completely city-based. Cities today offer many of the facilities of modern life that people enjoy, from opera houses and art galleries to pop music and fashion.

Yet almost from the beginning cities have had problems – poverty, overcrowding, crime, disease, and pollution. Large cities need huge supplies of food and could not survive without the surrounding countryside. They make huge demands on energy supplies, raw materials, and cheap human labour for their industries.

Many cities in developed countries have stopped growing as people move away from them, seeking more pleasant surroundings in the suburbs and semi-rural areas. In contrast, far greater numbers of people in developing countries who want to escape from poverty leave the countryside and move to cities. By the year 2000 more than half the human race will live in cities, compared with only 14 per cent in 1900.

Main airline routes linking cities

Cities are centres of knowledge, ideas, and information. They are home to most large libraries, newspaper and book publishing, and television and radio broadcasting.

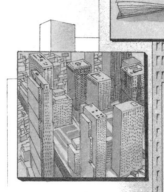

Money was once mainly just a tool of trade. Now money itself is traded. New York, Frankfurt, Tokyo, and other cities are powerful banking and finance centres whose decisions can affect the lives of millions of people worldwide.

Architecture – the design and construction of buildings – is an important urban art form. The ruins of many fine monuments show the glories of past city-based civilizations.

3000 BC

200 BC

CITIES AND CIVILIZATION

Every civilization has involved people living in cities. The link between cities and civilization is just as strong today. Cities can be places of opportunity, wealth creation, culture, and new ideas. But they could not exist without a network of support links providing energy, food, and communications.

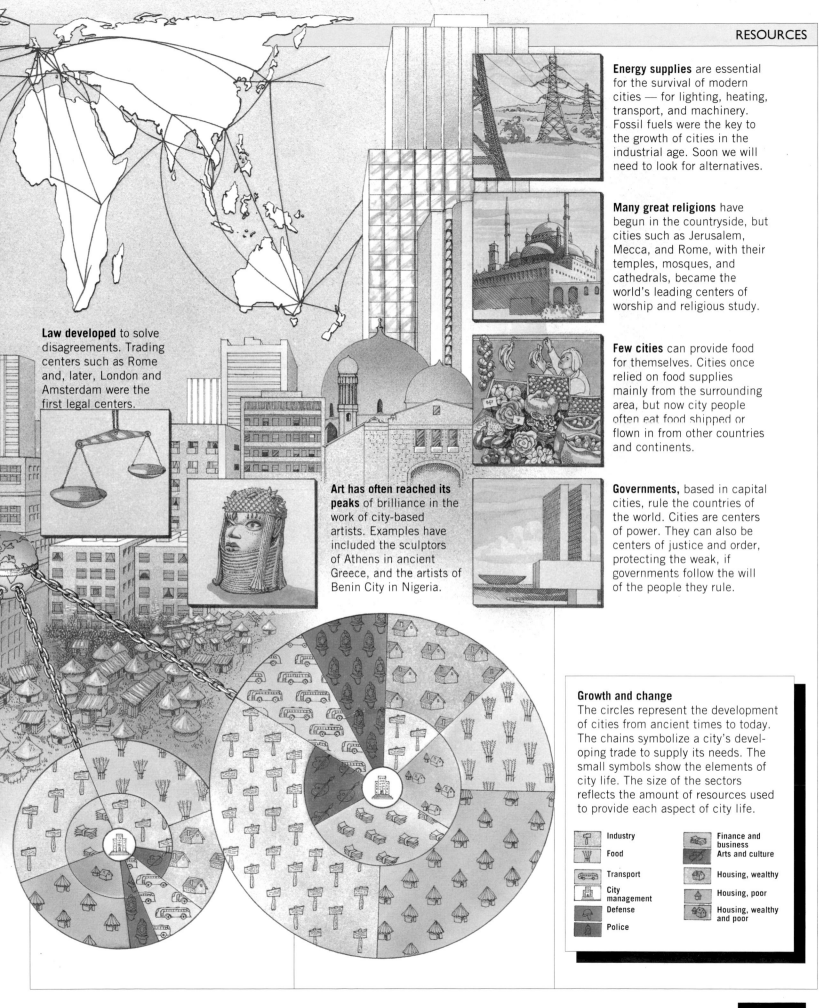

Energy supplies are essential for the survival of modern cities — for lighting, heating, transport, and machinery. Fossil fuels were the key to the growth of cities in the industrial age. Soon we will need to look for alternatives.

Many great religions have begun in the countryside, but cities such as Jerusalem, Mecca, and Rome, with their temples, mosques, and cathedrals, became the world's leading centers of worship and religious study.

Few cities can provide food for themselves. Cities once relied on food supplies mainly from the surrounding area, but now city people often eat food shipped or flown in from other countries and continents.

Governments, based in capital cities, rule the countries of the world. Cities are centers of power. They can also be centers of justice and order, protecting the weak, if governments follow the will of the people they rule.

Law developed to solve disagreements. Trading centers such as Rome and, later, London and Amsterdam were the first legal centers.

Art has often reached its peaks of brilliance in the work of city-based artists. Examples have included the sculptors of Athens in ancient Greece, and the artists of Benin City in Nigeria.

Growth and change
The circles represent the development of cities from ancient times to today. The chains symbolize a city's developing trade to supply its needs. The small symbols show the elements of city life. The size of the sectors reflects the amount of resources used to provide each aspect of city life.

Industry		Finance and business
Food		Arts and culture
Transport		Housing, wealthy
City management		Housing, poor
Defense		Housing, wealthy and poor
Police		

WORLD FACTORY

Are you good at making things? You may be a clever model maker, or skillful with a needle and thread or electrical circuits. It is natural to enjoy making things well, and sometimes our skills can earn money for us. But problems may develop if making goods and selling them become more important to us than anything else.

Before the Industrial Revolution began in the 18th century, people made furniture, clothes, and other goods on a small scale. They used mainly water power, animal power, and their own hands. Trade was mainly local. Modern industry developed as people began to burn coal to produce steam to power machines making more and more goods in factories.

Britain, France, Spain, Portugal, and the Netherlands had grown rich through conquest and slavery. They controlled much of Africa, Asia, the Caribbean, and Central and South America, and sent millions of Africans to work as slaves in the Americas. Britain led the world in making and trading goods around the world. Germany, the USA, and other countries followed on the road to industrialization. Countries such as Brazil are developing their industries in the same way today.

The inventions and new technologies of the 19th and 20th centuries — from electricity and conveyor belts to information technology (IT) and biotechnology — have transformed world industry.

DID YOU KNOW?

The biggest businesses
Huge global companies called multi-nationals control about a third of the world's major industries and employ millions of people. Their activities include mining and oil production, farming, scientific research, manufacturing, advertising, and marketing. The largest corporations, such as General Motors, are richer than many countries.

Manufacturing industry
Manufacturing – the large-scale production of finished goods from raw materials – is the main activity of modern industry. A constant flow of industrial products (such as chemicals, steel, and machinery) and consumer goods (such as cars, household items, and clothes) comes from the world's factories. Can we make manufacturing less environmentally damaging?

In the Americas industry's share of wealth creation is between 30% and 40%. The USA leads the world in manufacturing.

Industry, employment, and wealth
The importance of industry in creating wealth varies from region to region, as does the number of people working in services (retail, banks, offices, and so on) as opposed to farming. Industrial development depends on industrial research, and the amount of money spent on it. The money value of manufacturing (making goods from raw materials) reveals the importance of industry to a country's economy.

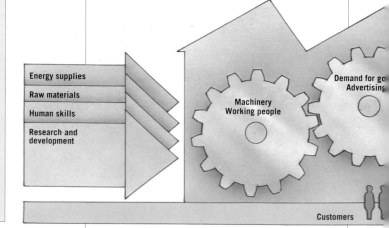

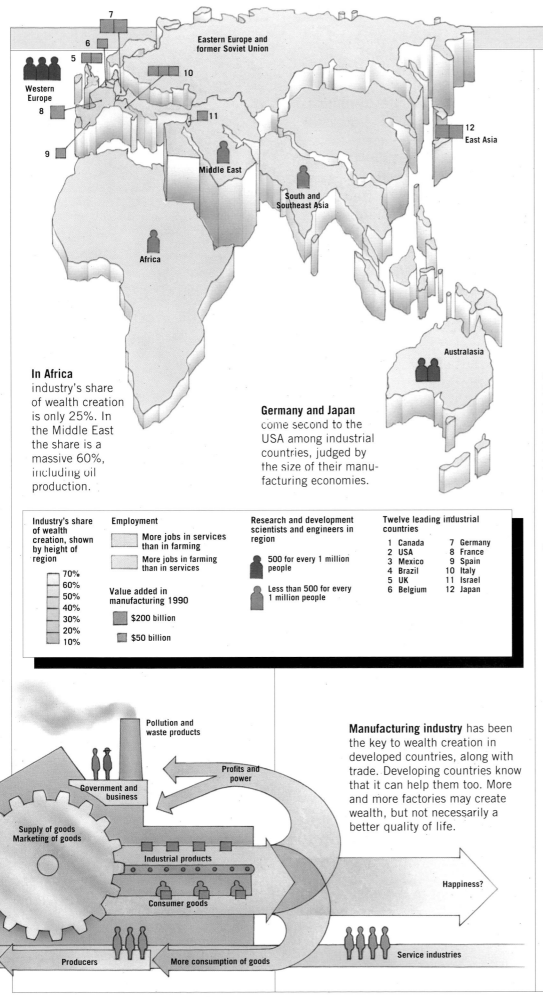

In Africa
industry's share of wealth creation is only 25%. In the Middle East the share is a massive 60%, including oil production.

Germany and Japan
come second to the USA among industrial countries, judged by the size of their manufacturing economies.

Eastern Europe and former Soviet Union

Western Europe

East Asia

Middle East

South and Southeast Asia

Africa

Australasia

Industry's share of wealth creation, shown by height of region	Employment	Research and development scientists and engineers in region	Twelve leading industrial countries
70% 60% 50% 40% 30% 20% 10%	More jobs in services than in farming / More jobs in farming than in services / Value added in manufacturing 1990 / $200 billion / $50 billion	500 for every 1 million people / Less than 500 for every 1 million people	1 Canada 7 Germany / 2 USA 8 France / 3 Mexico 9 Spain / 4 Brazil 10 Italy / 5 UK 11 Israel / 6 Belgium 12 Japan

Manufacturing industry has been the key to wealth creation in developed countries, along with trade. Developing countries know that it can help them too. More and more factories may create wealth, but not necessarily a better quality of life.

Pollution and waste products

Government and business

Profits and power

Supply of goods Marketing of goods

Industrial products

Consumer goods

Happiness?

Producers

More consumption of goods

Service industries

Research and development

We invest large amounts of money in researching and developing new products and technologies. A quarter of this money is for weapons research. Developed countries spend the most on research and development; developing countries have little money available.

Share of research and development spending in 1990

World total $175,000 million

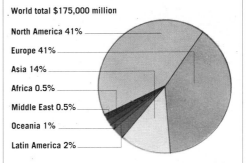

North America 41%
Europe 41%
Asia 14%
Africa 0.5%
Middle East 0.5%
Oceania 1%
Latin America 2%

The price of industrialization

Industry and world trade have brought many benefits to humankind. More people than ever have long, comfortable, and interesting lives, and enjoy goods and services unknown to their ancestors. Yet some people question whether the disadvantages of an industrialized world outweigh the advantages.

Much of the wealth that we "create," for example, comes from using up non-renewable resources, such as oil and minerals. Large-scale, modern industry can harm traditional communities and cause widespread environmental damage. The world's weapons armory has continued to grow through the arms trade. And although we now have many brilliant medical treatments, millions of men, women, and children still die from a lack of food and clean water.

The wealth gap between rich and poor has widened within countries and between the developed and developing worlds. If all countries produced and consumed in the way the developed world does today, our environment would soon become a wasteland.

COMMUNICATION

Communication means sending and receiving information, ideas, thoughts, and feelings. Many people today have a wide choice of communication technologies at their fingertips: newspapers and magazines, books, the telephone, radio, television, and computers. Computer and satellite communications have developed enormously in the last 20 years. We can now store all the material from a book such as this on a tiny microchip and send information across the world in seconds.

Modern communications can help solve problems. In developing countries, radio is a good way to communicate information about preventing disease and improving health, and about family planning practices. It is especially useful where many people do not read.

Like many young people, you probably spend a lot of time at a computer keyboard. You belong to one of the first "computer generations." Most people growing up 15 or 20 years ago did not have computer rooms at school or college, or a word processor at home. Even today, hundreds of millions of people in some parts of the world will never use a computer — or even a telephone.

FROM THE BIRTH OF LANGUAGE TO THE INTERNET

Speech was the first human system of communication. Over time people have invented a whole series of new ways to send and receive information and messages: long-distance signals and sounds, printing, the telegraph and telephone, radio and television, satellite technology, and computer networks. Each new technology has been a step in the transformation of communications. Today's Internet gives a person seated at a computer speedy access to an almost limitless range of other people, discussion groups, and information sources all over the world. "Interactive" programs and technologies promise a wide variety of future developments.

Speech and language are the basis of most human communication. Nearly all the world's languages belong to a small number of language groups. As early people increased in number and spread around the world, languages in the same group became different from each other. The first human writing may be cave-wall "picture stories" from about 30,000 BC. By 3300 BC people in the Middle East used a form of cuneiform, or word-picture writing, that is probably the long-distant ancestor of the Latin alphabet.

Computers are probably the most important and fastest-changing communications and information technology today. Early machines were large and expensive. Hundreds of millions of people and businesses now use cheaper, desktop computers.

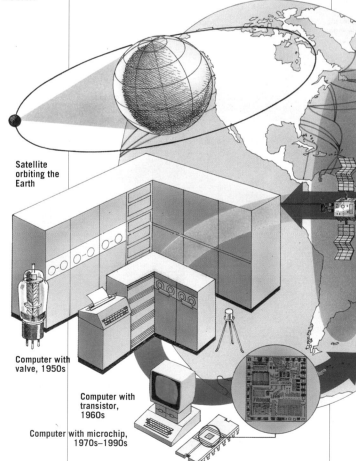

Satellite orbiting the Earth

Computer with valve, 1950s

Computer with transistor, 1960s

Computer with microchip, 1970s–1990s

Early systems of sending long-distance messages included drumbeats (a method still used in parts of Africa), beacon fires, flags, and knotted ropes.

The first printers used carved stone and wooden blocks. Printing using wooden movable type began in China and Northern Europe in the 15th century.

The telegraph and telephone, in the 19th century, were the first electrical forms of long-distance communication. Telephones now use satellite links.

"Wireless" radio followed soon after Marconi had invented the wireless telegraph in 1895. The first regular radio broadcasts, by the BBC, began in 1922.

With satellite technology we can map the Earth's surface and see what is happening to forests, farmland, lakes, rivers, and seas.

Yet not everyone benefits equally from modern communications networks. Fewer than one person in a hundred in developing countries has a television set. A few giant corporations own many newspapers and television and computer companies. These corporations, and some governments, have great control over the information we receive. People watch US-made television programs and films, for example, all over the world.

Another worry is that governments and businesses can use computers secretly to gather, store, and exchange private information about people.

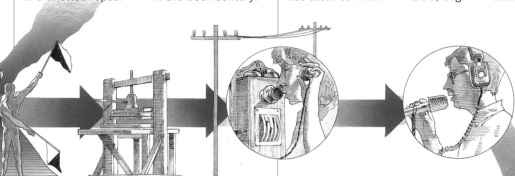

Thousands of satellites have gone into orbit since the first launch in 1957, but only a few hundred remain circling the Earth. We use them mainly for television and telephone links, weather forecasting, and geological and environmental monitoring.

Television was invented in the 1920s, and the first regular broadcasts began ten years later. TV is now one of our most powerful forms of communication. People in developed countries own over half the world's 850 million sets.

Remote sensing by satellite reveals information about the Earth that is much harder to see on the ground. Different rocks reflect sunlight differently. Pictures taken by satellite are color-coded on computer to show these differences, as here. Identifying rocks may reveal mineral deposits.

Undersea telephone cables

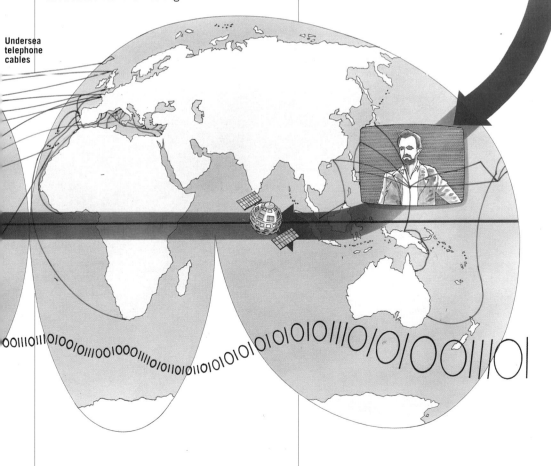

CHAOS IN THE CITY

Is there a neighborhood near where you live that you try to avoid, especially after dark? Most of us know such places. They are badly lit, dirty, ugly, and trouble seems to lurk in the shadows. You may find these areas unpleasant enough to walk through, but for the people living there, they are even worse. Many cities have large areas like this, and they present many problems worldwide.

About 2.4 billion people live in cities today. This is four times as many as 45 years ago. City populations are growing particularly fast in developing countries. In these countries almost half the city population increase results from people moving in from the country-side — at a rate of 75,000 each day worldwide.

The growing urban population
By the end of the 20th century, for the first time, half the world's people will live in urban areas (towns and cities). The proportion will rise to 60 percent by 2020, leaving just two out of every five people in the countryside.

2020 – 60% of world population in towns and cities

2000 – 50% of world population in towns and cities

Why do so many people migrate to the cities in developing countries? As large-scale farming, forestry, and other forms of development increase, natural resources, including land, become scarcer. Poor people who once earned a living off the land find it harder to survive. So they head for the cities looking for work.

Most newcomers join many other poor city dwellers in shanty-towns fringing the suburbs and business districts. Usually shelter is in shacks built from scrap metal, plastic, and cardboard. There is often no piped water, electricity, sanitation, or refuse disposal.

North America	Europe	
1 Los Angeles	20 London	
2 Chicago	21 Paris	
3 Detroit	22 Berlin	
4 Philadelphia	23 St Petersburg	
5 New York	24 Moscow	41 Calcutta
6 Mexico City	25 Madrid	42 Dhaka
7 Guadalajara	26 Milan	43 Bangkok
	27 Istanbul	44 Ho Chi Minh City (Saigon)
South America		45 Wuhun
8 Caracas	Africa	46 Xian
9 Bogota	28 Cairo	47 Beijing
10 Manaus	29 Lagos	48 Shenyang
11 Lima	30 Addis Abeba	49 Tokyo/ Yokohama
12 La Paz	31 Nairobi	50 Osaka
13 Belo Horizonte	32 Kinshasa	51 Seoul
14 São Paulo	Asia	52 Pusan
15 Santiago	33 Baghdad	53 Tianjin
16 Buenos Aires	34 Amman	54 Shanghai
17 Rio de Janeiro	35 Lahore	55 Hong Kong
18 Porto Alegre	36 Delhi	56 Taipei
19 Montevideo	37 Karachi	57 Manila
	38 Ahmadabad	58 Jakarta
	39 Bombay	59 Surabaya
	40 Madras	

GROWTH OF THE WORLD'S CITIES

In 1950 only seven of the world's cities had a population of more than five million. By 1990, ten cities contained more than ten million people. By the year 2010 there could be 60 cities of around five million inhabitants, and several giant cities of between 15 million and 20 million people. The map shows that almost all the world's fast-growing cities are in developing countries, to the south of the North-South divide. Mexico City could become the first city of 30 million inhabitants.

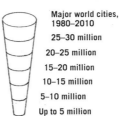

Major world cities, 1980–2010

25–30 million
20–25 million
15–20 million
10–15 million
5–10 million
Up to 5 million

Population growth to 2010
Population in 1995
Population in 1980

Life in a shantytown

Hunger, overcrowding, pollution, and sickness are common in shantytowns. So is underemployment. Many children have no schooling, and many families do not have access to health services. To survive and raise children in these terrible surroundings is a great struggle.

The governments of developing countries do not always do enough to help people in shantytowns. They may spend more money on motorways, airports, and business districts than on helping the poor improve their living conditions. People in poor neighborhoods may be treated like criminals by the police, especially if they are squatting on land belonging to others. When municipal authorities want to sell or build on land where there is a shantytown, the shacks get bulldozed to the ground.

Cities of the developed world

Cities in developed countries also have problems, although on a smaller scale. Many industries and businesses have shut down or moved out of town, often leaving derelict buildings behind. Higher-earning people have moved to the suburbs, where pleasant shops, schools, workplaces, and other facilities are a drive away. Inner-city services such as community housing, public transport, libraries, and parks are underfunded and neglected. Many once-prosperous city centers are now unpleasant, unsafe, and troubled by vandalism and crime.

*The **tumbledown houses** of a shantytown in Kennedy Town, west Hong Kong, cling precariously to a steep slope.*

HAVES & HAVE-NOTS

It is natural to enjoy spending money. Hardly anybody could live without it at all. Yet, because it is important to so many, money can have undesirable effects. It can turn friends into enemies. It also "breeds": those who have a lot of it seem to get more. Money means power in many places, and it has a great impact on our world.

HOME ACTION

It will take many generations to end poverty, but we can all play a part.

- Try to live more simply and spend less money on yourself.
- Where possible, buy fair-traded goods, which provide higher incomes for producers (at slightly higher cost to the customer).
- Give unwanted clothes, gifts, and so on to a local thrift shop.
- Support, or work as a volunteer for, an anti-poverty group.
- When you have money to save, use an "ethnical" bank or savings plan; that is, one that avoids making unfair profits from developing countries.
- Find out more about living conditions in poor countries and help spread the word.

The wealth gap between the rich, developed countries of the North (including Australia and New Zealand) and the poor, developing countries of the South is wide and growing wider. People in North America, Western Europe, and Japan are about 60 times richer, on average, than those in developing countries. With just 20 percent of the world's people, the North has 75 percent of its income.

How the rich got rich

What has produced the wealth gap? Many countries in the North once had empires and colonies in the South, and grew rich partly at their expense. They built up their industries at home using cheap raw materials from the countries they ruled. They sold goods, such as machinery and processed foods, to less developed countries for big profits. (Of course, some people stayed quite poor in the richer, industrial countries.) Rising profits and high consumption levels in the North have meant ever-larger debts in the South and have damaged environments worldwide.

A few developing countries, such as Brazil, South Korea, and India, have become wealthier by developing industry. But most of the developing world can never take this route. There are not enough raw materials, and the environment could not cope with the pollution. In many countries of Africa, most people are no better off than they were 30 years ago.

Within developing countries too, there is a gap between rich and poor. A few politicians, business people, and others live in comfort, but many are trapped in poverty.

THE POVERTY BOMB

More than 1 billion people worldwide live in total poverty. They lack decent living conditions, enough food, education, paid work, access to health or transport services and, in most cases, government help. As the map shows, all except a few of the very poorest people live in the developing countries of the South. Widespread severe poverty can have devastating effects — like a bomb exploding — leading to massive outbreaks of disease, environmental damage, and violent rioting.

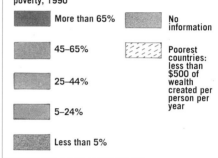

Percentage of a country's people living in worst poverty, 1990

- More than 65%
- 45–65%
- 25–44%
- 5–24%
- Less than 5%
- No information
- Poorest countries: less than $500 of wealth created per person per year

Aid and trade

In 1990 Northern banks and governments gave or lent the South $5.6 billion. Many loans depend on the involvement of Northern businesses. In 1990 Northern companies made profits of more than $13 billion from working in the South. Aid from development charities usually works better.

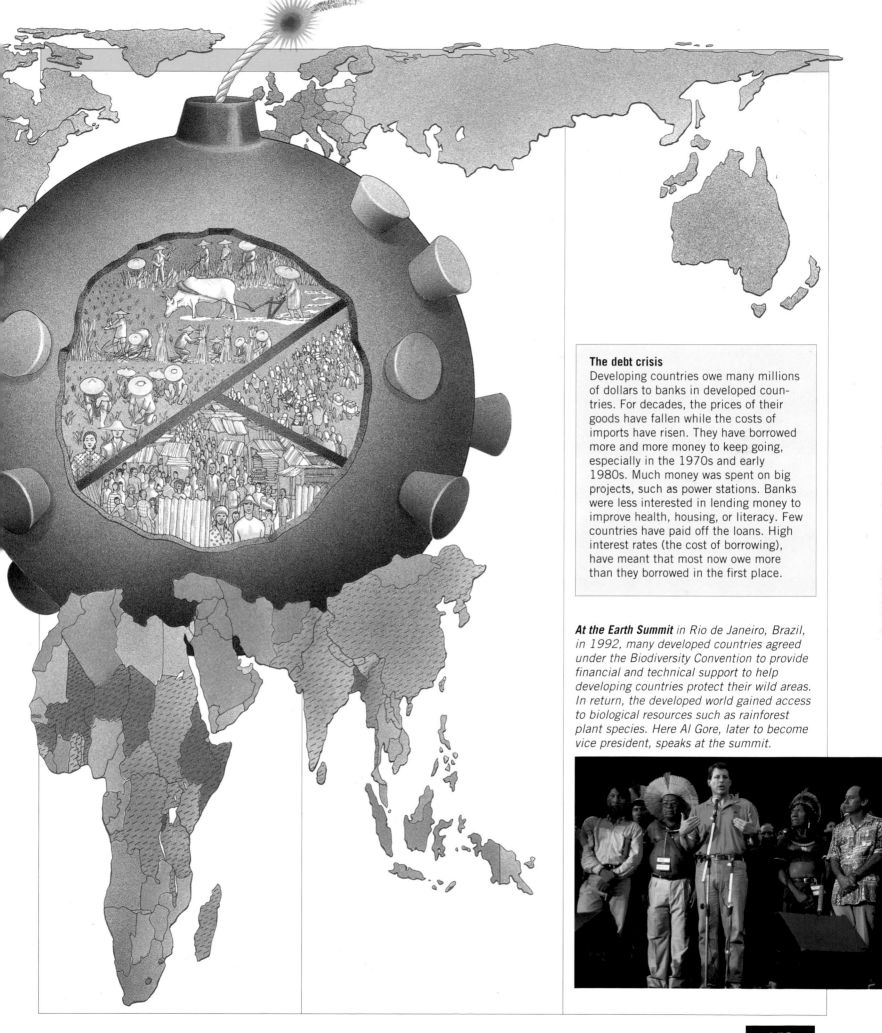

The debt crisis

Developing countries owe many millions of dollars to banks in developed countries. For decades, the prices of their goods have fallen while the costs of imports have risen. They have borrowed more and more money to keep going, especially in the 1970s and early 1980s. Much money was spent on big projects, such as power stations. Banks were less interested in lending money to improve health, housing, or literacy. Few countries have paid off the loans. High interest rates (the cost of borrowing), have meant that most now owe more than they borrowed in the first place.

At the Earth Summit in Rio de Janeiro, Brazil, in 1992, many developed countries agreed under the Biodiversity Convention to provide financial and technical support to help developing countries protect their wild areas. In return, the developed world gained access to biological resources such as rainforest plant species. Here Al Gore, later to become vice president, speaks at the summit.

WORLD AT WAR

Are you an aggressive person? Most likely not. You would probably try very hard to avoid becoming involved in a violent situation. Most people feel the same. Yet there has hardly been a time when the whole world was at peace, and it is far from peaceful today. Many people worry that environmental problems will lead to conflict, unless we solve them first.

Since 1945 there have been at least 170 wars. Most have taken place in developing countries, using weapons sold by developed countries. Twenty-two million people have died in these wars, and millions more have been injured or become refugees. Some thinkers argue that most wars are fought over land, raw materials, and wealth, and not because human beings are naturally aggressive.

The end of the Cold War between the West and the Soviet Union in 1989–90 brought the promise of peace. But it was followed by new wars, such as that in the former Yugoslavia. Many wars are "civil wars" between different groups of people in the same country. Civil wars often begin when some people have too much power over others, or because of struggles over resources such as land.

Soldiers have always died in war, but modern war kills more civilians (non-fighting citizens) than soldiers. During the 1980s, for example, 85 percent of the people who died in war were civilians.

Each year the world spends a massive $1 trillion on weapons and war. The price of a nuclear submarine would pay to educate children in 23 developing countries for a year. For the cost of a day's fighting in the 1991 Gulf War, we could have saved 5 million children's lives through health programs. Two days' worth of world "defense" spending would enable us to tackle the spread of deserts. Five hours' worth would fund the UN's Environment Program for up to 10 years, and seven months' worth would pay for Agenda 21, the UN action plan for sustainable development.

Casualties of war
Between 1945 and 1995 nearly 22 million people died in wars, most of them civilians.

REGION	CIVILIANS KILLED	SOLDIERS KILLED
Europe	290,000	70,000
South Asia	2,200,000	1,100,000
Far East	6,600,000	4,100,000
Middle East	440,000	600,000
Latin America	460,000	200,000
Africa	3,800,000	1,700,000
Total	13,790,000	7,770,000

The nuclear weapons that already exist could wipe out the human race. The USA, the UK, France, Russia, Israel, and China already have nuclear weapons. The governments of many other countries may try to develop them in the future.

Country with nuclear weapons

Country able to make nuclear weapons

Country hoping to make nuclear weapons

Landmines
Landmines are deadly. Laid just below the soil surface, they remain "live" for many years and explode when a person steps on them. Since 1970 landmines have killed or maimed more than a million people, mostly civilians. Up to 100 million landmines are scattered in in Angola, Bosnia, Cambodia, El Salvador, Georgia, Iraq, Laos, Mozambique, Nicaragua, Somalia, Vietnam, and other countries. An exploding mine can blow off a person's leg or kill outright. Clearing mines is slow, dangerous, and expensive. The UN Children's Fund and others believe they should be banned.

WAR AND THE PLANET
From Angola to Vietnam, Lebanon to the former Yugoslavia, millions of people live in surroundings devastated by war. Uranium mining (for nuclear weapons), chemical weapons production, and other war preparations cause further damage. Nuclear weapons testing since 1945 may have caused millions of cancer deaths. Scientists warn that a large-scale nuclear war could plunge us into a "nuclear winter," with smoke and dust blotting out the Sun. Crops would fail. Many people would die from radioactive poisoning, while the "survivors" would lack food, water, fuel, shelter, and medicines.

"We are so far from anywhere that the government doesn't even know that animals live here," says Yaqub Baloch.

"Here" is Kharochan, about as far south as you can go in Pakistan before ending up in the Rann of Kutch, an area of salt and mud-flats on the border of India and Pakistan. It is hot: the land is flat and barren, with a few acacias and thorn scrub. It is hard to imagine anyone making a living here. There are few roads, schools, or clinics. People survive by growing bananas and vegetables.

In 1992 Yaqub Baloch and his friends had an idea: "We heard on

▲ **In Kharochan** (main picture), villagers are working together to make life easier in a harsh region that has scorching temperatures and sparse vegetation, and is subject to sudden floods in the rainy season. Teams of people dig drainage channels or build walls of earth to protect the roads.

◄ **Villagers are trying** to protect their homes from flooding. Soil is piled up around the houses, and in the courtyards, and packed down to make a firm base, higher than the surrounding land.

▶ **Kharochan is so hot** that houses are built to allow as much air as possible to blow through the walls and keep them cool. The houses are often flooded during the monsoon, so everyone keeps most of their belongings off the ground.

the radio, and read in the newspapers, that there are village organizations working for change and improving life for people in their villages.

"We called a meeting of some friends, and put forward the idea that we should form such a group. There was a lot of debate, but finally 12 of us decided to form the *tanzeem* (community group). The first thing we did was to rebuild a section of road destroyed by floods.

"Then some friends told us that Oxfam might help us. So, after the floods in 1994, we wrote to them. Because of the emergency situation they provided money to buy food for 400 of the most needy people." The *tanzeem* worked to raise houses above flood level and build better flood defenses.

The community group has demonstrated that working together can get results. Its efforts provided food and jobs when both were in short supply. Yaqub says: "Now people have seen that there is a point to the *tanzeem*, and they are showing their support. If we work hard for ourselves, others may see our struggle and join hands with us."

◀ *People need to be able to move safely* from village to village during the monsoon season, or whenever there is flooding, so the roads are being raised above the highest flood level. The villagers work together in shifts, day and night, so that the work will get finished sooner.

ACTION FOR CITIES

Imagine a perfect city. What would it be like? In some ways it might be similar to the city you live in or one you know. But the chances are that you would want more parks and open spaces, cleaner streets, safer roads, an end to city poverty, and more friendly neighborhoods. It is possible to redesign our city surroundings for real.

People are already putting good ideas into practice to solve city problems. The aim is to make cities healthier, safer, "greener," and more people-friendly. City neighborhoods in both developed and developing countries need adequate, affordable housing; local shops, services, and markets; well-maintained schools and community centers; small-scale workplaces and local businesses; parks and other open spaces; and safe, pleasant roads.

In developed countries a partnership between local and central government, community groups, and private businesses provides the best mix of skills and resources. In developing countries neighborhood improvement programs need government funding and technical advice but should rely on the skills of local people.

CITY ACTION IN DEVELOPING COUNTRIES
Developing countries can involve local people in low-cost programs to improve poor neighborhoods. Given tools, technical help, loans, basic services, and legal rights to land, shantytown dwellers prove to be excellent neighborhood builders and managers.

Improving a shantytown
1 Laying water and sewage pipes.
2 Link-up to electricity supplies.
3 Locally run garbage collection.
4 Local people build houses, helped by government and development groups.
5 Community center and planning office, run by local people.
6 Old shantytown area.
7 Street lights and trees.
8 New market area with water well.

DID YOU KNOW?

Poor people take the lead
People in shantytowns in Latin America have a talent for getting organized. In 1985 an earthquake in Mexico City wrecked hundreds of homes in one poor neighborhood. Landlords wanted to redevelop the area. But local people, led mainly by women, set up a rebuilding program that the city council paid for. Homeless people in Lima, Peru, and in Buenos Aires, Argentina, have "invaded" unused land, and built homes, roads, schools, and community centers, organized garbage removal, planted trees, and started food cooperatives.

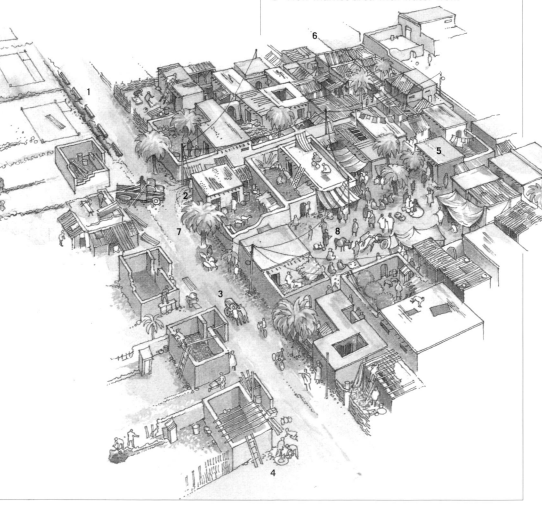

Many poor city dwellers *live in temporary homes with no services on unused or waste land. In Recife, in Brazil, an organization helps people to get the legal rights to the land they are living on. It then helps them build permanent homes to replace the temporary ones, as here, and get services such as water, sanitation, and electricity.*

Making big cities better

Easing the burden on cities in developing countries depends on improving living conditions in the countryside and small towns, thus reducing country-to-city migration.

Many governments spend far more money encouraging big business than they do on inner-city or shantytown renewal. This is because they think that wealth from big business will "trickle down" to help the poor. In the UK, the government has invested huge sums in London's Docklands. Yet this major new business district is close to some of the worst inner-city conditions in Western Europe. Developing countries too are often more interested in helping foreign companies build factories than in improving slum housing.

Governments need a fairer and "greener" approach to the creation of wealth. This means more spending on basic health services, welfare, and education; less special treatment for big business; tighter pollution controls; higher taxes on environmentally harmful products and activities; the promotion of energy efficiency and recycling; a switch to more environment-friendly forms of transport; more support for community groups; and better local democracy, so people can make decisions about their own neighborhoods.

CITY ACTION IN DEVELOPED COUNTRIES
Local communities have a say in the most succesful inner-city renewal pro-grams. These projects improve old buildings, encourage "self-build" housing communities, provide green spaces, create workshops, and promote environment-friendly forms of transport.

Renewing the inner city
1 New community center and nursery.
2 New energy-efficient housing.
3 Old houses upgraded.
4 Street improvements: speed bumps, trees, and landscaping.
5 Wall painting by local artist and children.
6 Neighborhood planning office and shops.
7 New park and playground.
8 New workshops and offices.
9 New local bus route.

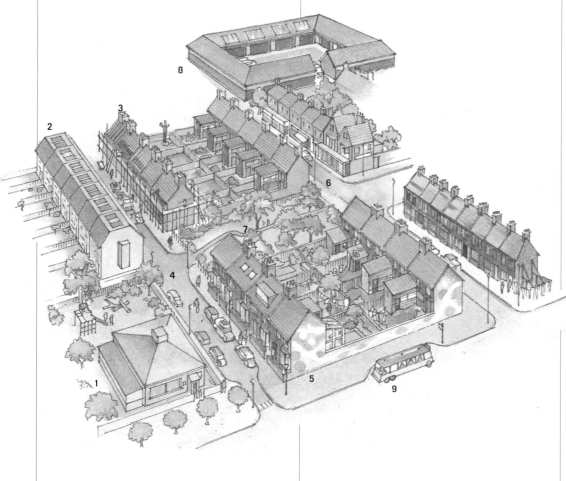

CLOSING THE GAP

What makes some countries, and some people, poor? There are those who say it is their own fault for not trying hard enough. Others argue that poverty just can't be helped. This chapter has tried to show that wealth and poverty are part of the same problem — injustice. If we could all agree on that, we would be halfway to doing something about it.

Joint efforts between people from North and South on development projects can be very successful. Here in West Africa, a US wildlife group, the Sierra Leone Ministry of Agriculture, and researchers from US and African universities come together to help the local people build a wildlife sanctuary and research station.

The fates of developed and developing countries are closely connected. High living standards in the North depend on the supply of raw materials from the South. Northern industries need Southern customers. Both "halves" of the world need each other to help protect the planet from environmental damage. But besides all this, can people in developed countries be happy knowing that millions of their fellow human beings are struggling in poverty?

Trade, aid, and development can help us close the wealth gap between developed and developing countries. But perhaps we need to change our idea of trade. More is not always better. Fairer and more

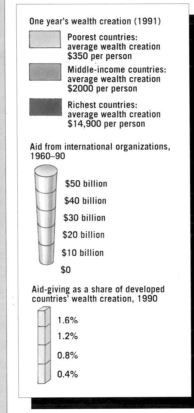

One year's wealth creation (1991)

Poorest countries: average wealth creation $350 per person

Middle-income countries: average wealth creation $2000 per person

Richest countries: average wealth creation $14,900 per person

Aid from international organizations, 1960–90

$50 billion
$40 billion
$30 billion
$20 billion
$10 billion
$0

Aid-giving as a share of developed countries' wealth creation, 1990

1.6%
1.2%
0.8%
0.4%

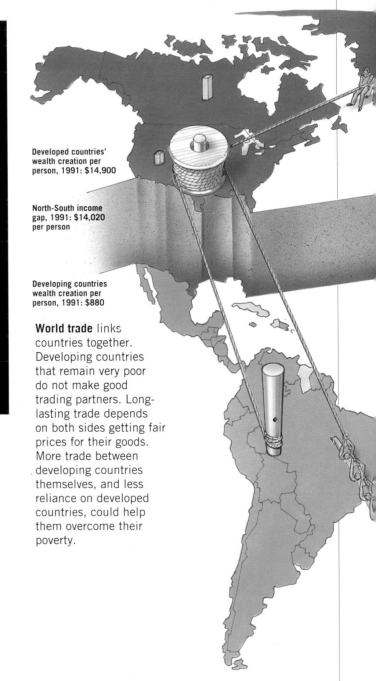

Developed countries' wealth creation per person, 1991: $14,900

North-South income gap, 1991: $14,020 per person

Developing countries wealth creation per person, 1991: $880

World trade links countries together. Developing countries that remain very poor do not make good trading partners. Long-lasting trade depends on both sides getting fair prices for their goods. More trade between developing countries themselves, and less reliance on developed countries, could help them overcome their poverty.

sensible trade would mean that countries where people go hungry never had to grow luxury foods to sell abroad, rather than food to feed their own people. And there would be fairer shares of trading profits.

Many people believe that aid to developing countries should also change. Too much money has been wasted on large-scale projects that fail to improve the lives of ordinary people. Aid has often made the rich richer and the poor poorer. We are learning to target aid money more carefully, so that the poorest people benefit most.

Both trade and aid can help pay for development. Yet forms of development that look impressive are not always effective. What use to a poor country are motorways, for example, if millions of its people cannot even afford a bicycle?

World leaders have met at many conferences to discuss ways of bridging the gap between rich North and poor South. A wide range of solutions is possible. Working together, we can win the war against poverty.

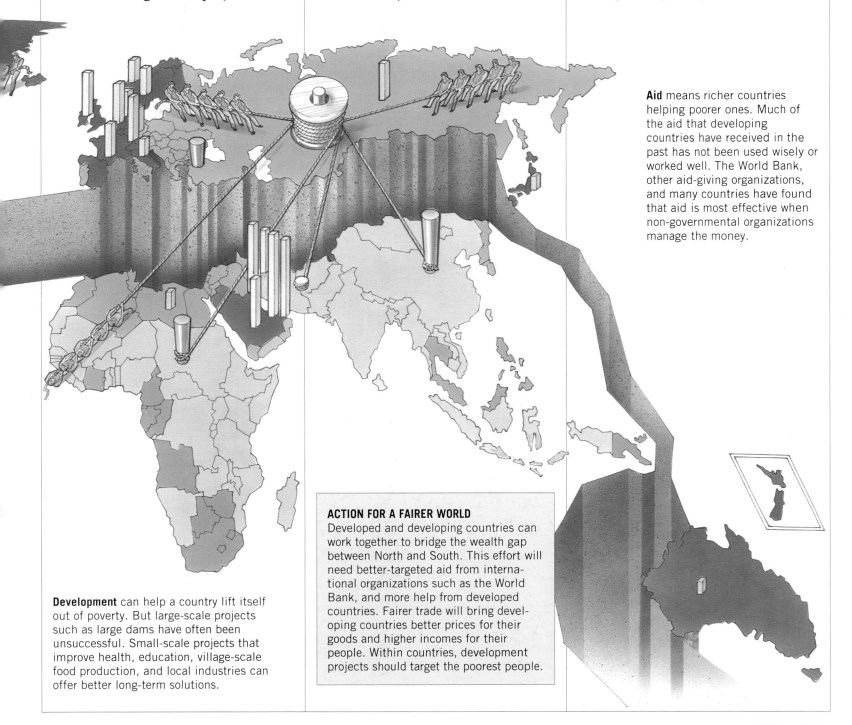

Aid means richer countries helping poorer ones. Much of the aid that developing countries have received in the past has not been used wisely or worked well. The World Bank, other aid-giving organizations, and many countries have found that aid is most effective when non-governmental organizations manage the money.

Development can help a country lift itself out of poverty. But large-scale projects such as large dams have often been unsuccessful. Small-scale projects that improve health, education, village-scale food production, and local industries can offer better long-term solutions.

ACTION FOR A FAIRER WORLD
Developed and developing countries can work together to bridge the wealth gap between North and South. This effort will need better-targeted aid from international organizations such as the World Bank, and more help from developed countries. Fairer trade will bring developing countries better prices for their goods and higher incomes for their people. Within countries, development projects should target the poorest people.

9
TOMORROW'S WORLD

"We must keep on striving to make the world a better place for all . . . each one contributing his bit, in his or her own way."
KEN SARO WIWA,
Nigerian environment and human rights campaigner, writing from prison in 1995, shortly before army rulers executed him

This book has taken us on a long journey, from the distant past when humankind first evolved, to the present and beyond. The story it tells is a mixture of triumph and disaster. The human race has had many glorious moments, but probably an equal number of disgraceful ones. Our story is still unfolding today, perhaps faster than ever. How much longer humanity has on this planet may depend on how realistically we judge ourselves and our actions. Many things are beyond human control. But the kind of world that future generations will inherit from us tomorrow depends largely on choices that we make today. Both as individuals and as members of the world community, the future is in many ways in our hands.

This spectacular building is home to a museum of modern cinema technology at Futuroscope, near Poitiers in France. It is an impressive example of the human ability to design and build complex structures. On the other hand, it could be seen as a symbol of the wastefulness of developed countries.

WORKING TOGETHER

When small children learn to walk, first they try to stand — and fall. Once they can stand, they take their first steps — and fall again. Gradually they learn to "toddle." Learning through trying, failing, and trying again is the key to human progress. When it comes to caring for the Earth, and our fellow men and women, there is still time for us to learn to do better.

Our ability as human beings to learn from our mistakes reflects our level of intelligence and enables us to progress. Human progress has always come about this way. In 1918, at the end of World War I, for example, countries that had been involved realized that they needed to work together for peace. This led to the founding of the League of Nations. The League failed and broke up in the 1930s, but after World War II a new effort set up the United Nations in 1945. The UN is far from perfect, but it is an improvement over the League of Nations. Much of its work shows how people from around the world can work together for the good of all.

A more recent sign of progress has been the growth of non-governmental organizations, or NGOs. Ranging from Friends of the Earth to the World Council of Indigenous Peoples, NGOs are dedicated to solving developmental, environmental, and human rights problems. They have linked up across the globe, building up a large, effective network of campaigners and problem-solvers. NGOs often act as the "voice" of ordinary people. Many governments, but not all, respect them. Fifteen hundred such groups met at the 1992 Earth Summit in Rio de Janeiro, Brazil.

At the same time, and linked to the NGOs, has been a growing movement working toward "grass-roots" change, that is, among ordinary people rather than governments.

Power to the people
Like a tall, strong, healthy tree, a community of people has long, deep roots. These roots link people to places, culture, history, and the rest of nature. Communities can provide a wealth of problem-solving knowledge and skills — given a chance. In the past we have often let powerful leaders make bad choices. A different approach is to let local communities take the lead in solving the problems that affect them, based on their experience, and to give them the power to act for themselves.

More and more people see that giant programs and "master-plans" are not always the answer to the world's problems. Better results can often come when local communities manage their own affairs. Community action in both developed and developing countries — from the villages of Kenya to inner-city Chicago, USA — has proved this.

A third form of progress is a new appreciation of the need to listen to the voices of women everywhere. Women are courageous and clever problem-solvers.

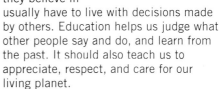

Education is the key to progress. It gives people better control over their lives and surroundings. Those who can read and understand can get the information they need to make choices. Those who do not or cannot speak out for what they believe in usually have to live with decisions made by others. Education helps us judge what other people say and do, and learn from the past. It should also teach us to appreciate, respect, and care for our living planet.

Democracy means that people have a real say in decisions that affect them. The right to vote in elections is important, and people have fought hard to win this right in many countries. Voting can send a strong message to political leaders. But for democracy to be successful, it needs healthy and well-educated communities of people who want to, and can, make decisions for themselves.

Since the 1980s, women have led peace and human rights movements in Europe and Latin America, and environmental movements in North America, Africa, and Asia. But women need to make their voices heard more clearly in politics and other areas where they have been ignored, or where their commitment to the family or their position in society puts them at a disadvantage or restricts their opportunities.

SIGNS OF HOPE

Thinking about your future, you may be excited about some things and worried about others. People feel the same way about the Earth's future. They hope we can end hunger and poverty, for example, but worry that we have already destroyed too much rainforest. This book has looked at what may go wrong and how we can fix it. Here are a few more reasons to be hopeful.

Millions of people around the world are trying to solve problems we all face. Successful businesses such as 3M follow strict environmental rules, while the UK-based Body Shop campaigns on human rights issues. "Green consumers," who try to consume less and buy environment-friendly products, help to change the way businesses and governments think. Concerned communities are demanding better pollution control, public health, and nature conservation. Those campaigning on human rights, democracy, and environmental issues are working together in every continent.

Achievements so far

Environmental groups played a leading part in the campaign for democracy in the Soviet Union and Eastern Europe in the late 1980s. In 1993 Al Gore became vice president — the first person in that position to make environmental issues his special concern. Many governments now encourage recycling, energy saving, and the protection of habitats and species. Since the 1992 Earth Summit, hundreds of programs for sustainable development have started.

Governments are working better together, mainly through the United Nations. Although countries often behave selfishly, the UN is probably our best hope for global action at this level. International cooperation has led to reductions in the use of ozone-damaging chemicals. And the Intergovernmental Panel on Climate Change is studying ways of preventing a runaway greenhouse effect.

The governments of many countries are changing their attitudes as they realize the need for teamwork in caring for the Earth. They are seeking new ways to give power to local communities and coming together in their efforts to tackle world problems.

Individuals and groups of people are learning about the problems we all face and taking action together to care for the planet. "Greener" lifestyles and membership in a whole range of pressure groups are two important ways of bringing about the necessary changes.

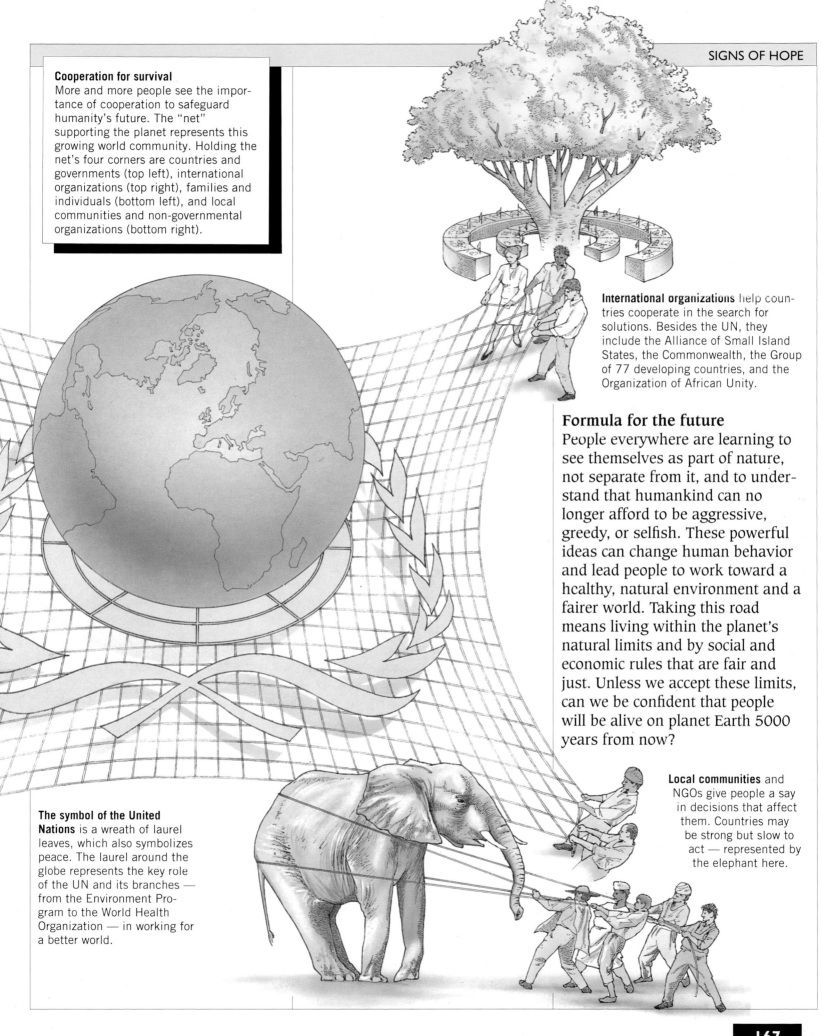

Cooperation for survival
More and more people see the importance of cooperation to safeguard humanity's future. The "net" supporting the planet represents this growing world community. Holding the net's four corners are countries and governments (top left), international organizations (top right), families and individuals (bottom left), and local communities and non-governmental organizations (bottom right).

International organizations help countries cooperate in the search for solutions. Besides the UN, they include the Alliance of Small Island States, the Commonwealth, the Group of 77 developing countries, and the Organization of African Unity.

Formula for the future
People everywhere are learning to see themselves as part of nature, not separate from it, and to understand that humankind can no longer afford to be aggressive, greedy, or selfish. These powerful ideas can change human behavior and lead people to work toward a healthy, natural environment and a fairer world. Taking this road means living within the planet's natural limits and by social and economic rules that are fair and just. Unless we accept these limits, can we be confident that people will be alive on planet Earth 5000 years from now?

The symbol of the United Nations is a wreath of laurel leaves, which also symbolizes peace. The laurel around the globe represents the key role of the UN and its branches — from the Environment Program to the World Health Organization — in working for a better world.

Local communities and NGOs give people a say in decisions that affect them. Countries may be strong but slow to act — represented by the elephant here.

REFERENCE SECTION

"We shall send [our young people] to the corners of the Earth to learn more. They shall lead us."
Declaration of the Five County Cherokee Native Americans, 19th century

More people than ever before are aware of the environmental dangers that threaten human survival, and of the kinds of choices we need to make to safeguard our future. Taking action is the next step. To make this book as useful as possible, we have included the following Reference Section. This provides additional background information, explanations of the maps and diagrams, definitions of a wide range of environmental and related terms, and a feature on official international organizations. To help readers extend their interest in global issues we have included details of organizations and campaigning groups that are actively involved in finding practical solutions to our problems, and a list of recommended books, magazines, study resources, and CD-ROM packages. Good luck.

Large-dish antennae *at a ground station on Earth send television and telephone signals up to an international communications satellite. This relays the signals to a receiving dish in the destination country. Better communications can help us to protect our environment.*

WORLD MAP: PHYSICAL

The rigid outer layer, or crust, of the Earth is like a giant jigsaw. Each huge piece, or plate, rests on molten rock. Over very long periods, and in reaction to forces beneath the Earth's crust, ocean and continental plates move apart, join together, slide past, under, and over each other, and break up and re-form. Collisions between plates have formed some of the Earth's great mountain chains.

Most volcanoes and earthquakes occur at the edges of plate margins. Volcanoes become active when magma (molten rock) from below the Earth's crust makes its way to the surface. Most active volcanoes are beneath the sea. Some of the world's main earthquake zones are at plate margins around the Pacific Ocean. Earthquakes result from sudden movements in, or just below, the crust, causing stresses and strains and forcing blocks of crust toward each other. The strain builds up, finally forcing the blocks to move.

Oceans cover more than two-thirds of the Earth. Below their surface are mountain ridges, deep trenches, level plains, and volcanoes. On the beds of the Atlantic and Pacific, mid-ocean ridges run for 44,400 miles around the planet. These are also plate margins, where plates are moving apart and magma rises up, forming new crust. The seafloor is gradually spreading away from the ridges as new crust forms.

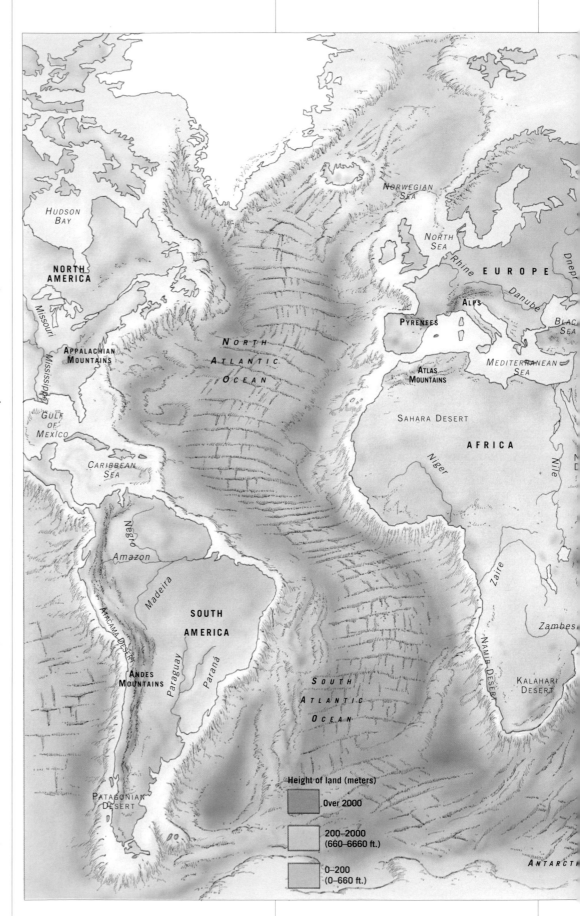

Height of land (meters)

Over 2000

200–2000
(660–6660 ft.)

0–200
(0–660 ft.)

ARCTIC OCEAN

Mackenzie

Lena

GOBI DESERT

BERING
SEA

Yenisey

Ob

SEA OF
OKHOTSK

ROCKY
MOUNTAINS

URAL MOUNTAINS

Amur

NORTH
AMERICA

ASIA

Yukon

ARAL
SEA

NORTH
PACIFIC
OCEAN

CASPIAN
SEA

KARA
KUM
DESERT

Huang He

SEA
OF
JAPAN

CAUCASUS
MOUNTAINS

HIMALAYAS

EAST
CHINA
SEA

ZAGROS
MOUNTAINS

THAR
DESERT

Brahmaputra

Chang Jiang
(Yangtze)

Indus

Ganges

Irrawaddy

ARABIAN
SEA

Mekong

SOUTH
CHINA
SEA

ARABIAN
DESERT

INDIAN
OCEAN

OCEANIA

GREAT SANDY
DESERT

SIMPSON
DESERT

SOUTH
PACIFIC
OCEAN

GIBSON DESERT

GREAT VICTORIA
DESERT

Darling

GREAT
DIVIDING
RANGE

Depth of ocean (meters)

0–1,000

1,000–5,000
(3300–16,500 ft.)

OCEAN

5,000–7,000
(16,500–23,100 ft.)

WORLD MAP: POLITICAL

CONTINENTS AND REGIONS

The world's land area consists of a number of main landmasses, which we call continents. In descending order of size, the seven continents are: Asia, 16,833,000 sq. mi.; Africa, 11,709,000 sq. mi.; North and Central America, 9,798,000 sq. mi.; South America, 6,798,000 sq. mi.; Antarctica, 5,149,240 sq. mi.; Europe, 4,052,000 sq. mi.; and Australia, 3,444,278 sq. mi.

We use the names of continents and regions as if they are simple geographical facts. But definitions can vary:

The Antarctic refers to the continent of Antarctica and its surrounding seas, that is, the South Polar region south of the Antarctic Circle.

The Arctic refers to the North Polar ice cap and the North Polar region north of the Arctic Circle.

Australasia consists of Australia, New Zealand, and the South Pacific islands. Sometimes the term Oceania is used, referring to not only Australasia but also the Central Pacific islands and the Malay islands of Southeast Asia.

The Caribbean region consists of the Caribbean Sea and its islands, but also usually Guyana on the South American coast.

Central America is the narrow strip of land connecting North America to South America — usually from the southern border of Mexico south to the northwestern border of Colombia.

Central Asia consists of the now independent Central Asian countries of the former Soviet Union, plus Mongolia, and sometimes northern China.

The East refers generally to Asia, as opposed to Europe and North America. From 1945 to 1990 the term also included the Soviet Union and Communist countries of Eastern Europe.

Eastern Europe usually means all the former Communist countries of Europe, to the east of what was West Germany.

The Far East refers to the countries of East Asia, including China, Japan, North and South Korea, and eastern Siberia, as well as countries in Southeast Asia, such as Malaysia.

Latin America consists of Central and South America and the Caribbean islands where most people speak Spanish or Portuguese. French-speaking Caribbean countries, such as Haiti, are sometimes included.

The Middle East (also called the Near East) is the eastern Mediterranean region, from Libya and Egypt in the west to Yemen in the south and Iran in the east.

North and **South** mean roughly "developed" and "developing." All developed countries apart from Australia and New Zealand are in the Northern Hemisphere; most countries in the Southern Hemisphere are developing ones.

North Africa consists of all African countries to the north of the Sahara Desert, notably Morocco, Algeria, Tunisia, Libya, and Egypt.

North America consists of Canada, Mexico, and the USA. Greenland, the world's largest island, is sometimes included.

Scandinavia means strictly Norway and Sweden, but more broadly can include Denmark, Finland, and Iceland.

The West means countries of the Western Hemisphere, seen as politically and historically different from the East. Politically, the term refers mainly to Western Europe and North America.

Western Europe generally refers to all European countries west of (and including) Germany and Austria. Greece, which belongs to the European Union, is often included.

LARGEST COUNTRIES BY SIZE AND POPULATION

Russia (officially called the Russian Federation) is the world's largest country in terms of land area; it covers 6,592,100 sq. mi., and extends from eastern Scandinavia and eastern Europe to northeast Asia. Then, in descending order, come: Canada, 3,830,840 sq. mi.; China, 3,704,440 sq. mi.; the United States of America, 3,614,170 sq. mi.; Brazil, 3,285,620 sq. mi.; Australia, 2,965,370 sq. mi.; and India, 1,222,395 sq. mi.

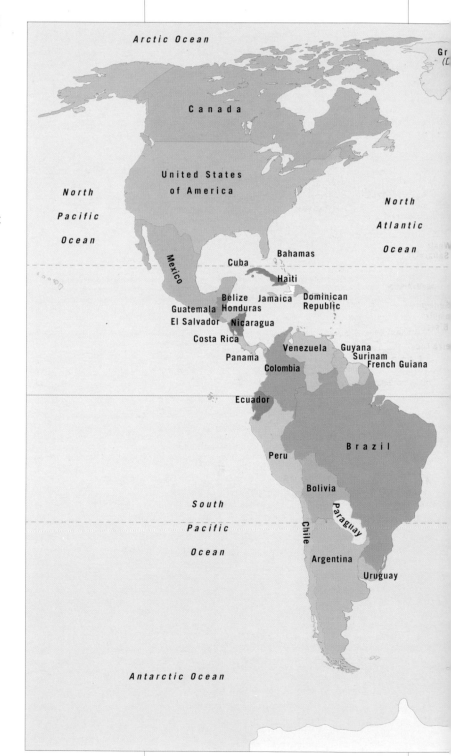

Norway
Finland
Sweden
Estonia
Latvia
Lithuania
Denmark
United Kingdom
Belarus
Ireland
Netherlands
Poland
Belgium
Germany
Ukraine
Luxembourg
Czech Republic
Liechtenstein
Slovakia
Switzerland
Slovenia
Austria
Hungary
Moldova
France
San Marino
Croatia
Romania
Monaco
Bosnia & Herzegovina
Yugoslavia
Andorra
Bulgaria
Italy
Albania
Macedonia
Portugal
Spain
Vatican City
Greece

According to UN figures (1995), countries with the largest populations are: China, 1.221 billion; India, 936 million; the USA, 263 million; Indonesia, 198 million; Brazil, 169 million; Russia, 147 million; Pakistan, 140 million; Japan, 125 million; Bangladesh, 120 million; and Nigeria, 112 million. The total population of developed countries, including the former Soviet Union and Eastern Europe, was 1.167 billion in 1995. The total population of developing countries was 4.550 billion, making a world population total of 5.717 billion.

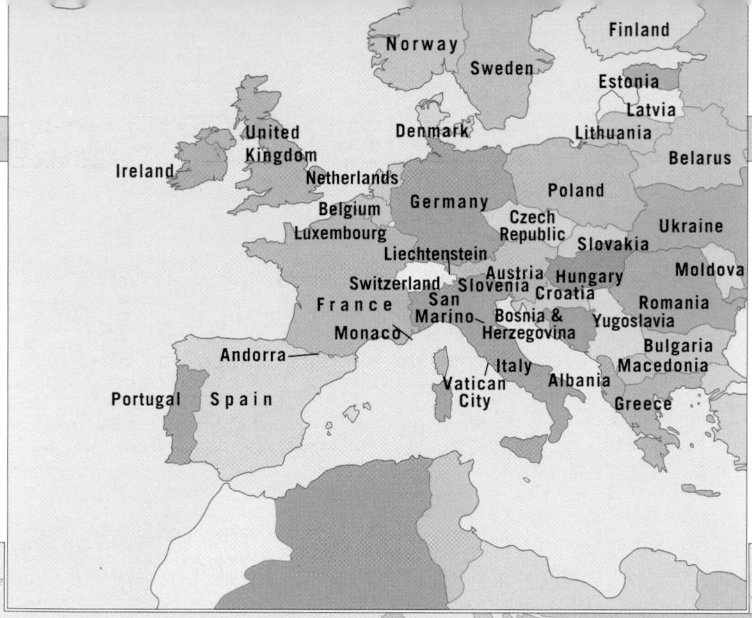

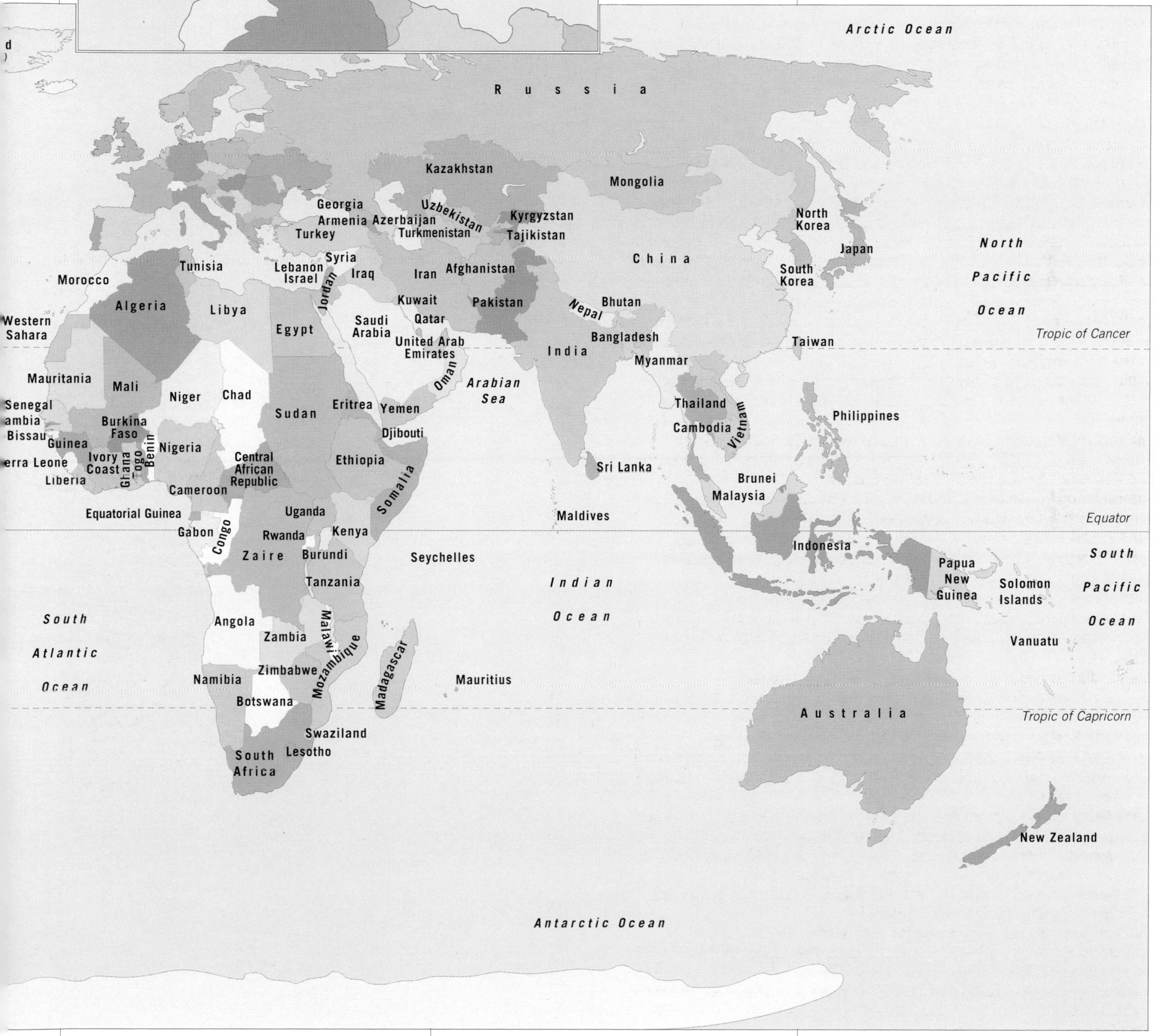

Arctic Ocean

Russia

Kazakhstan
Mongolia

Georgia
Uzbekistan
Armenia
Azerbaijan
Kyrgyzstan
Turkey
Turkmenistan
Tajikistan
North Korea
Japan

Tunisia
Syria
China
South Korea
North Pacific Ocean
Morocco
Lebanon
Iraq
Israel
Afghanistan
Jordan
Iran
Algeria
Libya
Kuwait
Pakistan
Nepal
Bhutan
Western Sahara
Egypt
Saudi Arabia
Qatar
United Arab Emirates
India
Bangladesh
Taiwan
Tropic of Cancer
Mauritania
Oman
Arabian Sea
Myanmar
Mali
Niger
Chad
Eritrea
Yemen
Senegal
Sudan
Thailand
Philippines
Gambia
Burkina Faso
Djibouti
Cambodia
Guinea Bissau
Benin
Nigeria
Vietnam
Guinea
Ivory Coast
Central African Republic
Ethiopia
Sri Lanka
Sierra Leone
Ghana
Togo
Liberia
Cameroon
Brunei
Equatorial Guinea
Uganda
Somalia
Maldives
Malaysia
Gabon
Congo
Kenya
Equator
Rwanda
Zaire
Burundi
Seychelles
Indonesia
Papua New Guinea
Solomon Islands
South Pacific Ocean
Tanzania
Indian Ocean
South Atlantic Ocean
Angola
Malawi
Zambia
Mozambique
Madagascar
Mauritius
Vanuatu
Namibia
Zimbabwe
Botswana
Australia
Tropic of Capricorn
Swaziland
South Africa
Lesotho

New Zealand

Antarctic Ocean

MAPPING THE WORLD

The ancient Babylonians, Egyptians, and Greeks all used maps. Today there are many complex ways of creating and presenting maps, including by computer.

All maps of the world distort landmasses in some way. The main difficulty that cartographers (mapmakers) face is the problem of accurately representing a sphere like the Earth, or part of its curved surface, on a flat piece of paper.

People attempt to solve this problem by "projecting" (throwing) the Earth's features onto a piece of paper as if the globe had a light inside it, making shadows of the features. Some maps represent surface area accurately, but distort shape, direction, and distance. Others show the correct shape, but distort area. Mapmakers choose the best projection (from more than 100) for their purposes.

The Mercator projection

The first accurate world map for navigators was devised by the Flemish geographer Gerardus Mercator in 1569. Still widely used, this cylindrical projection is accurate if you are traveling on "bearings." So, if you want to travel in a northeasterly direction, it is at the same angle anywhere on the map. Mercator represents accurately the shape of landmasses, but enlarges those nearer the poles. Greenland, for example, looks larger than South America although it is 12 times smaller.

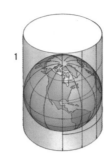

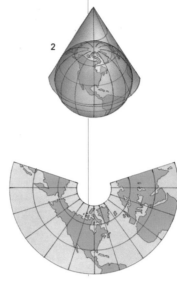
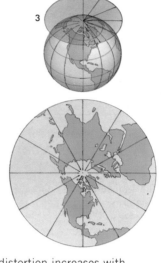

Cylindrical projections (**1**) are produced as if by wrapping a piece of paper around the equator to make a tube or cylinder, projecting the Earth's features on to the paper, and then laying the paper flat. Only at the equator, where the paper touches the globe, is the map fully accurate. Lines of longitude (north–south lines) do not come together to meet at the poles, as on a globe, but stay parallel from one end of the map to the other. This has the effect of stretching the shape and size of landmasses and seas near the poles.

A conical projection (**2**) imagines a piece of paper rolled into a cone shape and then placed over the globe like a hat, touching it along a line of latitude (an east–west line). Then the sheet is opened up, with the globe's features projected on to it. Conical maps show areas, distances, and directions quite accurately where the cone touches the globe. But distortion increases with increasing distance north and south of that line.

An azimuthal, or zenithal, projection (**3**) is made by imagining a sheet of paper kept flat and placed so that it touches the globe at one point, the center of the map. This kind of projection is accurate only at the central point, and is used mainly to map relatively small areas, such as a polar region, or to show distances from a central point.

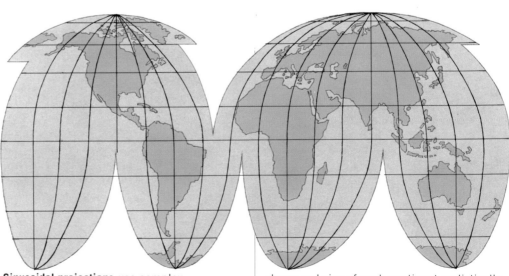

Sinusoidal projections use complex mathematical calculations to slice the globe vertically into several linked projections. This is as if the segments of an orange had been opened out. The resulting maps represent the shape and size of each continent realistically. But they do not show the correct distances between the continents. Projections that preserve accuracy of area at the expense of distance are called equal-area projections.

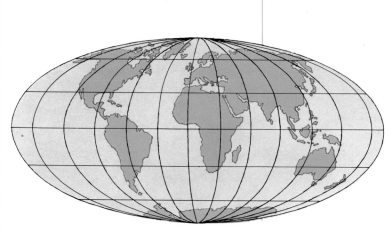

The Mollweide projection, named after its 19th-century German creator, shows the Earth as an ellipse (flattened circle). It represents the sizes of landmasses and seas accurately but distorts shapes, distances, and directions. The projection is mainly used for mapping continental drift and other features of world geography.

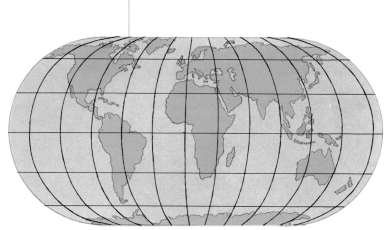

The Eckert projection is another cylindrical projection. Here size distortions are reduced by "stretching" and "squeezing" the land-masses in a north-south direction. Land near the equator is elongated, while land toward the poles is compressed.

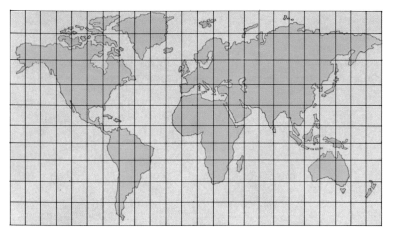

The Gall projection is a cylindrical one in which the cylinder has a smaller circumference than the globe. Thus, rather than touching the globe only at the equator, the cylinder sits "inside" it, meeting the surface at two lines of latitude equidistant between the equator and the poles. This reduces the exaggeration of areas and shapes toward the poles.

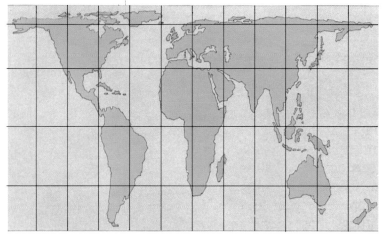

The Peters projection, also cylindrical, was devised by the German historian Arno Peters in the 1970s. He was concerned that many maps reduced the size and significance of regions in the South. His projection avoids distortions of area, but it does stretch (north to south) landmasses near the equator. Use of this projection has been associated with the movement for greater North-South equality.

The North and South Poles are most commonly mapped using azimuthal projections. In all azimuthal projections, lines of longitude radiate out from a central point, in this case the North or South Pole, and lines of latitude are concentric circles. Accuracy decreases away from the central point. Azimuthal projections can be used to map a whole hemisphere, or even the entire globe. But, more usually, they are used to map small-scale areas centered on, for example, a city, airport, or seismic station.

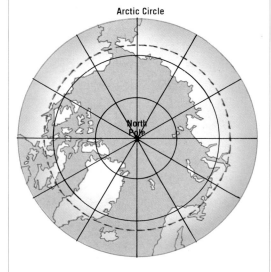

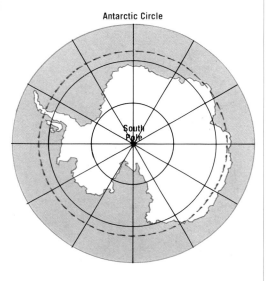

PRESENTING DATA

The *Atlas of Earthcare* uses a wide variety of diagrams and maps to present many kinds of information. Maps are an important feature of an atlas, and in this book they take various forms and present data in a range of different ways. Many of the maps are combined with other kinds of diagram.

The purpose of using maps and diagrams is to convey information in a clear, visually interesting, yet straightforward way. Diagrams that need long, complicated explanations are not much help. But well-designed graphics can often communicate information more clearly than a lot of words.

Here we look at the various forms of diagram used in the book. Some of these examples — from simple bar charts to combined maps and pictograms — appear in earlier chapters. We explain how each sort of diagram works and the kind of information that it is most suitable for.

Bar charts are useful for comparing things. The height of the bar shows an amount. The example here presents three kinds of information for one country, which can then be compared with others. Bar charts can also be horizontal.

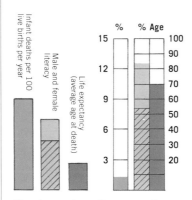

Histograms are graphs with bars to represent measurements of the same item at different stages. This shows the proportion of the total population of each age.

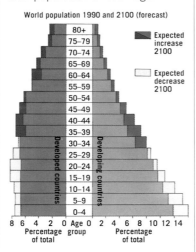

World population 1990 and 2100 (forecast)

Maps and histograms can be combined (left). Here targets for reducing carbon dioxide emissions are compared.

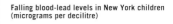

Line graphs such as that below show how some sets of information are related to others over time. Often these graphs have more than one line, and they may include different but relevant information.

Falling blood-lead levels in New York children (micrograms per decilitre)

African-Americans
Latinos

Falling US sales of leaded petrol in 1970s

Pie charts show the proportions of several items that make up a whole. The area of each slice of the "pie" represents the size of the share. In this example the segments indicate how much of a continent's total area is covered by crops, animal grazing, forest, and other land.

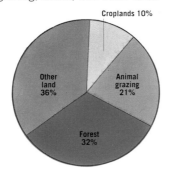

Croplands 10%
Other land 36%
Animal grazing 21%
Forest 32%

Exploded, three-dimensional pie charts help to show the size of each segment more clearly, and emphasize information about volume or weight. In this case we can see that nearly a third of the total world fish catch in 1990, weighing 107 million tons, was used for animal feed and fertilizer.

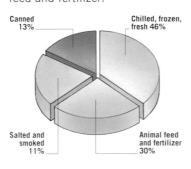

Canned 13%
Chilled, frozen, fresh 46%
Salted and smoked 11%
Animal feed and fertilizer 30%

Comparative pie charts bring together similar sets of data. In our example each pie represents a different amount of discharge. The segments within the pies allow us to compare each pollutant's path via New York City's river estuary to the sea in the 1980s (before discharges were banned).

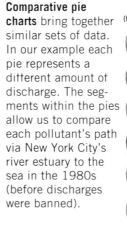

Discharge (tonnes per day)

Carbon 2600
Oil and grease 870
Nitrogen 520
Iron 230
Copper 14
Lead 13
Mercury 0.3
PCBs 0.01

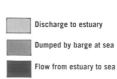

Discharge to estuary
Dumped by barge at sea
Flow from estuary to sea

Pie charts can draw attention to important points. This three-dimensional diagram strikingly illustrates how much less water a Bangladeshi villager uses each day (9 gal. [35 l]) than a UK city dweller (52 gal. [200 l]).

BANGLADESHI VILLAGER
Personal washing
Other
Washing dishes
Laundry
Cooking, drinking

UK CITY DWELLER
Toilet flushing
Leaks from mains and piping
Car washing
Watering garden
Washing dishes
Laundry
Cooking, drinking
Personal washing

Pictograms (pictorial diagrams) use pictures to represent data. They are best for giving simple information. This pictogram compares the size of four fleets of factory-fishing ships, measured by tonnage (the maximum weight of fish that the fleet can carry at one time).

Liberia 20,000 tons

Panama 50,000 tons

Japan 200,000 tons

Former Soviet Union 8,000,000 tons

Maps can present a huge range of data in addition to purely geographical information. The example here compares how women were represented in the legislatures (law-making bodies) of different countries in the 1980s.

- Not all adults can vote

Women as a proportion of members of legislature
- No information
- Less than 10%
- 11%–20%
- 21%–30%
- 31%–40%

Maps and pictograms can be combined to good effect. This map shows the state of the nuclear industry in Europe (excluding the former Soviet Union) in 1982 and 1990. To understand the map fully, we need to study the key first. Then it becomes clear at a glance which countries have most nuclear reactors, which built reactors during the 1980s, which rely most on nuclear power, and where nuclear accidents have occurred.

Pictograms can combine two or more images. In this example each log symbol and each firewood symbol represents the cutting of 260 million cubic yards of timber. Together they show the world's total wood consumption in 1975.

Shortage of firewood

Used for industry

Used for firewood

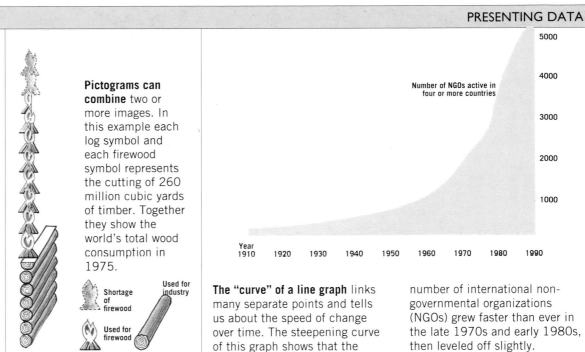

The "curve" of a line graph links many separate points and tells us about the speed of change over time. The steepening curve of this graph shows that the number of international non-governmental organizations (NGOs) grew faster than ever in the late 1970s and early 1980s, then leveled off slightly.

Number of NGOs active in four or more countries

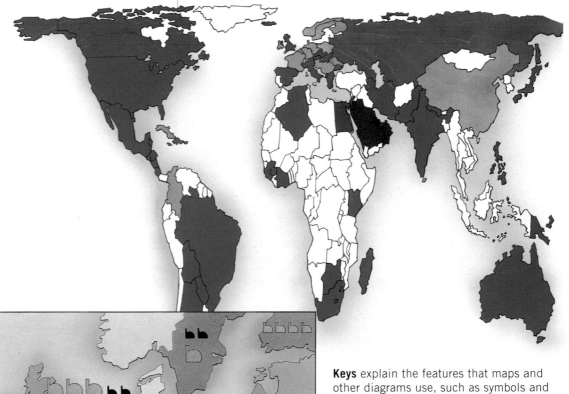

Keys explain the features that maps and other diagrams use, such as symbols and shading. In this case, the map uses the nuclear power station symbol in different sizes and colors to present a range of information.

Nuclear reactors working

1990 | 1982
10 reactors
1 reactor

Building plans canceled

Nuclear accident site

Amount of electricity from nuclear power
- More than 30%
- 11%–30%
- Up to 10%
- Unknown
- Nuclear industry starting

GLOSSARY

Abortion The termination of a pregnancy before birth.

Acid Any one of a group of liquid chemicals that corrode (eat away) materials by chemical action.

Acid rain Cloud, mist, rain, sleet, or snow formed when acid waste gases from fuel burning combine with water in the air.

Acidification An increase in the acidity of soil or water.

ACP African, Caribbean, and Pacific countries.

Agenda 21 The international program of action for sustainable development agreed at the 1992 Earth Summit.

Agribusiness Commercial farming based on large farms, heavy machinery, and chemicals.

Agriculture Farming.

Agrochemicals Human-made chemical fertilizers and pesticides used in modern farming.

Agroforestry Farming that combines trees and crops.

Aid Money grants and other assistance given by developed countries to developing ones.

AIDS Acquired immuno-deficiency syndrome, a condition in which the body loses its ability to defend itself against infections.

Albedo The reflective shininess of lighter-colored areas of the Earth's surface and clouds.

Algae Simple plant species, including seaweeds.

Alternative energy Another name for renewable energy.

Animal rights movement People and organizations that believe modern society treats animals badly and campaign for better treatment of animals.

Anthropology The study of humanity.

Apartheid The official South African government policy of racial segregation from 1948 to about 1990.

Appropriate development Development that improves the lives of poor people and causes no environmental damage.

Aquifer Underground rocks holding water.

Arable Connected with crop growing.

Arms conversion The conversion of weapons industries to non-military use.

Arms trade The large-scale buying and selling of weapons and other military equipment.

ASEAN Association of South-East Asian Nations.

Atmosphere The thin layer of gases surrounding the Earth.

Atom The smallest known part of any chemical that can combine with another chemical.

Aurochs A wild ox, now extinct, that was the probable ancestor of domesticated cattle.

Bacteria Tiny, one-celled organisms.

Bauxite The clay ore from which we obtain aluminum.

Big Bang The supposed beginning of the universe in a single cosmic explosion about 15,000 million years ago.

Biodegradable Able to decompose naturally.

Biodiversity Rich variety of life forms.

Biodiversity Treaty A worldwide agreement to preserve natural diversity signed at the 1992 Earth Summit.

Biogas Fuel gas made from plants or rotting refuse.

Biomass The living weight or chemical energy contained in plants or animals.

Biosphere The thin layer containing all living things surrounding the Earth.

Biosphere reserve A nature reserve where human activity can take place in one zone but other parts are kept free of people.

Biotechnology Modern techniques using the chemistry of life to make food, drugs, or other products.

Birth control Limiting the number of children born.

Birth rate The number of births each year per member of the population, or per 1000 people.

Blue-collar Connected with manual industrial work.

Bottom-up Development that focuses on helping the poorest people improve their lives.

Breed A group within a plant or animal species that human management has made different from the rest of the species.

Broadleaved Non-coniferous trees with broad rather than needle-shaped leaves.

Calorie A unit of heat, first defined as the heat needed to raise the temperature of 1 gram of water by 1°C.

Cancer A harmful tumor or growth that may spread from one part of the body to other parts.

Carbohydrate A natural substance containing carbon, hydrogen, and oxygen that animals need for food: for example, sugar or starch.

Carbon One of the most common chemical elements on Earth, and present in all living things.

Carbon dioxide A gas combining carbon and oxygen, produced by living things during respiration (e.g., through breathing), the rotting of organic matter, and fuel burning.

Carbon tax A tax that could be charged according to the amount of carbon released when fuel is burned.

Carcinogen A cancer-causing substance.

Carnivore An animal that eats other animals, birds, insects, etc.

Cash crop Farm produce grown for sale, often abroad, not for local use.

Catalytic converter A device fitted to the exhaust of a motor vehicle to reduce waste gases.

Cereal A member of the grass family of plants.

Cetaceans The whale and dolphin family of marine mammals.

CFCs Chlorofluorocarbons, the main ozone-destroying chemicals. They are human-made and do not occur in nature.

Chlorophyll The green coloring matter in plants that absorbs light energy during photosynthesis.

CHP Combined heat and power, a way of using fuel in power stations more efficiently by making use of waste heat.

CITES The Convention on International Trade in Endangered Species, the world's main agreement controlling the wildlife trade.

Citrus The family of fruits including oranges and lemons.

Civilian A non-military person; a non-fighter in a war.

Civilization A developed and complex human society.

Civil war A war between different groups of people within the same country.

Climate The usual weather conditions of an area.

Co-disposal The disposal of household solid waste together with dangerous factory waste.

Cold War The semi-warlike relationship between the US-led West and the Soviet Union's Eastern bloc between 1945 and the late 1980s.

Commercial Connected with buying and selling goods or services.

Commodity A traded cash crop or raw material.

Common Agricultural Policy (CAP) The European Union's system for organizing farming.

Communicate To pass on information or another form of message.

Communist Connected with the belief (communism) in a classless society in which the means of production are owned collectively rather than privately.

Community A group of organisms living in one area and interacting with each other. Applied to humans, the term suggests shared values or experience.

Complementary medicine Traditional, alternative, and especially Eastern medical treatments outside the usual Western approach to healing.

Compost Decayed plant matter, sometimes mixed with animal manure, used as fertilizer.

Coniferous Describing cone- and needle-bearing trees that are mostly evergreen.

Conservation The protection and management of natural resources and the environment.

Consumption The act of using up a resource or product.

Continent A large landmass.

Continental plate A giant segment of underlying rock on land.

Continental shelf The sea bed beneath shallow seas bordering continental landmasses.

Contraception Artificial or natural methods used by a man and a woman during sexual intercourse to prevent the conception of life in the woman's womb.

Convenience food Food that is quick and simple to prepare in the home but often less nourishing than fresher food.

Convention An international agreement.

Cooperative A form of organization in which people share ownership, management decisions, and income collectively.

Coral A small sea creature with a hard skeleton that attaches itself to a solid surface.

Coral reef A ridge in the sea formed by the skeletons of dead coral creatures.

Corporation A large business company.

Country A separate territory that rules itself independently.

Crop rotation The growing of different crops on the same piece of land from one year to the next in a repeating cycle, usually four years.

Crossbreeding Producing a new breed of plant or animal using parents of different breeds.

Crust The rigid outer part of the Earth.

Crustacean A class of mainly water-dwelling invertebrates with hard outer shells.

Cultivate To grow plants.

Culture The ideas, beliefs, technology, and lifestyles of a particular society or group of people.

Cuneiform An ancient form of writing using wedge-shaped characters.

DDT Dichloro-diphenol-trichloroethane, one of the earliest and strongest chemical pesticides, linked with some cancers and damage to wildlife, and now banned in developed countries.

Debt Something owed, especially money.

Debt crisis The problems of developing countries since the 1980s in repaying money lent by banks in developed countries.

Deciduous Describing trees and shrubs that lose all their leaves at the end of the growing season each year.

Decade Ten years.

Decompose To decay, to rot.

Decomposer Any organism that breaks down dead matter.

Deforestation The cutting or destruction of trees over a wide area.

Democracy Government by the people or their representatives with freedom of choice.

Deposit Any material that has been set down, such as silt or coal.

Desertification The appearance of desert-like conditions in once fertile areas.

Developed country A relatively wealthy country where large-scale industry, based on burning fossil fuels, is well established and usually the main source of jobs and wealth creation.

Developing country A relatively poor country where farming, rather than large-scale industry, is still the main way of life.

Development Growth or progress; in economics, change whereby a community or a country becomes more effective at meeting its needs.

Diet The amount and quality of food and drink that a person regularly consumes.

Dike A wall or embankment built to hold back water.

Dioxins A dangerous group of human-made chemicals, usually the by-products of other processes.

Distance learning Home-based study, at a distance from the school or college.

Diversity Difference and variety.

DNA Deoxyribonucleic acid, a complex, nucleic acid molecule laid out in a double helix (that is, like two spiral staircases) and containing chemically coded genetic information.

Domesticate To bring or keep animals or plants under control.

Dredge To drag a material up to the surface from the bed of a river, lake, or the sea.

Drought A severe lack of rainfall.

Drylands Areas of low rainfall.

Dumping Unloading or disposing of a substance.

Earth Summit The UN Conference on Environment and Development (UNCED), held in Rio de Janeiro, Brazil, in June 1992.

Ecology The relationships of living things, including humans, with each other and the environment.

Economy The activities involved in producing and consuming goods and services, and in managing resources and money.

Ecosystem A community of plants and animals that depend on each other in one habitat.

Ecotourism Tourism in which travelers pay to enjoy carefully the unspoiled natural environment, while the money they pay helps to fund conservation.

Emission The discharge of any substance into the environment.

Energy The ability of a living thing or a machine to be active or do work.

Energy efficiency Ways of producing and using energy from fuels that reduce waste to a minimum.

Environment The surroundings in which a plant or animal lives.

Equator An imaginary line around the surface of the Earth at an equal distance from the north and south poles.

Erosion The wearing away of soil or rock by, for example, ice, rainfall, or the wind.

Estuary The mouth of a river where fresh and sea water mix.

Ethnic minority A group of culturally similar people seen as in some way separate from the majority population.

EU European Union.

Eutrophication An overgrowth of plants in rivers, lakes, and seas caused by the presence of too many nutrients in the water.

Evaporate To rise up in small droplets (vapor) into the air.

Evergreen Trees and shrubs that produce and retain leaves throughout the year.

Evolve To develop gradually.

Evolution The development of species by the gradual change in animals or plants over many generations.

Export To sell to another country.

Extinct Having died out completely, leaving no living individuals.

Factory farming Raising animals close together in factory-like conditions.

Fair trade A program to help low-income producers by buying their goods or services directly from them, rather than through agents, and at better-than-usual prices.

Fallow Farmland left unused.

Family planning The use of birth control to limit the number and control the timing of births in a family.

FAO Food and Agriculture Organization of the United Nations.

Famine A severe shortage of food.

Fertile (Land or soil) having plenty of the nutrients that plants need for growth.

Fertilizer A substance that makes the soil more fertile when added to it.

Fish farming Raising fish in captivity for food.

Flood plain Level land beside a river that floods when the river overflows.

Fodder Food for domesticated animals.

Food chain A series of plants and animals, each of which serves as food for the next higher on the chain.

Food web A network of feeding relationships between plants and animals.

Forest death Severe forest damage caused by acid rain.

Forestry The management of forest lands.

Fossil The preserved remains of a plant or animal that lived millions of years ago.

Fossil fuels Coal, natural gas, and oil, created over millions of years by the decay of plant and animal remains.

Free trade Trade between people and businesses of different countries without government interference. In practice, trade is rarely free of government involvement.

Fuel Any substance burned to produce heat or power.

Fuelwood Firewood.

Fungi A group of plants without leaves or roots.

Fungicide A chemical for killing fungi that damage food crops.

GATT General Agreement on Tariffs and Trade.

GDP and **GNP** Gross domestic product and gross national product, two measures of the money value of work done in or by a country, usually in one year.

Gene A basic unit, or sequence, of DNA (in a chromosome) by which parents of any species pass physical features or behavior to their offspring.

Gene bank A place where living plant and animal matter can be stored in controlled conditions for long periods.

Generation A stage in the natural reproduction of animals or plants.

Gene revolution Major rapid changes in populations of food crops and animals resulting from scientific breeding.

Genetic Relating to genes.

Genetic diversity Variety and difference among organisms within a species population.

Geothermal Related to heat inside the Earth.

Ghost acres Land in developing countries used to provide developed countries with food and other produce.

Glacier A large mass of ice, formed from the compaction (firm pressing together) of snow on high ground, that flows slowly down a valley.

Global warming The probable raising of average temperatures on the Earth caused by the greenhouse effect.

Grains Cereal crops.

Grass roots Ordinary people, as opposed to politicians and business leaders.

Green consumer A person whose buying decisions as a customer depend on how the use or production of products or services affect the environment.

Greenhouse effect The trapping of the Sun's heat close to the Earth by gases in the atmosphere.

Greenhouse gas Any gas that increases the greenhouse effect.

Green politics Political activity, often involving Green parties, based on the belief that environmental protection should come first.

Green Revolution The changes in farming methods since the 1940s in many developing countries based on chemical fertilizers, pesticides, irrigation water, and specially bred crops.

Groundwater Underground water.

Gulf Stream A warm sea current flowing from the Gulf of Mexico northeast across the Atlantic Ocean to Northwest Europe.

Habitat A place where plants or animals live.

Half-life The time taken by radioactive materials to lose half their radioactivity.

Hardwoods Broad-leaved trees of hard wood, such as mahogany.

Harvest A season's crop when ready for collection and use.

HCFCs Hydrochlorofluorocarbons, replacement chemicals for ozone-destroying CFCs.

Heavy metal A metal that can be converted from one form to another but not destroyed.

Hectare A metric measure of land area, one-hundredth of a square kilometer.

Hemisphere Half the Earth, divided north and south or east and west.

Herbicide A pesticide for killing weeds.

Herbivore An animal that eats plants.

HFCs Hydrofluorocarbons, non-ozone-destroying replacement chemicals for CFCs.

High-tech Using up-to-date, complicated technology.

High-yield variety (HYV) A strain of a cereal crop bred by scientists to grow fast and produce large seed heads.

Human rights Rights that every human being is entitled to.

Humus Decayed remains of plant and animal matter in soil.

Hunter-gatherer A person whose way of life is based on food collection and hunting.

Hydroelectricity The use of the power of falling or running water to turn turbines to produce electricity.

Ice cap A thick mass of ice or snow permanently covering the land.

Illiterate Unable to read or write.

ILO International Labor Organization.

IMF International Monetary Fund.

IMO International Maritime Organization.

Immunize To protect a person medically against a disease.
Import To buy from another country.
Incineration The burning of garbage or other materials in a specially built furnace.
Indigenous Belonging naturally to a place.
Indigenous people People who have lived in a place, and close to the land, from the earliest times.
Industrial Revolution The 18th- and 19th-century development of large-scale industrial manufacturing in Western Europe and North America.
Industry Organized activity concerned with processing raw materials to produce things that people use, including food.
Infant mortality The rate of death among young children.
Infection An invasion of the body by harmful microbes.
Informal economy Casual and at times illegal work, sometimes called the "underground economy."
Information technology (IT) The use of computers to produce, store, and communicate information.
Inner city Poorer parts of a city close to the center.
Insecticide A chemical for killing insect pests.
Insulation A barrier to the movement of heat, sound, or electricity.
Integrated pest management (IPM) Using natural methods as far as possible to control farm pests.
Intensive farming Farming that uses the land to produce as much as possible.
Intermediate technology Cheap and simple technology suitable for use by poor people in developing countries. It should be used more in developed countries to conserve energy and help solve environmental problems. Bicycles are a good example.
Invertebrate An animal that lacks a backbone, such as an insect or a shellfish.
IPCC Intergovernmental Panel on Climate Change.
Irrigation The supply of water to farmland to improve crop growth.
IUCN World Conservation

Union (formerly called the International Union for the Conservation of Nature and Natural Resources).
IWC International Whaling Commission.
Kilocalorie A unit of heat used to measure the energy value of food.
Kilowatt 1000 watts.
Kilowatt-hour Energy equal to the work done by 1000 watts in one hour.
Krill A small shrimp-like sea creature.
Landfill The disposal of solid waste in the ground.
Landmine An explosive device placed in the ground that explodes when stepped on or driven over.
Larvae (plural of larva) The young of species having a different appearance and way of life from the adult.
Lava Hot molten rock from beneath the Earth's crust that reaches the surface, often via volcanoes.
Law of the Sea A series of international agreements for the protection and use of the sea.
League of Nations An international organization founded in 1920 to promote peace between countries, replaced by he United Nations in 1945.
Legume A pea- or bean-like plant or tree, bearing seeds in pods. Legumes are good for soil because they fix nitrogen (convert it into usable forms) and good to eat as they are high in protein and fiber.
LETS Local Exchange Trading Systems, a way of organizing work in a community based on a local "paper" currency rather than cash.
Life expectancy The average age at death of people in one area.
Literacy The ability to read and write.
Lithosphere The Earth's crust and upper mantle, made up of huge plates.
Litter The layer of decomposing leaves, twigs, and other natural waste matter on the floor of a forest.
Livestock Animals kept for food and other needs.
Logging Large-scale cutting of forest trees.
Low-tech Using as little complicated modern

technology as possible.
Magma Hot molten rock from deep inside the Earth.
Malaria A dangerous infectious disease carried by mosquitoes.
Malnutrition A poor level of nutrition resulting from a lack of food or a poor diet.
Mammal A class of warm-blooded vertebrate animals in which females have mammary (milk-producing) glands.
Mangrove A tropical evergreen tree or shrub growing by the sea.
Mantle The part of the Earth between crust and core.
Manufacturing Making products, especially factory goods, from raw materials.
Maritime Connected with the sea.
MARPOL International Convention for the Prevention of Pollution from Ships.
Mesh The links and gaps in a net.
Microbe Any tiny organism invisible to the naked eye.
Microchip A tiny semiconductor made out of silicon and carrying electronic circuits.
Migration Movement of people, animals, or plants from one place to settle in another. In birds and other animals this often occurs in a seasonal cycle.
Migration corridor A strip of protected land linking two or more nature reserves along which animals travel.
Mineral Any solid, non-plant and non-animal, naturally occurring material.
Monoculture Farming based on growing each crop separately, usually in large quantities.
Montreal Protocol The first agreement to limit the use of CFCs and other ozone-destroying chemicals, signed in Montreal, Canada, in 1987.
Mortality The number of deaths in a period of time.
Mortality rate The number of deaths per 1000 people per year.
Mulch A layer of half-decayed plant remains to protect the soil.
Multinational corporation A large business company active in several countries; also known as a transnational corporation.
NAFTA North American Free Trade Agreement.

Nation An independent country; a community of people with a common history or culture who are not organized as a country, e.g., Native American peoples.
National park A large area of land set aside for nature conservation.
NATO North Atlantic Treaty Organization.
NGO Non-governmental organization.
Newly industrializing country (NIC) Any one of a small group of countries that have developed their industries, especially for exporting goods, in recent years.
Nitrate A compound of the common chemical nitrogen, and an important substance in soil.
Nodule A small lump of a substance, usually rounded.
Nomad A person who travels from place to place with livestock to find pasture.
Non-governmental organization (NGO) An independent organization concerned with environmental issues, human rights, or similar problems.
Non-renewable Describes resources that are destroyed by being used only once, especially fossil fuels.
North The developed countries of Western Europe, North America, Japan, and Australasia.
Nuclear Related to the nucleus, the center of an atom.
Nuclear energy Energy production based on using changes in the center of atoms to generate heat.
Nuclear reactor The central part of a nuclear power station where nuclear energy is generated.
Nuclear waste The unwanted by-products of nuclear energy production.
Nuclear winter Possible conditions after a global war using nuclear weapons.
Nucleic acid A complex acid, such as DNA, occurring in living cells.
Nutrients Substances that plants need for growth.
Nutrition Nourishment with food.
OAS Organization of American States.
OAU Organization of African Unity.
Oceanic plate A giant segment of rock on the sea floor.

OECD Organization for Economic Cooperation and Development.
OPEC Organization of Petroleum-Exporting Countries.
Oral rehydration therapy (ORT) The taking of a simple salt-sugar-water solution by mouth to help recovery from diarrhea.
Ore Rock containing a useful mineral, usually a metal.
Organic Living.
Organic farming Farming without human-made chemicals, relying on natural methods.
Organism A living animal or plant.
Overfarming The cultivation of crops to the extent that the fertility of the soil is reduced or destroyed.
Overfishing Taking more fish from the sea than natural reproduction can replace.
Overgrazing Vegetation damage caused by domesticated animals stripping the ground of plant matter.
Overpopulation A situation in which there are too many individuals of a species for the environment to support.
Oxygen A gas that living things need for respiration (e.g. through breathing) and that green plants release during photosynthesis.
Ozone A form of oxygen naturally present in the upper atmosphere, also produced by a mixture of polluting gases in the lower atmosphere.
Ozone layer The layer of ozone in the upper atmosphere that filters out ultraviolet rays from the Sun.
Parasite A plant or animal that lives on or in the body of another organism and feeds off it.
Pastoralist A person who raises livestock for a living.
Pasture Land covered by grass or other vegetation suitable for grazing livestock.
PCBs Polychlorinated biphenyls, indestructible, dangerous human-made chemicals.
Peace dividend Money that the countries of North America and Europe, and the former Soviet Union have saved since the late 1980s by spending less on weapons and armies.
Peninsula Land almost surrounded by sea.

Percent(age) Out of every 100.

Permaculture Organic farming based on growing and raising together as many plant and animal species as possible.

Permafrost Permanently frozen ground in high-latitude regions that does not thaw even in summer and has been frozen for many years.

Pesticide A chemical used to kill animal or plant pests.

Photosynthesis The process by which plants use the Sun's energy to make their own food from carbon dioxide and water, releasing oxygen as a by-product.

Phytoplankton Tiny floating plants in the sea and fresh water.

Plankton Tiny life-forms floating in water.

Plantation A farmed area planted with one crop of trees or bushes.

Plutonium A radioactive substance produced in nuclear reactors and used to make nuclear weapons.

Polar Connected with the north or south pole.

Pollination The fertilization of plants by pollen.

Polluter pays The idea that a person or organization causing pollution should pay for cleaning it up.

Pollution Any substance that interferes with and harms natural processes when added to the environment.

Polyculture A number of different crops grown together.

Polytunnel A polythene tunnel in which crops grow.

Population A group of plants or animals of the same species in a certain area.

Prairie A treeless grassy plain.

Prehistoric Before people began to record history in writing.

Primary forest Forest in its original form that has not been cut down.

Primary health care Basic health care, advice, and treatment.

Primate Any individual or species belonging to an order of large-brained mammals including apes, monkeys, and humans.

Protein Any one of a large group of chemical compounds that all living things have within them.

Radiation Electromagnetic rays — from short wave-length rays such as x-rays, to long wavelength rays such as radio waves — and particles that travel through space. The higher-energy forms such as x-rays can pass through most materials.

Radioactive The quality of giving out atomic radiation.

Rainforest Species-rich forest in areas of heavy rainfall.

Raw material A substance used to make something else.

Reactor The central part of a nuclear power station that generates energy.

Recycling Using or processing materials (or energy) more than once.

Reforestation The replanting of trees and forests.

Refugee A person who flees from one country to another to escape danger or a severe problem.

Renewable Able to be used without reducing stocks of natural resources or causing pollution.

Renewable energy Energy that can be produced using natural processes such as tidal and wave movements, river flow, wind, and sunshine.

Reproduction Breeding, a process by which a plant or animal produces one or more individuals similar to itself.

Reserve An area set aside for conservation; the quantity of a resource that people know is available for use at reasonable cost.

Resistance The ability of crops or livestock to withstand pests or diseases.

Resource A natural material or process (such as water flow) that provides energy or materials for people to use.

Respiration A chemical process in which living things get energy from their food, usually using oxygen.

Road hump A raised strip extending across a road with the purpose of reducing the speed of traffic.

Rural Connected with the countryside.

Salinization Damage caused when soil becomes too salty.

Sanctuary A safe place.

Sanitation Equipment and facilities used to protect public health, especially with regard to toilets and water supplies.

Savanna Open tropical grassland with tall grass and scattered trees and bushes.

Scavenger A carnivore that does not hunt to kill but feeds on the remains of other animals' kills.

Seed bank A store of plant seed varieties.

Seismic Connected with earthquakes.

Selective breeding Breeding of plants or animals by people to develop chosen features.

Service industries Industries that provide services such as transport and banking, rather than goods.

Set-aside Farmland taken out of production as part of a government scheme to reduce output.

Sewage Waste matter carried away in sewers or drains.

Shantytown A town or part of a town or city where poor people live in cheaply built houses or shacks.

Shifting cultivation Farming that involves people clearing small patches of land and growing crops there for a few seasons and then moving on.

Slave trade The transporting of millions of Africans to the Americas from the 16th to 19th centuries.

Silt Fine mud or clay, especially on the bed of a river or lake.

Smog Air pollution caused by the mixture of smoke and fog.

Solar Connected with the Sun.

South The developing countries of Africa, Asia, the Caribbean, Central and South America, and the Pacific.

Species A complete group of living organisms that can breed together and produce offspring.

Starch A chemical substance, a carbohydrate, produced by plants and consumed by animals to produce energy.

Stratosphere The upper atmospheric layer, 6–30 miles above the Earth.

Subsidize To give financial help.

Subsistence farming Farming

for daily needs, not to sell produce for cash.

Subsoil The layer of soil below the topsoil.

Suburb An area, usually residential, on the edge of a town or city.

Sugar A chemical substance, a carbohydrate, consumed by animals to produce energy.

Sustainable Not reducing the ability of people in the future to meet their needs.

Sustainable development Development by which people meet their present needs without reducing the ability of future generations to meet future needs.

Terrace A flat area of land, often part of a series of flat "steps" constructed to allow farming on hillsides.

Thermal Connected with heat.

Third World A once widely used term for developing countries of the South.

Tick A small parasitic spider-like creature.

Tidal power Energy generated using the rise and fall of tides.

Topsoil The layer of soil nearest the land surface.

Toxin, toxic Poison, poisonous.

Trawler A ship that catches fish by dragging a large net through deep water.

Tropical Connected with the tropics, close to the equator.

Tropics The region of the Earth's surface on both sides of the equator.

Troposphere The lowest layer of the atmosphere, closest to the Earth.

Tundra Cold, treeless lands between the polar ice cap and northernmost forests.

Turbine A machine turned by liquid, steam, gas, or air pressure to produce energy.

Typhoon A small-scale but violent tropical storm.

Ultraviolet An invisible form of light that can tan and burn exposed human skin.

UN United Nations.

Underdevelopment The condition of a developing country that is not using its resources mainly for its own benefit and where people have a low material standard of living.

Underemployed Lacking enough work or the kind of work for which a person is qualified.

UNDP United Nations Development Program.

UNEP United Nations Environment Program.

UNESCO United Nations Educational, Scientific and Cultural Organization.

UNFPA United Nations Population Fund.

UNHCR United Nations High Commissioner for Refugees.

UNICEF United Nations Children's (Emergency) Fund.

Uranium A naturally found radioactive element used by the nuclear energy industry.

Urban Connected with towns and cities.

USSR Union of Soviet Socialist Republics, the Soviet Union (disbanded in 1991).

UV Ultraviolet.

Vapor A mass of small droplets of a liquid in the air.

Vegetation Living plants.

Vertebrate Any animal that has a backbone.

Vitamin Any one of a group of chemicals that animals need in small amounts.

WCED World Commission on Environment and Development, set up by the UN in the 1980s, which produced *Our Common Future* (the Brundtland Report).

Weather Daily conditions of temperature, cloud, rainfall, and so on, affecting a particular place.

West, Western Refers usually to North America and Western Europe but may include Australasia, Latin America, and other countries.

Wetlands Floodplains, mangroves, marshes, swamps, and mud-flats close to a river, a lake, or the sea.

White-collar Connected with non-manual work.

WHO World Health Organization.

Wholefood Food that has been processed as little as possible and is close to its natural state.

Wind farm A large number of wind-power machines set up together to produce electricity.

WTO World Trade Organization.

Yield The amount or quality of a crop.

Zooplankton Tiny floating animals in the sea or fresh water.

USEFUL CONTACTS

Abundant Life Seed Foundation
1029 Lawrence Street
Port Townsend, WA 98368
(306) 385-5660 Fax: (360) 385-7455

Alaska Coalition
408 C Street, N.E.
Washington, D.C.
(202) 547-1141 Fax: (202) 547-6009

America the Beautiful Fund
219 Shoreham Building, N.W.
Washington, D.C. 20005
(202) 638-1649
(800) 638-1687

American Conservation Association
30 Rockefeller Plaza, Room 5402
New York, NY 10112
(212) 649-5600 Fax: (212) 649-5921

American Forests
1516 P Street, N.W.
Washington, D.C. 20005
(202) 662-3300 Fax: (202) 662-7751
(800) 368-5745

American Oceans Campaign
725 Arizona Avenue, Suite 102
Santa Monica, CA 90401
(310) 576-6162 Fax: (310) 576-6170
(800) 8-OCEAN-0

American Rivers
801 Pennsylvania Avenue, Suite 400
Washington, D.C. 20003
(202) 547-6900 Fax: (202) 543-6142

American Wildlands
7500 E. Arapahoe Road, Suite 305
Englewood, CO 80101
(303) 773-1804

Atlantic Center for the Environment
55 S. Main Street
Ipswich, MA 01938
(508) 365-0038
Fax: (508) 356-8322

Audubon Naturalist Society of the Central Atlantic States
8490 Jones Mill Road
Chevy Chase, MD 20815
(301) 652-9188 Fax: (301) 951-7179

Camp Fire Conservation Fund
130 Camp Fire Road
Chappaqua, NY 10514
(914) 941-0199
Fax: (914) 923-0977

Center for Ecoliteracy
2522 San Pablo Avenue
Berkeley, CA 94701
(501) 845-4595
Fax: (510) 845-1439

Center for Environmental Study
143 Bostwick, N.E.
Grand Rapids, MI 49503-3201

Center for Marine Conservation
1725 DeSales Street, N.W., Suite 500
Washington, D.C. 20006
(202) 429-2003   Fax: (202) 872-0619

Charles Darwin Foundation for the Galapagos Isles
National Zoological Park
Washington, D.C. 20008
(202) 673-4705   Fax: (703) 538-6835

Coast Alliance
235 Pennsylvania Avenue, S.E.
Washington, D.C. 20003
Fax: (202) 546-9609

Coast Conservation Association
4801 Woodway, Suite 220W
Houston, TX 77056
(713) 626-4222 Fax: (713) 951-3801

Concern, Inc.
1794 Columbia Road, N.W.
Washington, D.C. 20009
(202) 328-8160 Fax: (202) 387-3378

Conservation International
1015 18th Street, N.W., Suite 1000
Washington, D.C. 20036
(202) 429-5660   Fax: (202) 887-5108

Conservation Technology Information Center
1220 Potter Drive, Room 170
Purdue Research Park
West Lafayette, IN 47906
(317) 494-9555 Fax: (317) 494-5969

Desert Protective Council
P.O. Box 2312
Valley Center, CA 92082-2312
(619) 397-4264

Earth Day 2000
116 Montgomery Street, #530
San Francisco, CA 94105
(415) 495-5987 Fax: (415) 543-1480
(800) 727-8619

Earth Day U.S.A.
Box 470
Peterborough, NH 03458
(603) 924-7720 Fax: (603) 924-7720

Earthsave Foundation
706 Frederick Street
Santa Cruz, CA 95062-2205
(408) 423-4069 Fax: (408) 458-0255

Earth Society Foundation
Box 780
Pine Plains, NY 12567
(518) 398-6187
Fax: (518) 398-6012

Ecologic Development Fund
c/o Shaun Pail
1130 Massachusetts Avenue
Cambridge, MA 02138
(617) 441-6300
Fax: (617) 441-6363

Ecovillage at Ithaca
Cornell University
Anabel Taylor Hall
Ithaca, NY 14853
(607) 255-8276 Fax: (607) 255-9985

Environmental Action Coalition
625 Broadway, 2nd Floor
New York, NY 10012
(212) 677-1601 Fax: (212) 505-8613

Environmental Action Foundation
6930 Carroll Avenue, 6th Floor
Takoma Park, MD 20912

Friends of the Earth
218 D Street, S.E.
Washington, D.C. 20003
(202) 544-2600 Fax: (202) 543-4710

Friends of the Everglades
101 Westwood Drive, #2
Miami Springs, FL 33166
(305) 888-1230

Friends of the River
909 12th Street, #207
Sacramento, CA 95814
(916) 442-315 Fax: (415) 771-0301

Friends of Trees Society
P.O. Box 1064
Tonasket, WA 98855
(509) 485-2705 Fax: (509) 485-2705

Gaia Institute
Cathedral of St. John the Divine
1047 Amsterdam Avenue at 112th Street
New York, NY 10025
(718) 885-1906 Fax: (718) 885-0882

Global Action and Information Network
740 Front Street, Suite 355
Santa Cruz, CA 95060
(408) 457-0130 Fax: (408) 457-0133

Global Coral Reef Alliance
324 No. Bedford Road
Chappaqua, NY 10514
(914) 238-8788 Fax: (914) 238-8768

Global Response
P.O. Box 7490
Boulder, CO 80306-7490

Great Lakes United
Buffalo State College
Cassety Hall
1300 Elmwood Avenue
Buffalo, NY 14222
(716) 886-0142 Fax: (716) 886-0303

Greenpeace U.S.A.
1436 U Street, N.W.
Washington, D.C. 20009
(202) 462-1177 Fax: (202) 462-4507

Green World Center
P.O. Box 45
Highgate Springs, VT 05460

Interfaith Council for the Protection of Animals and Nature
4290 Raintree Lane, N.W.
Atlanta, GA 30327
(404) 814-1377

International Center for the Solution of Environmental Problems
5335 Lovett Boulevard
Houston, TX 77006
(713) 527-8711 Fax: (713) 527-8025
International Ecology Society
1471 Barclay Street
St. Paul, MN 55106-1405
International Mountain Society
P.O. Box 1978
Davis, CA 95617-1978
(916) 752-8330 Fax: (916) 752-9592
International Union for Conservation of Nature and Natural Resources
1400 16th Street, N.W.
Washington, D.C. 20036
(202) 797-5454
Isaak Walton League of America
IWLA Conservation Center
707 Conservation Lane
Gaithersburg, MD 20878
(301) 548-0150
Keep America Beautiful
9 W. Broad Street
Stamford, CT 06902
(203) 323-8987 Fax: (203) 325-9199
Kids for a Clean Environment
P.O. Box 158254
Nashville, TN 37215
(615) 331-7381
(800) 952-3223
Land Trust Alliance
1319 F Street, N.W., Suite 502
Washington, D.C. 20004-1106
National Audubon Society
700 Broadway
New York, NY 10003
(212) 979-3000 Fax: (212) 353-0377
National Coalition for Marine Conservation
3 W. Market Street #100
Leesburg, VA 22075-2901
(703) 777-0037
National Tree Society
P.O. Box 10808
Bakersfield, CA 93389
(805) 589-6912 Fax: (805) 589-7135
(800) SAY-TREE
North American Coalition on Religion and Ecology
5 Thomas Circle, N.W.
Washington, D.C. 20005
(202) 462-2591 Fax: (202) 234-0307

North American Conference on Christianity and Ecology
P.O. Box 40011
St. Paul, MN 55104
(612) 698-0349
National Wildlife Federation
1400 16th Street, N.W.
Washington, D.C. 20036-2266
Nature Conservancy
1815 No. Lynn Street
Arlington, VA 22209
(703) 841-5300 Fax: (703) 841-1283
Oxfam America
26 West Street
Boston, MA 02111-1206
(617) 482-1211
Fax: (617) 728-2594
Rainforest Action Network
450 Sansome Street, Suite 700
San Francisco, CA 94111
(415) 398-4404
Fax: (415) 398-2731
(800) 989-RAIN
Rainforest Alliance
650 Bleeker Street
New York, NY 10012
(212) 677-1900
Ranger Rick's Nature Club, National Wildlife Federation
8925 Leesburg Pike
Vienna, VA 22184-0001
(703) 790-4274
River Netword
P.O. Box 8787
Portland, OR 97207-8787
(503) 241-3506
Fax: (503) 241-9256
(800) 423-6747
Seacoast Anti-Pollution League
P.O. Box 1136
Portsmouth, NH 03802-1136
(603) 431-5089
Sierra Club
730 Polk Street
San Francisco, CA 94109
Fax: (415) 776-0350
Soil and Water Conservation Society
7515 N.E. Ankeny Road
Ankeny, IA 50021
(515) 289-2331
Fax: (515) 289-1227
(800) 843-7645

Student Conservation Association
P.O. Box 550
Route 12A, River Road
Charlestown, NH 03603-0550
(603) 543-1700 Fax: (603) 543-1828
Student Environmental Action Coalition
P.O. Box 1168
Chapel Hill, NC 27541-1168
(919) 967-4600 Fax: (919) 967-4648
(800) 700-7322
Thornton W. Burgess Society
6 Discovery Hill Road
East Sandwich, MA 02537
(508) 888-6870 Fax: (508) 888-1919
Tree Musketeers
136 Main Street
El Segundo, CA 90245
(310) 322-0263 Fax: (310) 322-4482
(800) 473-0263
Treepeople
12601 Mulholland Drive
Beverly Hills, CA 90210
(818) 753-4600 Fax: (818) 753-4625
United States Committee for the United Nations Environment Program
2013 Q Street, N.W.
Washington, D.C. 20009
(202) 234-3600 Fax: (202) 332-3221
Urban Initiatives
530 West 25th Street
New York, NY 10001
(212) 620-9773 Fax: (212) 727-9894
Wildlife Habitat Council
1010 Wayne Avenue, Suite 920
Silver Spring, MD 20910
(301) 588-8994 Fax: (301) 588-4629
World Environment Center
419 Park Avenue South, Suite 1800
New York, NY 10016
(212) 683-4700
Fax: (212) 683-5053
Worldwide Network, Women in Development and Environment
1331 H Street, N.W., Suite 903
Washington, D.C. 20005
(202) 347-1514
Fax: (202) 347-1524
World Wildlife Fund
1250 24th Street, N.W.
Washington, D.C. 20037
(202) 293-4800
Fax: (202) 293-9211

FURTHER READING

MAGAZINES
Audubon (monthly)
The Environmental Magazine (bimonthly)
International Wildlife (bimonthly)
National Wildlife (bimonthly)
Nature Canada (quarterly)
Sierra (monthly)
Wildlife Conservation Magazine (bimonthly)

GENERAL REFERENCE FOR YOUNG PEOPLE
Deane Edwin Abrahamson (ed.), *The Challenge of Global Warming*, Island Press, 1989.
Steven Anzonvin (ed.), *Preserving the World Ecology*, The H.W. Wilson Company, 1990.
David Bedds, *The Third World: Development and Interdependence*, Oxford University Press, 1995 edn.
David J. Bellamy, *The Roadside*, C.N. Potter, 1988.
Elizabeth T. Billington, *The Rock Pool*, C.N. Potter, 1988.
David Burnie, *How Nature Works*, Dorling Kindersley Eyewitness, 1991.
Mary Daegling, *Monster Seaweeds*, Dillon, 1986.
Madeleine Dunphy, *Here Is the Tropical Rainforest*, Hyperion, 1994.
Jon Erickson, *Greenhouse Earth: Tommorrow's Disaster Today*, Tab Books, 1990.
John Famdon, *Dictionary of the Earth*, Dorling Kindersley, 1994.
John Famdon, *How the Earth Works*, Dorling Kindersley Eyewitness, 1992.
Nance Fyson, *Rich World, Poor World*, Oxford University Press, 1991.
Edward Johnson, *United Nations – Peacekeeper?*, Wayland *Global Issues* series, 1995.
Dwight Kuhn, *More Than Just a Vegetable Garden*, Silver Press, 1990.
Marjorie Lamb, *2 Minutes a Day for a Greener Planet*, Harper & Row, 1990.
Patricia Lauber, *Who Eats What?*, Harper-Collins, 1995.
Emilie Lepthien, *Tropical Rain Forests*, Children's Press, 1993.
Nancy Luenn, *Squish!*, Altheneum, 1994.
Fiona Macdonald, *Rain Forest*, Raintree Steck-Vaughn, 1994.
Vicki McVey, *The Sierra Club Kid's Guide to Planet Care & Repair*, Sierra Club Books for Children, 1993.
E. Jaediker Norsgaard, *Nature's Great Balancing Act*, Dutton, 1990.
Steve Pollock, *Ecology*, Dorling Kindersley, 1993.
Alvin & Virginia Silverstein, *Life in a Tidal Pool*, Little, Brown, 1990.

Frank J. Staub, *America's Prairies*, Carolrhoda Books, 1994.
Jenny Tesar, *Endangered Habitats*, Facts On File, 1992.
Rose Wyler, *Puddles and Ponds*, J. Messner, 1990.

An annual *Resources for Schools and Youth Groups* catalog is available from Oxfam (for address and telephone number, see page 183). This lists materials from a wide range of publishers and other organizations. These include:
Backbone of Development, 1994.
Be My Guest: An Introduction to Tourism's Impact, Tourism Concern.
Can You Be Different?, 1994.
Changing Places, Oxfam, 1991.
The Coffee Chain Game, 1994.
Colonialism, Conflict and Community, 1994.
Dammed Water: Nigeria, IBT, 1995
Developing Geography: Ghana, 1995.
Doing It Ourselves.
Education for Development, Hodder & Stoughton and UNICEF, 1995.
Fala Favela, Catholic Fund for Overseas Development, 1991.
The Final Frontier? Land, Environment and Pastoralism in Kenya, 1994.
Mangla: A Study of Change and Development in Mirpur, Azad and Kashmir, Pakistan, 1995.
Moving Stories: A Young Person's Guide to Refugees in Today's World, British Red Cross, 1995.
Peters Projection World Map.
Refugees: We Left Because We Had To, Refugee Council, 1995.
A Right to a Roof, Council for Education in World Citizenship, 1994.
Shifting Sands: Agriculture, Development, and Environmental Change in India's Thar Desert, 1994.
Southern Perspectives on Development, 1996.
Summing up the World: Mathematical Activities with a Global Perspective.
The Trading Game, Christian Aid, 1993.
Triumph of Hope: Eritrea's Struggle for Development, 1994.
Understanding Global Issues.
"We All Have the Right . . .," poster set, 1995.
Where We Live, Birmingham DEC, 1992.
Women Make a Difference, poster set, Oxfam, 1993.
Worlds behind the Music, 1995.

YOUNG PEOPLE'S FICTION, MYTH, AND POETRY RELATED TO THE ENVIRONMENT
Anita Desai, *The Village by the Sea*, Heinemann, 1982.
Gaye Hicilmaz, *Against the Storm*, Viking, 1990.
Graham Salisbury, *Blue Skin of the Sea*, Scholastic, 1994.
Robert Swindells, *Brother in the Land*, Oxford University Press, 1984.
Forest Peoples of South America, Africa, and Southeast Asia, Cambridge University Press, 1994.

ADULT BOOKS
Steven Anzovin (ed.), *Preserving the World Ecology*, H.W. Wilson, 1990.
William H. Baarschers, *Eco-Facts & Eco-Fiction: Understanding the Environmental Debate*, Routledge, 1996.
Frank Barnaby (ed.), *The Gaia Peace Atlas*, Pan Books, 1988.
Julian Berger, *The Gaia Atlas of First Peoples*, Robertson McCarta, 1990.
Rachel Carson, *Silent Spring*, Penguin Books, 1965.
Paul Ekins, *Wealth beyond Measure: An Atlas of New Economics*, Gaia Books, 1992.
Niles Eldredge, *The Miner's Canary*, Prentice Hall, 1991.
Michael Frome, *Chronicling the West: Thirty Years of Environmental Writing*, The Mountaineer's Books, 1996.
Linda Gamlin, *Life on Earth*, Gloucester Press, 1988.
Robert Garner, *Environmental Politics*, Prentice Hall, 1996.
Herbert Girardet, *The Gaia Atlas of Cities: New Directions for Sustainable Urban Living*, Gaia Books, 1994.
Global Human Rights Report on Societies in Danger, Beacon Press, 1993.
Peter Harper, Jeremy Light, and Chris Madsen, *The Natural Garden Book*, Gaia Books, 1994.
Roger Hart, *The Children's Community Participation Handbook: Involving Children in Sustainable Development*, Earthscan and UNICEF, 1996.
Ron Hirschi, *Save Our Oceans and Coasts*, Delacorte Press, 1993.
William M. Lafferty and James Meadowcroft, *Democracy & the Environment: Problems & Prospects*, Ashgate Publishing Co., 1996.
Mark Lambert, *Farming and the Environment*, Steck-Vaughn, 1991.
Miles Litvinoff, *The Earthscan Action Handbook for People and Planet*, Earthscan, 1990.
James Lovelock, *Gaia: The Practical Science of Planetary Medicine*, Gaia Books, 1991.

Jan McHarry, *Reuse, Repair, Recycle: A Mine of Creative Ideas for Thrifty Living*, Gaia Books, 1993.

Norman Myers (ed.), *The Gaia Atlas of Planet Management*, Gaia Books, 1994 edn.

Joni Seager, *The State of the Environment Atlas*, Penguin Books, 1995.

Pat Simmons, *Words into Action: Basic Rights and the Campaign against World Poverty*, Oxfam, 1995.

UNICEF, *The State of the World's Children 1996*, Oxford University Press, 1995.

Paul Wapner, *Environmental Activism & World Civic Politics*, State University Press of New York, 1996.

Kevin Watkins, *The Oxfam Poverty Report*, Oxfam, 1995.

Jonathan Weiner, *The Next One Hundred Years*, Bantam Books, 1990.

Philip Whitfield, *Can the Whales Be Saved?*, Viking Kestrel, 1989.

Robert Muir Wood, *Atlas of the Natural World,* Facts On File, Inc., 1990.

CD-ROM SOFTWARE

The Big Green Disc. Looks at major environmental issues, such as global warming and pollution.

Encarta '95 (Microsoft). An all-embracing encyclopedia.

Energy Resources (Bradford Technology) Investigates energy sources and uses.

Exploring Plant Sciences (Attica Cybernetics) Survey of the plant kingdom and uses of plants.

ITN European Atlas (Attica Cybernetics) Maps and country profiles.

Last Chance to See (Softline). The record of a search for endangered species.

Lifemap series (Time Warner Interactive). Focuses on different major groups of animals.

Mammals (National Geographic Society) An encyclopedia of 400 mammals with text, photographs, and film clips.

Nature in Motion (Andromeda). A voyage through the world's natural habitats.

Ocean Life (Suneria Educational). Explores marine wildlife.

Sim City 2000 (Interplay Ltd). Plan your own city of the future – a simulation game.

World Guide (Third World Institute and Oxfam). Statistics and texts on global issues and the world's countries compiled by researchers and journalists in developing countries. Also available in book form.

World Reference Atlas (Dorling Kindersley). Country profiles and gazetteer.

Zoo Guides (Kim Tec). The world's wildlife, including many endangered species.

Worldwatch Database Disk 1996 (Worldwatch Institute). Graphs, tables, and data on the state of our planet and human environmental impacts.

OFFICIAL INTERNATIONAL ORGANIZATIONS

Official international organizations are groupings of countries controlled and financed by country governments. Besides the United Nations — the main international organization to which almost all governments belong — there are many other official groupings. The addresses of all the following organizations, and more details about them, are available from *The Europa World Year Book*, published every year by Europa and available in reference libraries.

THE UNITED NATIONS
The United Nations was set up in 1945 with its headquarters in New York. Member countries (185 at the start of 1996) send representatives to the General Assembly to discuss issues and vote on decisions and recommendations. The Security Council is the main UN decision-making body; it has five permanent members — China, France, Russia, the UK, and the USA — and ten other elected members. The Economic and Social Council makes UN policy relating to economic, social, cultural, educational, health, and human rights matters. The International Court of Justice, based in The Hague, Netherlands, settles inter-country disputes. The Secretariat, led by the Secretary-General, manages the UN's daily affairs.

Other United Nations bodies
Commission on Sustainable Development Set up in 1992 to monitor progress on the Earth Summit's Agenda 21. Based in New York.
Food and Agriculture Organization Set up in 1945 to improve food production, distribution, and living conditions in developing countries. Based in Rome.
General Agreement on Tariffs and Trade Set up in 1946 to expand world trade. Based in Geneva. The World Trade Organization took over its work in 1995.
Intergovernmental Panel on Climate Change Set up in 1988 to study and advise governments about climate change and global warming. Based in Geneva.
International Atomic Energy Agency Set up in 1957 to promote peaceful uses, and prevent military uses, of nuclear energy. Based in Vienna.
International Bank for Reconstruction and Development (The World Bank) Set up in 1944 to help countries rebuild their economies after World War II. Today, mainly lends money to developing countries. Based in Washington, D.C.
International Fund for Agricultural Development Set up in 1976 to help poor rural people in developing countries. Based in Rome.
International Labor Organization Joined the UN system in 1946. Aims to improve working conditions and living standards among poor people. Based in Geneva.
International Maritime Organization Set up in 1959 to improve shipping safety and reduce sea pollution from ships. Based in London.
International Monetary Fund Set up in 1944 to make short-term loans to countries and keep the world economy in balance. Based in Washington, D.C.
Office of the UN Disaster Relief Coordinator Set up in 1971 to direct and co-ordinate disaster-relief activities. Based in Geneva.
Office of the UN High Commissioner for Refugees Set up in 1951 to solve refugee problems. Based in Geneva.
UN Children's (Emergency) Fund Set up in 1946 (reorganized in 1953) to meet the emergency needs of children and help provide long-term health and welfare services. Based in New York.
UN Commission on Human Settlements Set up in 1977 to help countries house their populations. Based in Nairobi.
UN Conference on Trade and Development Set up in 1964 to promote trade and economic growth among developing countries. Based in Geneva.
UN Development Program Set up in 1966 to help developing countries improve quality of life and living standards among their people. Based in New York.
UN Environment Program Set up in 1972 to monitor the state of the world environment and promote environmentally helpful activities. Based in Nairobi.
UN Educational, Scientific and Cultural Organization Set up in 1945 to increase international co-operation through education, science, and culture. Based in Paris.
UN Population Fund Set up in 1967 to increase awareness of, and help solve, population problems. Based in New York.
World Food Program Set up in 1961 to provide food aid and emergency relief to developing countries. Based in Rome.
World Health Organization Set up in 1948 to improve levels of health worldwide. Based in Geneva.

World Meteorological Organization Joined the UN system in 1950. Helps countries co-operate in producing and using information about the weather. Based in Geneva.
World Trade Organization Set up in 1995 to promote a new era of "free trade." Based in Geneva.

OTHER OFFICIAL INTERNATIONAL ORGANIZATIONS
Alliance of Small Island States A grouping of mainly Caribbean, Pacific, and Indian Ocean islands. Set up in 1990 to campaign for action to prevent sea-level rises resulting from global warming that could cause disastrous floods in the member countries.
Association of South-East Asian Nations A regional trading group of six member-countries — Brunei, Indonesia, Malaysia, the Philippines, Singapore, and Thailand — set up in 1967.
Caribbean Community and Common Market A regional grouping set up in 1973 to increase cooperation in many areas of activity. Most Caribbean countries are members.
Commonwealth Set up in 1931 to link together the United Kingdom and its former colonies. The population of the 49 member countries totals nearly a quarter of humanity.
Commonwealth of Independent States Set up in 1992 by all the independent countries of the former Soviet Union except for Estonia, Latvia, and Lithuania.
Council of Europe Set up in 1949 to promote unity between European countries. Membership includes all the countries of Western Europe and most Eastern European countries, including Russia. Active in promoting democracy and human rights.
European Bank for Reconstruction and Development Set up in 1991 to help countries of Eastern Europe reform and develop their economies.
European Union Began as the European Coal and Steel Community in 1952. It became the European Economic Community, or "Common Market," in 1957. There were originally six member countries: Belgium, France, (West) Germany, Italy, Luxembourg, and the Netherlands. Since then Austria, Denmark, Finland, Greece, Ireland, Portugal, Spain, Sweden, and the UK have joined. In November 1993 it became known as the European Union. Works in a wide range of areas, including trade and economic policy, agriculture, employment, environmental protection, and human rights.
Group of Seven The "rich countries' club" of Canada, France, Germany, Italy, Japan, the UK, and the USA. Also includes the European Union. Meets every year to discuss economic and political matters.

Group of Seventy-Seven A grouping of developing countries that first met in 1964 to discuss economics and development. The original 75 member countries have grown to about 130.

International Whaling Commission Set up in 1946 to promote sustainable whaling by 40 member governments. Iceland left in 1992.

Islamic Conference Organization A grouping of 44 Islamic countries set up in 1971.

Nordic Council Set up in 1952 to promote cooperation between Nordic countries. Members are Denmark, Finland, Iceland, Norway, and Sweden.

North American Free Trade Agreement A trade agreement signed between Canada, Mexico, and the USA in 1992.

North Atlantic Treaty Organization A defense organization joining certain countries of Western Europe and North America, set up in 1949. Members are Belgium, Canada, Denmark, France, Germany, Greece, Iceland, Italy, Luxembourg, the Netherlands, Norway, Portugal, Spain, Turkey, the UK, and the USA.

Organization for Security and Cooperation in Europe Set up in 1994 after regular conferences on security, economics, science, technology, and human rights in Europe. Has 53 member-countries.

Organization for Economic Cooperation and Development A grouping of 24 developed countries set up in 1961 to promote economic growth and expansion of trade.

Organization of African Unity Set up in 1963 to increase unity among African countries, to oppose colonialism, and to raise living standards in member countries. Morocco left in 1985, but all other African countries belong, making 52 members in all.

Organization of American States Set up by 30 North, Central, and South American countries in 1948 to promote peace, cooperation and development.

Organization of Petroleum-Exporting Countries Set up in 1960 by oil-producing countries to control oil prices and production levels. OPEC has 12 members.

Unrepresented Nations' and Peoples' Organization Set up in 1991 to represent the world's ethnic-minority and oppressed peoples. Funded and controlled by member peoples. Among the many peoples represented are the Aboriginals (Australia), Kurds (Middle East), Tibetans, and Adivasis (indigenous peoples of India and Bangladesh).

World Conservation Union Set up in 1948 to promote the protection and sustainable use of natural resources. It has more than 500 members, including non-governmental organizations, independent experts, and country governments.

ACKNOWLEDGMENTS

SOURCES OF DATA
Lester Brown and others, *State of the World*, Norton and Worldwatch Institute, New York, annual.
The Ecologist, various issues.
Steve Elsworth, *A Dictionary of the Environment*, Paladin, 1990.
Michael Keating, *The Earth Summit's Agenda for Change: A Plain Language Version of Agenda 21 and the Other Rio Agreements*, Center for Our Common Future, Geneva, 1994.
Geoffrey Lean and Don Hinrichsen, *Atlas of the Environment*, Helicon, 1992.
Miles Litvinoff, *The Earthscan Action Handbook for People and Planet*, Earthscan, 1990.
Norman Myers (ed.), *The Gaia Atlas of Planet Management*, Gaia Books, revised edn, 1994.
Joni Seager, *The State of the Environment Atlas*, Penguin Books, 1995.
Paul Smith and Kiki Warr, *Global Environmental Issues*, Hodder & Stoughton and the Open University, 1991.
The Times Atlas, Times Books, 7th edn, 1988; and *The Times Concise Atlas of the World*, Times Books, 5th edn, 1987.
United Nations Development Program, *Human Development Report 1994*, Oxford University Press, 1994.
United Nations Population Fund, *The State of World Population 1995*, UNFPA, 1995.
The World: A Third World Guide 1995/96, Third World Institute (Montevideo, Uruguay) and Oxfam, 1995.
World Resources Institute, *The 1994 Information Please Environmental Almanac*, Houghton Mifflin, Boston, 1993.

ACKNOWLEDGMENTS
The author and publishers wish to thank the following individuals and organizations for their help during the preparation of this book: Bangladesh High Commission, London; Books for a Change bookshop, London; British Wind Energy Association; Maggie Fealdman; Tim Hancock, Saferworld; Roger Kohn, International Maritime Organization; Julian Lewis, International Institute for Environment and Development; Ann Luzeckyj, UK Committee for UNICEF; Alex Marshall, United Nations Population Fund; the Pesticides Trust; Paul Rogers, Department of Peace Studies, Bradford University.

The publishers would like to thank Koos Neefjes, Amanda Barker, and Fred Martin for their helpful comments on the text. Bender Richardson White would like thank John Stidworthy for help in planning the book, and Liz Clayton and Anna Coryndon at Oxfam for producing the *Gaia Watch* articles and supplying photographs.

Illustrations David Ashby; Norman Barber (Linden Artists); Martin Camm (Linden Artists); Jim Channel (Linden Artists); Stefan Chabluk; David Cook; Bill Donohoe; Eugene Fleury; Chris Forsey; Aziz Khan; David Mallot; Gary Marsh; Francesca Pelizzoli; John Potter; David Salariya; Ann Savage; John Shipperbottom; Rob Shone; Nicky Snell (Virgil Pomfret Agency); Clive Spong (Linden Artists); Roger Stewart (Virgil Pomfret Agency); Alan Suttie; George Thompson; Shirley Willis.

Photographs The publishers would like to thank the following for permission to reproduce photographs: page **4** Wildlife Matters. **5** Lionel Bender. **6–7** Holt Studios International/Silvestre Silva. **12** Overseas Development Administration, London. **14–15** Hilary Coulby/Oxfam. **18** Sarah Errington/Oxfam. **21** Jeremy Hartley/Oxfam. **23** Rob Cousins/Oxfam. **25** Jeremy Hartley/Oxfam. **26–27** (main) Sean Sprague/Oxfam; (rest) Keith Bernstein/Oxfam. **28** Environmental Picture Library/Jeff Libman. **30–31** Holt Studios International/Inga Spence. **34** Penny Tweedie/Oxfam. **39** Sean Sprague/Oxfam. **42–43** (all) Geoff Sayer/Oxfam. **45** Geoff Sayer/Oxfam. **46–47** Zefa/Stockmarket/Tom Stewart. **48** Environmental Picture Library/Roger Grace. **54** Environmental Picture Library/David Sims. **58–59** (bottom left) Matthew Mawson/Oxfam; (rest) Jeremy Hartley/Oxfam **61** Shahidul Alam/Oxfam. **64** Zefa/Goebel. **66–67** Environmental Picture Library/Martin Bond. **68** Tim Malyon/Oxfam. **73** Larry Boyd/Oxfam. **77** Jon Magno/Oxfam. **78** Greenpeace/NASA/Environmental Picture Library. **79** Environmental Picture Library/Katherine Miles. **85** Environmental Picture Libary/Nigel Dickinson. **86–87** (main) Geoff Sayer/Oxfam; (left) Rajendra Shaw/Oxfam; (top right) Sean Sprague/Oxfam; (bottom right) Jeremy Hartley/Oxfam. **91** ETSU. **92–93** Zefa/Weigl. **100–101** (all) Sarah Errington/Oxfam. **102** Jeremy Hartley/Oxfam. **104–105** Zefa/Wisniewski. **107** Holt Studios International/Inga Spence. **112** (all) Wildlife Matters. **113** (left) Roshini Kempadoo/Oxfam; (right) Jeremy Hoare/Wildlife Matters. **116–117** (all) Dr J.F. Oates. **118** Dr J.F. Oates. **122–123** David Keith Jones/Images of Africa. **128** Julio Etchart/Oxfam. **132** Nancy Durrell-McKenna/Oxfam. **134** Howard Davies/Oxfam. **136–137** (main) Kay Willis/Oxfam; (rest) Mike Goldwater/Oxfam **142–143** Kim Richardson/Alba Publishing. **144** Raqu/Oxfam. **149** US Geological Survey. **151** Environmental Picture Libary/Leslie Garland. **153** Environmental Picture Library/H. Girardet. **156–157** (main) Maryam Iqbal/Oxfam; (rest) Liz Clayton/Oxfam **159** Mike Goldwater/Oxfam. **160** Dr J.F. Oates. **162–163** Lionel Bender. **168–169** British Telecom.